Edward Johnston Vernon, Rasmus Kristian Rask

A Guide to the Anglo-Saxon Tongue

A Grammar After Erasmus Rask, Extracts in Prose and Verse, with...

Edward Johnston Vernon, Rasmus Kristian Rask

A Guide to the Anglo-Saxon Tongue
A Grammar After Erasmus Rask, Extracts in Prose and Verse, with...

ISBN/EAN: 9783337254780

Printed in Europe, USA, Canada, Australia, Japan

Cover: Foto ©Thomas Meinert / pixelio.de

More available books at **www.hansebooks.com**

A GUIDE
TO THE
ANGLO-SAXON TONGUE:
A GRAMMAR
AFTER ERASMUS RASK;

EXTRACTS IN PROSE AND VERSE, WITH NOTES, ETC.

FOR THE USE OF LEARNERS.

𝔚ith an 𝔄ppendix.

BY

EDWARD JOHNSTON VERNON, B.A.
MAGDALENE HALL.

Antiquam exquirite Matrem.

LONDON:
JOHN RUSSELL SMITH,
36, SOHO SQUARE.
MDCCCLXXII.

TO

JOHN DAVID MACBRIDE ESQ. D.C.L.

Principal of Magdalene Hall,

ETC. ETC.

IN TOKEN OF

RESPECT AND ESTEEM

PREFACE.

ANGLO-SAXON was spoken by our forefathers in England for more than five hundred years; from it have sprung the greater part of our local and family names, very many of our old, and almost all our provincial words and sayings, and fifteen twentieths of what we daily think, and speak, and write. No Englishman therefore altogether ignorant of Anglo-Saxon can have a thorough knowledge of his own mother-tongue, while the language itself, to say nothing of the many valuable and interesting works preserved in it, may in copiousness of words, strength of expression, and grammatical precision, vie with modern German.*

The present object is to furnish the learner, if it may be, with a cheaper, easier, more comprehensive, and not less trustworthy guide to this tongue than may hitherto have been within his reach.

The first six chapters are mainly abridged from the Grammar of the late Professor Rask of Copenhagen, as edited by Mr. Thorpe, whom the compiler has to thank for leave to make use of his praiseworthy labours, and for obliging answers to queries.

* See Thorpe's Advertisement to Rask's Grammar

Some alterations and additions seemed called for by the progress of the study since the publication of that work, whence its improved cultivation in this country must be dated. Illustrations from the kindred new Teutonic dialects German and Dutch, with some from Greek and Latin, old and provincial English &c. have taken the place of the Scandinavian* references as fitter for the English learner. A view, however narrow and imperfect, of languages more or less nearly akin, can hardly fail, it is hoped, to awaken in the understanding student, a wish to know something more of comparative philology, hitherto so unworthily slighted among ourselves, and so laboriously and skilfully worked out by the Germans.

The hyphen is used throughout to divide the parts of compound words from each other, as also prefixes, and when needful, case-endings and other terminations, from roots; in this as in other tongues, the beginner must accustom himself to parse not only every word in a phrase, but every syllable in a word.

Some rules for gender have been attempted, and a list of exceptions to the general rule of its agreement with the German, together with comparative tables of the cardinal numbers, and of the chief tenses, are added.

The accent, sometimes misplaced or left out by Rask, and too often altogether neglected by others, has been carefully attended to.

---

* Some acquaintance with Icelandic and the other old northern tongues, above all Gothic, which shows the originals of the A. S. inflections, quantity &c., is of course needful for a *perfect* knowledge of Anglo-Saxon.

The Syntax is in great part new; the examples mostly gathered from the compiler's own reading.

The Extracts in prose and verse are fitted by explanatory notes for use without a dictionary; an analysis of the narrative verse, partly shortened from Rask, and a literal version of the poetry, are also given. The purpose here being to teach pure Anglo-Saxon only, the selections are all from writers of a good age; one well grounded in the language in its perfect state, will not find it hard to bring down his knowledge of his native tongue, through Semi-Saxon, and old and middle English, to our own time.

The Appendix contains lists of words likely to be confounded by learners, together with a number of additional notes. For the length to which the latter have run some apology may be needed, but it seemed best not to lose the opportunity of bringing in, however irregularly, some matter which may be useful.

To Mr. J. M. Kemble, Editor of Beówulf &c., who shares with Mr. Thorpe the honour of making his countrymen independent of foreigners for a right knowledge of their old national language and literature, sincere thanks are due for much very kind, and most valuable help and advice touching the accent, gender, and other hard and weighty points, on which opinions from such an authority cannot be too highly prized. Obliging hints, and the loan of scarce books from other quarters, must also be thankfully acknowledged.

The compiler, feeling what scanty justice has been done to these various and welcome aids, must add that for those faults both of doing, and of leaving undone, which he cannot hope to have avoided, he alone has to answer. Should this imperfect attempt however, by making the speech of the Anglo-Saxons somewhat easier and more attractive than heretofore to their children, give any of these a better knowledge of the real structure, and true spirit, and a greater love for the power and worth of that tongue, which bids fair one day to overspread the whole earth, some time and labour will not have been spent in vain.

CONTENTS.

	Page.
Preface	v

CHAPTER I.—LETTERS.

1. Alphabet &c.	1
2. Accent	2
3. Pronunciation	3
4. Spelling	4
5. Change of Letters	5
6. Correspondence of do.	7

CHAPTER II.—NOUNS.

1. Genders	8
2. Inflection	10
3. Simple Order, or Declension I.	12
4. Complex Order. Declension II. Class 1.	14
5. — — — — — 2.	14
6. — — — — — 3.	16
7. Complex Order. Declension III. Class 1.	17
8. — — — — — 2.	18
9. — — — — — 3.	19

CHAPTER III.—ADJECTIVES.

1. Inflection	20
2. Definite Declension	21
3. Indefinite Declension I.	22
4. — — II.	23
5. Comparison	24
6. Irregular do.	25

CHAPTER IV.—PRONOUNS.

	Page.
1. Personal	27
2. Possessive	29
3. Demonstrative	30
4. Interrogative	31
5. Indefinite	32
6. Cardinal Numbers	33
7. Ordinal do.	35

CHAPTER V.—VERBS.

1. Conjugation	37
2. Chief Tenses	38
3. Simple Order, or Conjugation I.	39
4. Conjugation I. Class 1.	41
5. — — — 2.	42
6. — — — 3.	45
7. Complex Order	46
8. Conjugation II. Class 1.	48
9. — — — 2.	50
10. — — — 3.	53
11. Conjugation III.	54
12. Conjugation III. Class 1.	55
13. — — — 2.	58
14. — — — 3.	59
15. Anomalous Verbs	60
16. Auxiliaries &c.	62

CHAPTER VI.—FORMATION OF WORDS.

1. Prefixes	63
2. Nominal Terminations	65
3. Adjectival do.	67
4. Verbal do.	68
5. Particles	69
6. Composition	71

CHAPTER VII.—SYNTAX.

		Page.
1. Syntax		73
2. Syntax of Nouns		74
3. — — Adjectives		76
4. — — Verbs		78
5. — — Prepositions		87
6. — — Conjunctions		92
7. — — Interjections		96

CHAPTER VIII.—PROSE EXTRACTS.

1. S. Matthew, XII. 1—13.	98
2. S. Mark, VI. 32.	100
3. S. Luke, XX. 9—25.	104
4. S. John, VII. 14—28.	107
5. Genesis, XLV.	109
6. Exodus, XXIII.	113
7. Saxon Chronicle	117
8. Apollonius	121
9. Boëthius, XVII., XXXIV. 10.	129

CHAPTER IX.—VERSE EXTRACTS.

1. Narrative Verse	135
2. Boëthius, Metre XII.	141
3. Cædmon, parts of Cant. II. and XVI.	145
4. Beówulf, parts of Cant. V., XXII., XXVII.	153

APPENDIX.

1. Words spelt alike, but differing in accent, pronunciation, and meaning	1
2. Words spelt and accented alike, but differing in meaning	167
3. Other words likely to be confounded by learners	174
4. Additional Notes	180

ABBREVIATIONS &c.

A. S. Anglo-Saxon.
Comp. compare.
D. Dutch.
F. French.
G. German.
Goth. Gothic.
Gr. Greek.
L. Latin.
lit. literally.
O. old English in general
P. provincial.
S. Scottish, the ancient English dialect of the Lowlands of Scotland, and part of the north of England.
Numbers, applied to a noun, denote the declension and class; to a verb, the conjugation and class; to an adjective, the indefinite declension.

GUIDE

TO THE

ANGLO-SAXON TONGUE.

CHAPTER I.

Sect. I.—*The Alphabet, &c.*

The A. S. letters are 24, viz.

A	a	[A]	N	n		
Æ	æ	[Æ]	O	o		
B	b		P	p		
C	c	[C]	R	r	[ɼ]
D	d	[ð]	S	s	[ſ]
E	e	[e]	T	t	[t̄]
F	f	[ꝼ]	U	u		
G	g	[L ȝ]	W	w	[ƿ Ƿ]
H	h	[ꞕ Ƕ]	X	x		
I	i		Y	y		
L	l		Þ	þ		
M	m	[ᛘ]	Ð	ð		

The characters between brackets were written by the Anglo-Saxons, but being for the most part mere corruptions of the Roman forms are now seldom printed.

In later times k was used for c; v and z occur in foreign names only. The abbreviations ꝫ for *and*, ꝥ for þ æ t; *the, that,* and others were in use; in general ¯ shows that m or n is left out.

II.—*Accent.*

The accent (′) over a vowel shows it to be long. The A. S. accented vowels are mostly long by nature; as, l á r *lore* (G. lehre), b ǽ r *bier* (G. bahre), g r é n *green* (G. grün), w í d *wide* (G. weit), g ó d *good* (G. gut), r ú m *room, space* (G. raum), f ý r *fire* (G. feuer). Some have become long by contraction, g, h, ng, or n, being left out; as, smeagan, sme á n *to consider,* sleahan, sleán *to slay,* gangan, gán *to go,* fangan, fó n *tu take:* in f í f *five,* t ó ð *tooth,* m ú ð *mouth,* and the like, the kindred tongues show the omitted n; as, πεντε, L. quinque, G. fünf; ὀ-δους, ὀ-δοντ-ος, L. dens,(¹) G. zahn; G. mund: a few from the omission of a vowel; as, tae, t á *toe.* From the examples above and below, it will be seen that in English a long or double vowel, and in German a long or double vowel, or diphthong, commonly answers to an A. S. long or accented vowel, while short vowels in general correspond in like manner. The accent serves at the same time, though never used for that purpose merely, to distinguish many words of like spelling but different meaning and sound; as, ac *but,* ác *oak;* m æ s t *mast,* m ǽ s t *most;* wende *turned,* went, wénde *weened;* i s *is,* í s *ice;* for *for,* fór *journey;* ful *full,*

(¹) In A. S. as in Greek, *ns* does not occur in the same syllable.

fúl *foul;* hyrde *herd, keeper,* hýrde *heard.*([2]) Without due attention therefore to the accent, A. S. cannot be rightly written, pronounced, nor understood.([3])

III.—*Pronunciation.*

The pronunciation is as follows:—

a has the sound of our *a* in *ah;* F. &c. short *a.*

á is longer and broader, like G. &c. long *a*, approaching our *au* and *aw.*

au and aw sound nearly like *ow* in *now*, but more open, like G. and Italian *au.*

æ is pronounced like *a* in *glad.*

ǽ nearly as *a* in *dare;* G. *eh;* F. close *é.*

e sounds like *e* in *send, rather*, when thus placed; before a consonant followed by a vowel it resembles the *ea* in *bear*, but is shorter, like F. open *è.* Before a or o it sounds as *y;* at the end of a syllable it is very lightly sounded, like the F. unaccented *e,* or the G. *e* final.

é is pronounced like *ǽ.*

i and y answer to *i* in *dim.*

i before another vowel to *y.*

í and ý to *ee* in *deem.*

o to short *o* in *not;* F. open *o.*

ó to long *o* in *note;* F. close *ó.*

ow is sounded as *ow* in *now.*

([2]) Comp. G. mast, meist; wandte, wähnte; ist, eis; für, fuhr; voll, faul; hirt, hörte.

([3]) The more advanced student will find comparison with the Gothic and other ancient dialects the only sure guide to the A. S. quantity.

u as *u* in *full.*

ú as *oo* in *fool.*

The consonants are pronounced as in English, with the following exceptions:—

c is always hard like *k*; cw stands for *qu*, which was however used in later times.

f between two vowels, or at the end of a syllable, sounds like *v.*

g is never soft; when placed however between two of the vowels æ, e, i, or y, or at the beginning of a syllable before e or i, followed by another vowel, it has the sound of *y*.([1])

cg is usually written for *gg*.

h is always strongly aspirated; at the end of a syllable or before a hard consonant it is guttural, like the G. *ch,* the S. *ch* in *loch,* and the Irish *gh* in *lough.*

hw anwers to our *wh*; h occurs also before *l, n* and *r.*

w sometimes, as in E., stands before *r*; likewise before *l.*

þ *(tha)* is our hard *th*, as in *thing.*

ð *(eth)* our soft *th*, as in *other.*

þ usually begins, ð ends a syllable, but they were and are often confounded.

IV.—*Spelling.*

The A. S. spelling was very variable; the following are the commonest changes:—

[1] It is likely that g before e or i, and (like h) at the end of a syllable, was guttural, as it often is in German, and always in Dutch.

CHANGE OF LETTERS.

á — ǽ and ǽ — á; þám, þǽm; þǽre, þáre.
a — ea; waldan, wealdan *to wield, rule.*
a — o and o — a; man, mon(²) *man;* on, an *on.*
ea — e and e — a; ceaster, cester (³) *town;* fela, feala *many;* eá — é; teáh, téh *drew.*
i — y, eo; hit, hyt *it:* him, heom *them.*
í — ý, íe, eó; hí, hý, híe, heó *they.*
eo — u, y, e; sweord, swurd *sword;* seolf, sylf, self *self.*
eó — ú, ý; sweótol, swútol, swýtol *manifest.*
g — h; sorg, sorh *care, sorrow.*
ng, nc, ngc; sang, sanc, sangc *song:* n and g are often transposed, &c.; þegen, þegn, þeng, þen *servant, thane:* g is sometimes added or cast off at the end of a word; as, hwý, hwýg *why?* hefig, hefi *heavy:* it is often left out before d or ð; mægden, mæden *maiden,* mægð, mæð *tribe.*
cs, sc, hs, x; ácsian, áscian, áhsian, áxian *to ask (ax).* (⁴)

V.—*Change of Letters.*

Other changes of letters take place in inflection and derivation; the German synonyms often undergo the like, the English sometimes.

a is changed into æ, and *vice versâ;* grafan *to grave,* (G. graben); þú grǽfst *thou gravest,* (G. du gräbst);

(²) P. *mon* for *man, lang* for *long,* and the like.
(³) L. castra; hence Chester, -cester, &c. in local names.
(⁴) See also nouns II. 2., and irregular comparison.

bæð *bath*, (G. bad); baðu *baths* (G. bäder.)(¹)

a into e; man, *man* (G. mann); men (²) *men* (G. männer).

á into ǽ; hál *hale, whole*, ge-hǽlan *to heal*.

ea into e or y; neah *nigh*, nehst nyhst *nighest, next*.

e, o, eo, u into i or y; ren *rain*, rinan *to rain*; storm *storm* (G. sturm); styrman *to storm* (G. stürmen); weorc *work* (G. werk), wyrcan *to work* (G. wirken); hunger *hunger*, hyngrian *to hunger*.

eá, eó, ú, into ý; leás *loose*, (G. los); a-lýsan *to re-lease* (G. er-lösen); neód *need* (G. noth); nýdan *to force* (G. nöthigen); scrúd *shroud*, scrýdan *to shroud*.

ó into é; dóm *doom*, déman *to deem, doom*.

bb into f; a-hebban *to exalt*, a-hafen *exalted* (⁴).

c and cc into h; sécan *to seek*, ic sóhte *I sought*; feccan *to fetch*, (ge-)freht *fretcht* (⁵).

g into h and *vice versâ*; wrígan *to cover*, ic wráh *I covered*; beorh *mountain*, plur. beorgas (⁶).

s into r (⁷); freósan *to freeze*, (ge-)froren *frozen*.

ð into d (⁸); sníðan *to cut* (G. schneiden), sniden *cut* (G. ge-schnitten).

Several other changes take place in the formation of imperfects I. 3. and complex; likewise in nouns II. 2., III. 1. 3. and in adjectives.

(¹) See Verbs II. 3., and Nouns III. 1.
(²) See Nouns III. 2.   (³) See irregular comparison.
(⁴) See Verbs II. 3.   (⁵) See Verbs I. 2, 3.
(⁶) See Verbs III. 1, 2.   Nouns II. 2.
(⁷) See Verbs III. 3.   (⁸) See Verbs II. 1, and III. 2.

VI.—*Correspondence of Letters.*

' Attention to the correspondence of A. S. with English and German letters helps not only to recognise words already known in a kindred tongue, but to settle their derivation, spelling, and quantity. Thus—

á answers to E. long o; G. ei, l. e; bán([9]) *bone,* G. bein; máre([10]) *more, greater,* G. mehr.

eá to E. l. e; G. l. o, a, au : streám *stream,* G. strom; sceáp *sheep,* G. schaf; ge-leáfa *be-lief,* G. g-laube.

ea to E. short a, l. o; G. s. a: scearp *sharp,* G. scharf; ceald *cold,* G. kalt.

æ to E. and G. a, e: gæst *guest,* G. gast; fæst *fast,* G. fest.

ǽ to E. l. e, a, o; G. l. a, ei: sǽd *seed,* G. saat; hǽr *hair,* G. haar; mǽst([11]) *most,* G. meist.

é to E. l. e; G. l. ü, ä: céne *bold, keen,* G. kühn; wénan *to ween, imagine,* G. wähnen.

í to E. l. i; G. ei: síde *side,* G. seite.

eo to E. a, o, u, e; G. e, ie: deorc *dark,* sweord *sword,* G. schwert; ceorl *churl,* G. kerl; feoll *fell,* G. fiel.

ó to E. oo; G. l. u: flór *floor,* G. flur.

eó, eów to E. l. e; G. l. ie, eu: deóp *deep,* G. tief; deór *dear,* G. theuer; cneów *knee,* G. knie.

ú to E. ou, ow, oo; G. l. au, u: mús *mouse,* G. maus; cú *cow,* G. kuh; rúm *room, space,* G. raum.

([9]) S. *bane.*   ([10]) S. *mair.*   ([11]) S. *maist.*

ý to E. l. i, e; G. l. eu, au, ö: fýr *fire*, G. feuer;
brýd *bride*, G. braut: hýran *to hear*, G. hören.

c (before a soft vowel) to E. and G. ch, k: cyle *chill*,
G. kühle; stician *to stick*, G. stechen.

cc to E. tch, ck; G. ck: streccan *to stretch*, G.
strecken; liccian *to lick*, G. lecken.

sc to E. sh, sk; G. sch: scyld *shield*, G. schild; disc
dish, *table*, G. tisch; tusc *tusk*.

g (before a soft vowel sometimes) to E. y, G. j: gear
year, G. jahr; girstan-dœg *yester-day*.

r and s are often transposed: forst *frost*, G. frost:
bridd (*young*) *bird*; flacse *flask*, G. flasche.

CHAPTER II.

I.—*Nouns. Gender.*

The genders, as in Greek, Latin, German, &c. are
three, viz. neuter, masculine, feminine; the first two,
as in those tongues, closely resembling each other, the
last differing widely from both. A. S. nouns in general
agree in gender with the corresponding German; as,

Neuter: { wíf   G. weib *woman, wife.*
         { cild   G. kind *child.*
Masculine: mona   G. mond *moon.*
Feminine: sunne G. sonne *sun.*
The chief exceptions are:—

  Neut. eár   G. ähre   (f.) *ear of corn.*
  — fæsten   G. feste   (f.) *fastness.*
  — fyðer   G. feder (f.) *feather, wing.*

Neut.	mód	G. muth	(m.)	*mind, mood.*
—	twig	G. zweig	(m.)	*twig.*
—	wǽpen	G. waffe	(f.)	*weapon.*
—	wésten	G. wüste	(f.)	*waste, desert.*
—	wín([1])	G. wein	(m.)	*wine.*
Masc.	cræft	G. kraft	(f.)	*power, craft, art.*
—	ende	G. endə	(n.)	*end.*
—	feld	G. feld	(n.)	*field.*
—	here	G. heer	(n.)	*army.*
—	lust	G. lust	(f.)	*lust, pleasure.*
—	mere([2])	G. meer	(n.)	*mere, lake, sea.*
Fem.	bóc	G. buch	(n.)	*book.*
—	hǽlu([3])	G. heil	(m.)	*health, salvation.*
—	heorte([4])	G. herz	(n.)	*heart.*
—	ge-sýhð	G. ge-sicht	(n.)	*sight.*
—	turf	G. torf	(n.)	*turf.*
—	wiht	G. wicht	(m.)	*wight, being.*

Moreover, all A. S. nouns ending in -dóm, -hád, and -scipe are masculine, while G. nouns in -thum are some neuter, some masculine, in -heit and -schaft feminine; A. S. in -nes (-nys, -nis) feminine, G. in -niss some neuter, some feminine.

Some words are of more than one gender; thus flód([5]) *flood* is neut. (II. 1.) and masc. (II. 2.); sǽ *sea* masc. (II. 2.) and fem. (I. 3.); bend *band, bond* masc. (II. 2.) and fem. (II. 3.); lác *gift, office*, &c. all three (II. 1. 2. 3.), but oftenest neuter.

([1]) Οἶν-ος masc. L. vin-um, neut. ([2]) L. mare, neut.
([3]) L. sal-us, fem. ([4]) Καρδ-ια fem. L. cor, neut.
([5]) G. *fluth* fem.; *see* masc. and fem.; *band* neut. and masc.

FURTHER RULES FOR GENDER.

I. Nouns ending in -tl, -ed, -incle, and diminutives in -en; likewise all having the nominative and accusative alike in both numbers are neuter.

II. Nouns in -a, -m, -ls, -að, -oð, -e (from verbs) and -ling; likewise all forming the genitive singular in -a, or the nominative plural in -as are masculine.

III. Nouns in -æð, -uð, -ð (after a consonant) -eo, -u (of quality from adjectives) -e (from adjectives) -ung, and -leást are feminine.

IV. The gender of compound words depends on that of the last part; thus wíf-man *woman* is masculine.([1])

II.—*Declension.*

Nouns are divided into two Orders, the Simple and the Complex;([2]) the former having one Declension of three Classes for the three Genders, the latter two Declensions of three Classes each([3]).

The Simple Order, answering to the Greek and Latin pure nouns, contains those ending in an essential vowel; viz. -e in the neuter, -a in the masculine, and -e in the feminine. The Complex Order, answering to the Gr. and L. impure nouns, comprises all ending in a consonant, together with some in an unessential -e or -u.

([1]) By the same rule G. frauen-zimmer *female* is neut.; manns-person *man* fem.

([2]) In Grimm's system Simple Nouns are called weak; Complex, strong.

([3]) For the grounds of this division, see Rask's Grammar, pp. 26—30.

Table of the Inflection of Nouns.

Simple Order.

Declension I.

	I. Neut.	II. Masc.	III. Fem.
		Singular.	
Nom.	-e	-a	-e
Accus.(⁴)	-e	-an	-an
Abl. & Dat.	-an	-an	-an
Gen.	-an	-an	-an

Plural.

Nom. & Acc.	-an
Abl. & Dat.	-um
Gen.	-ena

Complex Order.

	Declension II.			Declension III.		
	I. Neut.	II. Masc.	III. Fem.	I. Neut.	II. Masc.	III. Fem.
		Singular.			Singular.	
Nom.	—	—(-e)	—	—(-e)	-u	-u
Accus.	—	—(-e)	-e	—(-e)	-u	-e
A. & D.	-e	-e	-e	-e	-a	-e
Gen.	-es	-es	-e	-es	-a	-e
		Plural.			Plural.	
N. & A.	—	-as	-a	-u	-a	-a
A. & D.	-um	-um	-um	-um	-um	-um
Gen.	-a	-a	-a(-ena)	-a	-a	-a(-ena)

(⁴) On this arrangement see Rask, Preface p. 54.

RULES FOR DECLENSION.

I. All Nouns have the nominative and accusative alike in the plural.

II. All Nouns form the ablative and dative plural in -um, often changed to -on, and sometimes again to -an.

III. The ablative and dative are always alike in each number.

IV. Neuters, as in Greek, Latin, and German, have the nominative and accusative alike in each number.

V. Feminines vary the nominative and accusative singular; but form the ablative, dative, and genitive singular alike.

VI. The Simple Order forms its genitive plural in -ena, the Complex in -a. (¹)

III.—*Simple Order, or Declension I.*

The First Declension contains a few neuters ending in -e, all masculines in -a, and all feminines in -e; the nominative plural is formed in -an (²). The three Classes are so much alike that they may be shown at one view.

(¹) Participial nouns form it in -ra (see II. 2.) like indefinite adjectives. Complex feminines (II. 3. and III. 3.) sometimes have a Simple gen. plural.

(²) G. nouns forming their plur. in -en (-n) are Simple, all others Complex.

Examples—eáge *eye*, steorra *star*, tunge *tongue*.

	Class I.	Class II.	Class III.
		Singular.	
	Neuter.	Masculine.	Feminine.
Nom.	eág-e	steorr-a	tung-e
Accus.	eág-e	steorr-an	tung-an
Abl. & Dat.	eág-an	steorr-an	tung-an
Gen.	eág-an	steorr-an	tung-an
		Plural.	
N. & Acc.	eág-an	steorr-an	tung-an
Abl. & Dat.	eág-um	steorr-um	tung-um
Gen.	eág-ena	steorr-ena	tung-ena.

In like manner are declined eáre *ear*, clíwe *clew*; hearra *lord*, guma *man*, wyrhta *wright, workman*, tíma *time*, draca *dragon*, hlísa *fame*; hlæfdige *lady*, cirice (circe) *church*, wuce *week*, eorðe *earth*, wíse *wise*, way([2]) &c. Also some contracted nouns; as, freá *lord* (masc.) tá *toe*, beó([3]) *bee* (fem.), making freán &c. plural tán, táum, taena; beón, beóna &c. Æ' *law*, sǽ *sea*([4]), and eá *river* (likewise fem.) are indeclinable, except sometimes gen. eás([5]), nom. plural eán.

([2]) Manna *man* and heofone *heaven* are much less common than man III. 2. and heofon II. 2.
([3]) G. zehe, biene, not contracted.
([4]) Sǽ is also declinable, as II. 2.
([5]) All A. S. nouns originally formed the genitive in -s; see p. 70, n. 4.

IV.—*Complex Order. Declension II.*

Class I.

The Second Declension, first Class, contains many neuters ending in one or more consonants.

Examples—leáf *leaf,* word *word.*

SINGULAR.

Nom. & Acc.	leáf	word
Abl. & Dat.	leáf-e	word-e
Gen.	leáf-es	word-es

PLURAL.

Nom. & Acc.	leáf	word
Abl. & Dat.	leáf-um	word-um
Gen.	leáf-a	word-a.

Thus are declined eár *ear of corn,* hús *house,* deór ([1]) *beast,* ge-hát *promise,* hors *horse,* spel *story, spell,* wíf *woman, wife,* bearn *child, bairn,* lamb *lamb &c.;* feoh ([2]) *fee, money,* cattle makes feo, feos.

V.—Class II.

The Second Declension, second Class, comprises all regular masculines ending in a consonant, all complex ones in -e, and a few in -u (-o); the plural is formed in -as; some monosyllables change æ to a in the plural.

([1]) Hence *deer*—" Rats and mice, and such small *deer.*"
([2]) Comp. L. pec-us, pec-unia; our *fee* is *money* only, G. vieh *cattle* only.

Examples—dǽl *part, deal*, ende *end,* dæg *day.*

Singular.

N. & A.	dǽl	end-e	dæg
A. & D.	dǽl-e	end-e	dæg
Gen.	dǽl-es	end-es	dæg-es

Plural.

N. & A.	dǽl-as	end-as	dag-as
A. & D.	dǽl-um	end-um	dag-um
Gen.	dǽl-a	end-a	dag-a.

Thus also cyning (cing) *king,* smið *smith,* stán *stone,* weg *way,* freo-dóm *freedom,* munuc-hád *monkhood;* mete *meat,* rǽdere *reader,* weorðscipe *worship;* stæf([2]) *staff, letter,* mæg *kinsman,* &c. Participial nouns in -end usually have the nominative and accusative sing. and plur. alike, and make -ra in the gen. plural. Freónd *friend,* and feónd *foe, fiend* have plur. frýnd, fýnd, freónd, feónd, or freóndas &c. Dissyllables in -el (-ol), -en (-on), and -er (-or) are contracted in the oblique cases and plural; thus engel *angel,* dryhten *lord,* ealdor *prince,* make engle, engles, englas &c. dryhtne &c. Heofen (-on) *heaven* has abl. and dat. heofene, heofone, or heofne and so on. Monað (monð) *month* forms monðe &c. Winter *winter* has abl. and dat. wintra, nom. pl. wintras, or winter. Feld *field,* ford *ford,* and sumer (-or) *summer* make abl. and dat. felda, forda, sumera.

([2]) Comp. G. stab, stäbe; &c. G. buch-stab is *letter.*

Fæder *father* is seldom varied in the singular, and never contracted. Nouns in -h, and -u (-o), change them to g and w; as, beáh *ring*, beáge, beáges &c.; bealu *bale, injury*, bealwe, and the like: a few drop the -h; as, feorh *life*, feore &c. Those in -sc often take x (cs) in the plural; as, fisc *fish*, fixas &c.; sometimes throughout; fix, fixe &c.

VI.—Class III.

The Second Declension, third Class, contains all regular feminines ending in a consonant; the plural is formed in -a.

Examples—stefen (stefn) *voice*, spraéc *speech*.

	Singular.	
Nom.	stefen	spraéc
Acc.	stefn-e	spraéc-e
A. & D.	stefn-e	spraéc-e
Gen.	stefn-e	spraéc-e
	Plural.	
N. & A.	stefn-a	spraéc-a
A. & D.	stefn-um	spraéc-um
Gen.	stefn-a(-ena)	spraéc-a(-ena).

Thus are declined sáwel *soul*, wylen *female slave*, frófer *comfort*, ge-samnung *assembly*, écnys *eternity*, lág *law*, stów *place*, þeód *people*, lár *lore*, myrð *mirth*, bén *prayer*, &c. Dissyllables in -el (-ol), -en, -er (-or), are contracted in the oblique cases, and often in all; as, sáwl, wyln, frófr. A single final consonant after a short vowel is doubled; as syn *sin,* accus. &c. synne. The gen. plur. is sometimes in -ena. Nouns in -ung sometimes form the abl. and dat. in -a. Hand *hand,* makes accus. hand, abl. and dat. handa. Miht *might,* tíd *time, tide,* woruld *world,* have the accus. like the nom.; woruld sometimes makes gen. worldes. (¹) Niht *night,* and wiht *wight* remain unchanged in the accus. singular, and nom. plural.

VII.—*Declension III.*

Class I.

The Third Declension, first Class, contains all complex neuters in -e, all in -u, all neuter dissyllables in er (-or), -el (-ol), and -en, some in ed (-od), and many monosyllables in a consonant. The plural is in -u (-o), often changed to -a; some monosyllables change æ, and a few ea, into a in the plural.

Examples—treów *tree,* ríce *realm,* fæt *vat, vessel.*

	Singular.		
N. & A.	treów	ríc-e	fæt
A. & D.	treów-e	ríc-e	fæt-e
Gen.	treów-es	ríc-es	fæt-es
	Plural.		
N. & A.	treów-u	ríc-u	fat-u
A. & D.	treów-um	ríc-um	fat-um
Gen.	treów-a	ríc-a	fat-a.

(¹) See page 13, n. 5 above.

So likewise scip *ship*, lim *limb*, deófol(¹) *devil*, wæter *water*, ge-writ *writing, writ*; wíte *punishment*, e-mǽre *boundary*, spere *spear*, melu *meal, flour*; æð *bath*, glæs (²) *glass*, geat *gate*, &c.

Dissyllables are mostly contracted; thus, heáfod *head*, tácen *token*, wunder *wonder*, make heáfde, heáfdes &c. tácne, wundre &c.; nýten *beast, neat*, weofod *altar*, &c. are usually not. Those in -en sometimes double the n in the oblique cases; as, wésten *desert*, wéstenne &c. Cild *child*, cealf *calf*, and æg *egg*, form their plural cildru (-a) (³), cealfru, ægru; the first however often has cild or cilde. Þýstru *darkness*, lendenu *loins*, &c. have no singular. Nouns in -u take w, and are usually contracted, forming the plural in -a; as, searu *array, ambush*, searwe, searwes; plur. searwa &c.

VIII.—Class II.

The Third Declension, second Class, comprises masculines in -u (-o), forming their plural in -a, some irregulars (masc. and fem.) in -er (-or), changing their vowel in the ablative and dative, and making -u (-o, -a) in the plural, a few (masc.) changing their vowel as above, and in the nominative and accusative plural, &c.

(¹) Deófol is often masculine.
(²) Comp. G. fass, fässer; glas, gläser.
(³) Hence *childr-en*. P. *child-er*; comp. G. kind, kind-er; kalb, kälb-er; ei, ei-er: D. kind, kind-er-en: kalf, kalv-er-en; ei, eij-er-en.

NOUNS—COMPLEX ORDER. 19

Examples—sunu *son*, bróđer *brother*, man *man*.

SINGULAR.

N & A.	sun-u	bróđer	man
A. & D.	sun-a	bréđer	men
Gen.	sun-a	bróđer	mann-e

PLURAL.

N. & A.	sun-a	bróđr-u	men
A. & D.	sun-um	bróđr-um	mann-um
Gen.	sun-a	bróđr-u	mann-a.

So too are declined wudu *wood*, sidu *custom*, medo *mead, metheglin;* móder *mother*, dóhter *daughter*, sweoster *sister:* fót *foot*, and tóđ *tooth*, follow man making fét, téđ. (⁵) Sun-ena is rare.

Leóde (G. leute) *people*, Dene *Danes*, Engle *Angles, Englishmen*, and a few more in -e with no singular, make leódum, leóda, &c.

IX.—CLASS III.

The Third Declension, third Class, contains all feminines ending in -u or -o, also some irregulars which change their vowel, &c. The former sometimes make the genitive plural in -ena.

Examples—denu *vale*, bóc *book*, burh *burgn, town.*

SINGULAR.

Nom.	den-u }	bóc	burh
Acc.	den-e }		
A. & D.	den-e	béc	byrig
Gen.	den-e	béc	burḡ-e

(⁵) Comp. G mann, männer; fuss, füsse; zahn, zähne.

		Plural.	
N. & A.	den-a	béc	byrig
A. & D.	den-um	bóc-um	burg-um
Gen.	den-a (-ena)	bóc-a	burg-a.

Like denu are declined lufu *love,* gifu *gift, grace,* snóru *daughter-in-law,* caru *care,* lagu *water,* &c. Mænigeo (-u) *many, multitude,* yldo *age, eld,* brǽdo *breadth,* and some others in -o are indeclinable, except abl. and dat. plur. mænigum. Duru *door* makes abl. and dat. sing. dura. Collectives in -waru, as burh-waru *town's-folk,* form plur. -ware, gen. -wara or -warena. Mús *mouse,* lús *louse,* cú *cow,* gós *goose,* bróc *breeches,* follow bóc, making plur. mýs *mice,* lýs *lice,* cý *kye,* gés([1]) *geese,* bréc. Cú sometimes has gen. sing. cús,([2]) gen. plur. cúna. Turf *turf,* and furh *furrow,* follow burh, making tyrf, &c.

CHAPTER III.

I.—*Adjectives*

As in German &c. have a Definite and an Indefinite inflection: the former is used when the adjective is preceded by the definite article, by any other demonstrative, or by a possessive pronoun; the latter always else. There are three Declensions, one for the Definite form, agreeing closely with the Simple Order, two for the In-

([1]) Comp. G. buch, bücher; maus, mäuse; laus, läuse; kub, kühe; gans, gänse.

([2]) See page 70, n. 4.

ADJECTIVES.

definite, answering, though not so exactly, to the Complex Order of Nouns.

II.—*Definite Declension.*

Example—(gód *good*) þæt gód-e (³) &c. *the good.*

SINGULAR.

	Neut.	Masc.	Fem.
Nom.	þæt gód-e	se gód-a	seó gód-e
Acc.	þæt gód-e	þone gód-an	þá gód-an
Abl.		þý gód-an	þý gód-an
Dat.		þám gód-an	þǽre gód-an
Gen.		þæs gód-an	þǽre gód-an

PLURAL.

N. & A. þa gód-an
A. & D. þám gód-um
Gen.   þára gód-ena.

This declension is used for all adjectives, participles, and pronouns in general; participles present however take -ra instead of -ena in the genitive plural. Monosyllables commonly change æ to a throughout; as, smæl *small,* þæt smale, se smala, seó smale *the small,* and so on. Adjectives in -h, as heáh *high,* usually change it to g when the case-ending is a vowel, as, þæt heág-e, &c.; otherwise the h is dropt; as, abl. &c. heán. Those in -u (-o), as near-u *narrow,* take w throughout; as, þæt near-we, &c. (⁴)

(³) Comp. Nouns I. 1, 2, 3.   (⁴) Comp Nouns II. 2, 3. III. 1.

III.—*Indefinite Declension I.*

Example—gód(¹) *good.* gut

SINGULAR.

	Neut.	Masc.	Fem.
Nom.	gód	gód	gód
Acc.	gód	gód-ne	gód-e
Abl.	gód-e		gód-e
Dat.	gód-um		gód-re
Gen.	gód-es		gód-re

PLURAL.

	Neut.	Masc. & Fem.
N. & A.	gód(-u)	gód-e
A. & D.	gód-um	
Gen.	gód-ra.	

Thus are declined adjectives ending in -e, -el (-ol), -isc, and -wís; likewise most monosyllables, all participles present, participles past of the Simple Order, superlatives and pronouns; as, wyrð-e *worth, worthy,* dýg-el *dark,* sprec-ol *talkative,* menn-isc *human,* ge-wís *sure,* sóð *true, sooth,* leóht *light,* heard *hard,* seóc *sick,* wrec *wretched,* fæst *fast,* &c.

Those in -e drop it when a syllable of inflection is added; wyrð-ne, wyrð-um, wyrð-re, &c.

Adjectives in -h and -u follow the rules given above; accus. masc. heá-nne, nearo-ne; abl. &c. fem. heá-re, near-we or near-e; gen. plur. heá-ra, near-wa or near-a.

(¹) Comp. Nouns II. 1, 2.

IV.—*Indefinite Declension II.*

Example—smæl(²) *small*

Singular.

	Neut.	Masc.	Fem.
Nom.	smæl	smæl	smal-u
Acc.	smæl	smæl-ne	smal-e
Abl.		smal-e	smale
Dat.		smal-um	smæl-re
Gen.		smal-es	smæl-re

Plural.

	Neut.	Masc. & Fem.
N. & A.	smal-u	smal-e
A. & D.		smal-um
Gen.		smæl-ra.

Thus are declined monosyllables with æ (except fæst) &c., most adjectives with derived endings, and participles past of the Complex Order; some of both the latter, however, follow Declension I. As, læt *late, slow,* swær *heavy,* glæd *glad,* bær *bare,* swǽs *sweet, dear,* til *good,* eád-ig *blessed, prosperous,* fær-lic *sudden, dangerous,* ge-sib-sum *peaceable,* mæg-er *meagre,* hlutt-or *clear,* fæg-en *glad, fain.* Some dissyllables are contracted in certain forms, as, hál-ig *holy,* hál-ge, hál-ges, &c., but gen. plur. hál-igra and the like.

(¹) Comp. Nouns III. 1, 3.

V.—*Comparison.*

The Comparative and Superlative Degrees are regularly formed by adding -or and -ost (¹), (E. and G. *-er* and *-est*), to the indefinite form; as, leóf, leóf-or, leóf-ost *dear, dear-er, dear-est* (G. lieb, lieb-er, lieb-est): æ usually becomes a; as, smæl, smal-or, smal-ost, *small, small-er, small-est.* (G. schmal, schmäl-er, schmäl-est.) The ending -or is however only adverbial; as an adjective the Comparative is formed in -re, -ra, -re, whether used definitely or indefinitely; as, (þæt) leóf-re, (se) leóf-ra, (seó) leóf-re (*the*) *dearer;* (G. das &c. lieb-re) (þæt) smæl-re &c. (*the*) *smaller;* (G. das &c. schmäl-re). The Superlative has both the definite and indefinite inflections, the former in -ost, or -est, (also the adverbial form), the latter in -oste, -osta, -oste, or -este &c.; as, leóf-ost *dearest,* þæt leóf-oste, or leóf-este &c. *the dearest;* (G. das &c. lieb-ste.)

Table of Comparison.

Positive.	Comparative.	Superlative.
	Adjective.	
heard		heard-ost
hard	(þæt) heard-re	hard-est
þæt heard-e	(*the*) hard-er	þæt heard-oste
the hard		*the hard-est*
	Adverb.	
heard-e	heard-or	heard-ost
hard-ly	*hard-li-er*	*hard-li-est.*

(¹) Comp. the L. comparative -ior; Gr. superlative ιορ-ος, &c.

VI.—*Irregular Comparison.*

The following adjectives are irregularly compared; the change of a into e; æ into a; eá into ý, or é; ea, eo, u, into y, answers to that of the German a into ä, o into ö, u into ü: in English but few traces of this remain. The forms in -me ([2]) (-ma, -me) are old superlatives, afterwards used as positives, and then again compared. The words between brackets are adverbs, peculiarly formed.

Positive.	Comparative.	Superlative.
lang ([3])	lengre (léng)	lengest —
long	*longer*	*longest*
strang	strengre (strangor)	strengest
strong	*stronger*	*strongest*
hræd (hraðe)	hrædre (hraðor)	hraðost
quick, rath	*quicker (rather)*	*quickest*
eald	yldre	yldest
old	*elder*	*eldest*
neáh	nearre (near, nyr)	nyhst, nehst, next
nigh	*nigher*	*nighest, next*
heáh	hýrre	hýhst, héhst
high	*higher*	*highest*
eáð	eáðre (éðre, éð)	eáðost
easy	*easier*	*easiest*
feor	fyrre (fyr)	fyrrest
far	*further*	*furthest*
geong	gyngre	gyngest
young	*younger*	*youngest*

([2]) Comp. L. superlatives in -mum (-mus, -ma).

([3]) Comp. G. lang, länger, längst; alt, älter, ältest; nahe, näher, nächst; hoch, höher, höchst; jung, jünger, jüngst; fort, fürter; sanft, sänfter, sänftest; eher, erst; gut, wohl, besser, best; mehr, meist, &c.

Positive.	Comparative.	Superlative.
sceort	scyrtre	scyrtest
short	*shorter*	*shortest*
(forð, furð)	furðre (furðor)	
(*forth*)	*further*	
sóft	séftre (séft)	séftest
soft	*softer*	*softest*
ǽr (¹)	ǽrre (ǽrer, -or)	ǽrest (-ost)
early (*ere*)	*carlier, sooner*	(*erst*) *first*
gód (wel)	betere (bet)	betest, betst
good (*well*)	*better*	*best*
yfel	wyrse (wyrs)	wyrrest, wyrst
evil	*worse*	*worst*
micel	máre (má)(²)	mǽst
great, mickle	*greater, more*	*greatest, most*
lytel (lyt)	læsse (læs)	læst
little	*less*	*least*
forme (fore)		fyrmest, fyrst
former, fore		*foremost, first*
læt, læteme (late)	lætre (lator)	latost, lætemest
late, slow	*later, latter*	*latest, last*
síð, síðeme	síðre (síðor)	síðost, síðemest
late, (*since*)		
norðeme, (norð)(³)	(norðor)	norðemest
northern, north		*northmost*
úfeme (úp)	úfere (úfor)	ýfemest
high (*up*)	*upper*	*upmost*
æfteme (æfter)	æftre	æftemest
aft, after	*after*	*aftmost*

(¹) Hence O. *or*; " or ever.

(²) For in á r, to which we have returned ı *more*; O. was *mo*

(³) Some of these are often formed in -weard; as, n röe-weard *northern, north-ward*, úfe-weard (úp-we -ward.

Positive.	Comparative.	Superlative.
hindeme	hindere	hindemest
hind	*hinder*	*hindmost*
inneme (inn)	innere (innor)	innemest
inner (in)	*inner*	*inmost*
úteme (út)	útre (útor)	ýtemest
outer (out)	*outer, utter*	*outmost, utmost*
midd, midme		midmest
mid		*midmost*
niđeme(niđer)	niđre (niđror)	niđemest
low (down)	*nether*	*nethmost.*

CHAPTER IV.

I.—*Pronouns—Personal.*

THE personal Pronouns are ic *I,* þú *thou,* hit, he, heó *it, he, she.* The two first are the only A. S. words with a dual number.

SINGULAR.

	N.	ic (⁴)		þú (⁵)
	A.	me		þe
	A.&D.	me		þe
	G.	mín		þín

	DUAL.	PLURAL.	DUAL.	PLURAL.
N.	wit (⁶)	we	git	ge
A.	unc	ús	inc	eów
A.&D.	unc	ús	inc	eów
G.	uncer	úre	incer	eówer

(⁴) Comp. *ἐγ-ω, με,* &c. L. eg-o, me ; G. ich, mir, wir, (D. wij) uns, unser.

(⁵) Comp. (Dor.) *τυ, τε*; L. tu, te ; G. du, dir, euch, &c. D. gij, &c.

(⁶) Remark a peculiar construction with the dual:—wit Scilling *wæ twn,* viz. *I and Scilling* ; healf þæs cinges, healf uncer Brentinges, *half the king's, half mine and Brenting's.*

	Sɪɴɢᴜʟᴀʀ.	
Neut.	Masc.	Fem.
N. hit (¹)	he	heó
A. hit	hine	hí
A. & D. him		hire
G. his		hire

Plural.

N. & A. hí
A. & D. him
G. hira

Meh, mec (L. mihi, G. mich) and þeh, þec (G. dich) sometimes occur for me and þe: likewise the poetical úsih, úsic, and eówih, eówic for ús and eów; and uncit and incit, for unc and inc.

There being, as in English, no reflective pronoun, the personals are used instead; as, ic me reste *I rest me (myself);* þa þeówas wyrmdon híg, *the servants were warming them (-selves).* Sylf *self, same,* declined as an adjective both definitely and indefinitely (I.), and agreeing with the pronoun or noun, gives a strong reflective sense; as, ic sylf or sylfa *I myself;* fram me sylfum *of myself;* þú sylf *thou thyself;* we sylfe *we ourselves,* &c.; seó sylfe· tíd *the same time.*(²) Sometimes the pronoun stands in the dative before sylf; as, (ic) me sylf *I myself;* him-sylf *he himself.* (³)

(¹) Comp. ὁ, ἡ, ὅν, οἱ, αἱ; L. id, is, ea, eum, ejus, ii; G. es, ihn, ihm, ihr; D. het, hij, &c.

(²) Comp. G. ich selber, wir selben, die selbe zeit, &c.

(³) Like F. *moi-même, lui-même;* hence seemingly *my-self, thy-self* &c.: *self* is properly no more a noun than αὐτος, L. ipse, or F. même.

II.—*Possessives.*

The Possessive Pronouns are formed, as in German, from the genitives of the two first persons; as, mín (G. mein) *mine, my;* þín (G. dein) *thine, thy;* uncer, úre (G. unser) *our;* incer, eówer (G. euer) *your:* like other Pronouns in general, they are declined as indefinite adjectives I. Those in -er are usually contracted; as uncre, eówres, and the like. U're forms úrum, úres, &c; but remains unchanged in the whole feminine singular. The poetical úser (ússer) for úre is thus declined:—

	Neut.	Masc.	Fem.
		Singular.	
N.	úser	úser	úser
A.	úser	úserne	ússe
A. & D.	ússum		ússe
G.	ússes		ússe
		Plural.	
N. & A.	ússe, úser		
A. & D.	ússum		
G.	ússa		

The genitive of the third person is used unchanged; his, *its, his,* hire *her,* hira *their.* To make these reflective, the genitive of sylf agreeing with the pronoun, or the indefinite adjective ágen *own,* agreeing with the noun, must be used; as, þín sylfes bearn *thine own son;* tó his ágenre þearfe *to his own need.* Sín occurs in poetry as a possessive of the third person; not however like G. sein, for L. ejus, but for L. suus only.

III.—*Demonstratives.*

The Demonstrative Pronouns are þæt, se, seó *that*, likewise the relative *which, who, that,* and the article *the;* (1) and þis, þes, þeós *this.*

	Neut.	Masc.	Fem.		Neut.	Masc.	Fem.
N.	þæt(2)	se	seó		þis(3)	þes	þeós
A.	þæt	þone	þá		þis	þisne	þás
Abl.	þý		þý		þise		þisse
D.	þám		þǽre		þisum		þisse
G.	þæs		þǽre		þises		þisse
N. & A.	þa				þás		
A. & D.	þám				þisum		
G.	þára				þissa		

þæne, þǽm, þáre, þǽra, are sometimes used for þone, þám, þǽre, þára; likewise þǽs for þás; the s in þise, &c. is often doubled; þissere and þissera occur also for þisse and þissa. The indeclinable þe is used for all cases of þæt, se, seó, as a relative; combined with it it forms þæt-te (4) *that which*, se-þe *he that*, seó-þe *she that*. þæt, se, seó is sometimes repeated in a sentence, standing first as a demonstrative, and next as a relative; but þe commonly stands as

---

(1) Comp. the threefold use of G. das, der, die.

(2) Comp. τό, ὁ, ἡ, τον, τα, τοι, ται; G. das, den, dem, der, des, &c. D. dat, &c. From seó comes *she* (G. sie); from þa *they*, þǽm *them*, þǽra *their*.

(3) Comp. G. dies, &c.; þás and þǽs have become *those* and *these.*

(4) Þætte is also *that* (conjunction) G. dass.

relative in the second place; as, þæt micle ge-teld þe Moises worhte, *the great tent that Moses made.*

Þe is sometimes used along with hit, &c. as a relative; as, þe þurh hine *through whom.*

Swá is sometimes used (like G. so) as an indeclinable relative.

Ylc *same,* follows the indefinite declension.

Swylc *such,* is often repeated, standing in the second place adverbially; as, Ælc þing on-gitan swylc swylce hit is *to understand each thing so as it is.*

IV.—*Interrogatives.*

The Interrogative Pronouns are hwæt, hwá? *what? who?* hwylc? *which?* hwæðer *whether? which?* The first has no plural, and is thus declined:

	Neuter.	Masc. & Fem.
Nom.	hwæt	hwá
Acc.	hwæt	hwone (hwæne)
	Abl.	hwý
	Dat.	hwám (hwǽm)
	Gen.	hwæs (⁵)

It answers to L. quis not qui, and is never used as a relative: with a neuter adjective it governs the genitive; as, hwæt yfeles? *what evil?* it is also (like G. et-was, was) used not interrogatively, for *somewhat, a little;* as, hwæt lytles *some little.*

(⁵) From hwúm and hwæs, are *whom* and *whose.*

V.—*Indefinites.*

The Indefinite pronouns are swá-hwæt(-swá) *what-so-ever*, swá-hwá (-swá) *who-so-ever*, swá-hwylc (-swá) *which-so-ever*, ǽg-hwæt (ge-hwæt), ǽg-hwylc, &c. *whatsoever, &c.* which follow the declension of the chief word in the compound. Others are ælc, *each, every one*, eall *all*, ǽnig *any*, nǽnig *none whatever*, án-lipig (ǽn-lipig) *single, alone*, &c. Ge-noh *enough* is sometimes indeclinable. A'n *one, a*, and sum *some, a, a certain*, serve for the indefinite article, which is however often not expressed: sum placed after a genitive cardinal number implies one above it; as, fíf-tyna sum *one of sixteen, one with fifteen others*. Manig (mænig) *many* sometimes has nom. and accus. plur. manega. Fela *much, many* is indeclinable: feáwa (feá) *few*, sometimes has abl. and dat. plur. feáwum, gen. feára; both often govern a genitive plural; as, mádma fela *many treasures;* feá worda. *few words.* Man (*man*) is used (like G. man, and F. on) (¹) indefinitely for *one, they;* as, Me man sægde *they told me* (G. man sagte mir). From wiht (wuht) *creature, being*, (*wight, whit*) are formed á-wiht (á-wuht) contracted to áwht, áht *anything, ought;* and nán-wiht (-wuht) náwht, náht(²) *nothing, nought.* Other indefinite Pronouns are óðer (-or) *other, second* (L. alius, and alter for secundus), áwðer, áðer *one of two* (L. alter duorum), náwðer (náðor), *neither of two* (L. neuter), ǽgðer

(¹) Formerly hom, from L. homo.
(²) Hence *not*, like G. nicht from ne-wicht.

PRONOUNS. 33

either, each of two. O'ðer forms its oblique cases fem. sing. óðre; it sometimes follows indefinite. Decl. II.

VI.—Comparative Table of Cardinal Numbers.

Greek.	Latin.	Dutch.	A. S.	English.	German.
ἑν	un-um	een	án	one	ein
δυο	duo	twee	twá	two	zwei
τρια	tria	drie	þreo	three	drei
κεττορε (³)	quatuor	vier	feower	four	vier
πεντε	quinque	vijf	fíf	five	fünf
ἑξ	sex	zes	six	six	sechs
ἑπτα	septem	zeven	seofon	seven	sieben
ὀκτω	octo	acht	eahta	eight	acht
ἐννεα	novem	negen	nigon	nine	neun
δεκα	decem	tien	tyn	ten	zehn

Dutch.	A. S.	English.	German.
elf	endlufon	eleven	eilf
twaalf	twelf	twelve	zwölf
der-tien	þreo-ttyne	thir-teen	drei-zehn
veertien	feower-tyne	fourteen	vierzehn
vijftien	fíf-tyne	fifteen	funfzehn
zestien	six-tyne	sixteen	sechzehn
zeventien	seofon-tyne	seventeen	siebzehn
achtien	eahta-tyne	eighteen	achtzehn
negentien	nigon-tyne	nineteen	neunzehn
twin-tig	twen-tig	twen-ty	zwan-zig
dertig	þry-ttig	thirty	drei-ssig
veertig	feower-tig	forty	vierzig

(³) Æol. for τεσσαρα.

Dutch.	A. S.	English.	German.
vijftig	fíf-tig	fifty	funfzig
zestig	six-tig	sixty	sechzig
zeventig	hund-seofon-tig	seventy	siebzig
tachtig (¹)	hund-eahtatig	eighty	achtzig
negentig	hund-nigontig	ninety	neunzig
honderd	{ hund, hundred, hund-teontig }	hundred	hundert
	hund-endlufontig 110		
	hund-twelftig 120		
duizend	þúsend	thousand	tausend.

A'n, like all other pronouns, follows indef. Decl. I., sometimes making accus. masc. ænne; thus too nán *none*. Used definitely, áne, ána, áne, and standing after its noun, &c., it means *alone*. Twá(²) and þreo are thus declined:—

	Neut.	Masc.	Fem.	Neut.	Masc.	Fem.
N. & A.	twá (tú)	twegen(³)	twá.	þreo	þrý	þreo
A. & D.	twám (twǽm)			þrym		
G.		twegra (twega)		þreora.		

Bá, begen, bá *both*, follows twá; prefixed to twá it forms bá-twá (bú-tú) (⁴) which is indeclinable. The numbers feower to twelf inclusive, when used absolutely, have a nom. in -e, &c.; as, ealle seofone *all seven;* án of þám twelfum *one of the twelve;* án

(¹) The t- is probably a remnant of the prefix hond- retained before the vowel.

(²) S. *twa.* G. zwei, zwo.   (³) *Twain.* G. zween.

(⁴) Hence *both,* G. beide; comp. Italian ambe-due.

þissa fífa *one of these five.* Those above eahta usually govern a genitive. Twentig and the others in -tig make abl. and dat. -tigum, gen. -tigra. Hund prefixed to the tens after sixtig (answering to -κοντ-α, L. -gint-a) is sometimes dropt when hund *hundred* goes before; as, scipa án hund and eahtatig, *of ships one hundred and eighty.* Hund *(hundred)* follows II. 1; hundred and þúsend, III. 1.

Units are placed before tens, as, six and fíftig, *six and fifty.* In numbers above a hundred, the smaller stands last, and the noun is repeated; as, Hundteontig wintra and seofon and feowertig wintra, *a hundred winters and seven and forty winters.*(⁵)

Wintre affixed to numbers forms adjectives denoting age; as, fram twı-wintrum cilde, *from the child of two years.*

VII.—*Ordinal Numbers.*

þæt forme, se forma, seó forme	*first*
þæt, se, seó óđer	*second*
þæt þry-dde, se þry-dda, seó þry-dde (⁶)	*thir-d*
feor-þe, -þa, -þe	*four-th*
fíf-te, -ta, -te	*fifth*
six-te, — —	*sixth*
seofo-þe, -þa, -þe	*seventh*
eahtoþe — —	*eighth*
nigoþe	*ninth*

(⁵) The northern nations reckoned time by winters.
(⁶) Comp. τρι-τος, L. ter-tius, G. dri-tte, vier-te, &c.

teóþe	*tenth*
endlyf-te	*eleventh*
twelfte	*twelfth*
þry-tteóđe	*thir-teenth*
feower-teóđe	*fourteenth*
fíf-teóđe	*fifteenth*
six-teóđe	*sixteenth*
seofon-teóđe	*seventeenth*
eahta-teóđe	*eighteenth*
nigon-teóđe	*nineteenth*
twentig-ođe	*twenti-eth*
þryttigođe	*thirtieth*
feowertigođe	*fortieth*
fíftigođe	*fiftieth*
sixtigođe	*sixtieth*
hund-seofontigođe	*seventieth*
hund-eahtatigođe	*eightieth*
hund-nigontigođe	*ninetieth*
hund-teontigođe	*hundredth*
hund-endlufontigođe	110*th*
hund-twelftigođe	120*th*

Units combined with ordinal tens stand first when cardinals, last when ordinals; as, án and þryttigođe *one and thirtieth;* þý twentigođan dæge and þý feorđan dæge Septembris, *on the twenty and fourth day of September.*

Healf *half* placed after an ordinal number (like G. halb) reduces it by half; as, óđer-healf (lit. *second-half*) *one and a half,* (G. andert-halb) ; þridde-healf (lit. *third-half*) *two and a half* (G. dritte-halb).(¹) A'n, twá, þreo, form ǽn-e *once*, twɪ-wa (tu-wa) *twice*, þry-wa *thrice*; with the other cardinals, and all the ordinals, síð *a time* is used in the ablative for the same purpose; as, feower, fíf, &c. síðum or síðon *four, five, &c. times*; (þý) forman, óðre, þryddan, &c. síðe *the first, second, third, &c. time*.

CHAPTER V.

I.—*Verbs. Conjugation.*

There are two Orders of Verbs, as of Nouns; viz. the Simple and the Complex; (²) the former containing pure or open Verbs answering to the Greek in -αειν, -εειν, and -οειν, and to the Latin in -are, -ēre, and -ire; the latter impure or close Verbs, answering to the Greek regulars, and to the Latin in -ĕre, &c.(³) The Simple Order forms its imperfect by adding -ode (-ede), -de, or -te to the root; the participle past by adding -od (-ed), -d, or -t: in the Complex the imperfect becomes monosyllabic and changes its vowel; the participle past ends in -en.(⁴) The former is divided into three Classes forming one Conjugation; the latter into two Conjugations of three Classes each.

(¹) Comp. ἡμισυ-τριτος, L. sesqui-alter, -tertius.
(²) Simple Verbs are by Grimm termed Weak, Complex Strong.
(³) See Rask's Grammar, pp. 67—70.
(⁴) E. and G. verbs in general follow the A.S., though complex forms have in each not seldom become simple.

II.—*Comparative View of the Chief Tenses.*

Simple Order, or Conjugation I.

Examples—luf-ian *to love,* G. lieb-en; hýr-an *to hear,* G. hör-en; tell-an *to tell, reckon,* G. zühl-en.

	Present.	Imperfect.	Part. past.
Class I.	ic luf-ige *I love* G. ich lieb-e	— luf-ode — *lov-ed* — lieb-te	(ge-)luf-od *lov-ed* ge lieb-t
Class II.	hýr-e *hear* G. hör-e	hýr-de *hear-d* hör-te	(ge-)hýr-ed *hear-d* ge-hör t
Class III	tell-e *tell* G. zähl-e	teal-de *tol d* zähl-te	(ge-)teal-d *tol-d* ge-zähl t.

Complex Order.—Conjugation II.

Examples—brec-an *to break,* G. brech-en; heald-an *to hold,* G. halt-en; drag-an *to draw, drag,* G. trag-en.

	Present.	Imperfect.	Part. past.
Class I.	brec-e *break* G. brech-e	bræc *brake* brach	(ge-)broc-en *brok-en* ge-broch en
Class II.	heald-e *hold* G. halt-e	heóld *held* hielt	(ge-)heald-en *hold-en* ge-halt-en
Class III.	drag e *draw* G. trag-e	dróh *drew* trug	(ge-)drag-en *draw-n* ge-trag-en.

Conjugation III.

Examples—bind-an *to bind*, G. bind-en; drîf-an *to drive*, G. treib-en; clûf-an *to cleave*, G. klieb-en.

	Present.	Imperfect.	Part. past.
Class I.	bind-e *bind* G. bind-e	band *bound* band	(ge-)bund-en *bound-en* ge-bund-en
Class II.	drîf-e *drive* G. treib-e	drâf *drove* trieb	(ge-)drif-en *driv-en* ge-trieb-en
Class III.	clûf-e *cleave* G. klieb-e	cleâf *clave* klob	(ge-)clof-en *clov-en* ge-klob-en.

III.—Simple Order, or Conjugation I.

	Class I.	Class II.	Class III.
	Indicative Mode.		
	Present.		
Sing.	ic luf-ige (¹)	hýr-e	tell-e
	þú luf-ast	hýr-st	tel-st
	he luf-að	hýr-ð	tel-ð
Plur. we, ge, hí	luf-iað	hýr-að	tell-að
	luf-ige	hýr-e	tell-e
	Imperfect.		
Sing.	ic luf-ode	hýr-de	teal-de
	þú luf-odest	hýr-dest	teal-dest
	he luf-ode	hýr-de	teal-de
Pl. we, ge, hí	luf-odon	hýr-don	teal-don

(¹) Comp. *love, lov-est, lov-eth*; G. lieb-e, lieb-est, lieb-et, &c. L. am-o, -as, -at, &c.

SUBJUNCTIVE MODE.
Present.

	Sing. luf-ige	hýr-e	tell-e
	Plur. luf-ion	hýr-on	tell-on

Imperfect.

	Sing. luf-ode	hýr-de	teal-de
	Plur. luf-odon	hýr-don	teal-don

IMPERATIVE MODE.

	Sing. luf-a	hýr	tel-e
Plur.	{ luf-iađ	{ hýr-ađ	{ tell-ađ
	{ luf-ige	{ hýr-e	{ tell-e

INFINITIVE MODE.

Pres.	luf-ian	hýr-an	tell-an
Gerund.	tó luf-igenne	—hýr-enne	—tell-anne
Part. pres.	luf-igende	hýr-ende	tell-ende
P. past	(ge-) luf-od	(ge-) hýr-ed	(ge-) teal-d.

The first form of the present indicative, and of the imperative plural, is used when the pronoun comes first, or is left out; as, we lufiađ *we love,* hýrađ *hear;* the second when the pronoun follows close; as, telle ge *tell ye?* The subjunctive plural sometimes ends in -an or -en; as, lufian, hýrden, and the like. The gerund, which is always preceded by tó, and seems to be a kind of dative of the infinitive, answers to our infinitive present, active and passive, and to the Latin supines, infinitive future, active and passive, &c.; as, Come þú ús tó for-spillanne? *camest thou to destroy us?* L. nos perditum. Hwæđer is éđre tó cweđanne? *whether is easier to say?* L. facilius dictu. Eart þú se-þe tó cumenne eart? *art thou he that is (art) to come?*

L. qui venturus est. Heó býd tó lufigenne (¹) *she is (must be, or ought) to be loved*, L. amanda est. The infinitive of the first Class is often formed in -igan, sometimes in -igean, for -ian, and g is put in or left out in some other forms with little or no change of pronunciation. The Gerund of the third Class sometimes makes -enne for -anne. Ge- may be prefixed to any part of verbs in general, but is oftenest used with the imperfect, and especially with the participle past, though not, as in German, to be considered the sign of the latter.(²)

IV.—Class I.

Like lufian are conjugated:

Present.	Imperfect.	Part. past.	
hatige	hatode	(ge-)hatod	*hate*
losige	losode	losod	*be lost*
clypige	clypode	clypod	*call, clepe*
fullige	fullode	fullod	*baptize*
fúlige	fúlode	fúlod	*rot*
cunnige	cunnode	cunnod	*try*
wacige(³)	wacode	wacod	*watch*
hangige(⁴)	hangode	hangod	*hang*
hýrige	hýrode	hýrod	*hire*
hergige	hergode	hergod	*harry*
macige	macode	macod	*make*
bletsige	bletsode	bletsod	*bless*

(¹) Hence the phrases "house to let," "he is to blame," &c.
(²) Ge- is seldom used before another prefix.
(³) Neut. L. vigilare; act. weccan.
(⁴) Neut. L. pendēre; act. hangan, hón.

E 2

Some verbs of this Class, especially those having e for their vowel, form their imperfect and part. past in -ede and -ed, as well as -ode and od; as, herian *to praise*, seglian *to sail*, ge-fremian *to profit*, which make herede, (ge-)hered, or herode, herod; seglede, and the like: -ode and -od are sometimes changed into -ade and -ad. Swerian *to swear*, borrows some tenses from a complex form, making imperf. swerede or swór swore; imp. subj. swóre; imper. swera or swere; part. past (ge-)sworen *sworn*. Folgian, fyligan, or fylian *to follow*, has imperf. folgode, fyligde, or fylide; imper. folga or fylig.

V.—*Class II.*

The second Class forms its imperfect and participle past in -de and -ed, or in -te and -t, according to its characteristic letter; the hard consonants, viz. t, p, c, x, requiring -te and -t; the soft, viz. d, đ, f, g, w, l, m, n, r, s, taking -de and -ed; as,

Present.	Imperf.	Part. past.	
méte	métte	(ge-)mét	*meet*(*met*)
lette	lette	lett	*let, hinder*
dyppe	dypte	dypt	*dip*(*-t*)
tǽce	tǽhte	tǽht	*teach*(*taught*)
lixe	lixte	lixt	*gleam*(*-ed*)
lǽde	lǽdde	lǽded	*lead*(*led*)
sende	sende	send	*send*
cýđe	cýđde	cýđed	*make known*
ge-lýfe	ge-lýfde	ge-lýfed	*believe*(*-d*)

VERBS—SIMPLE ORDER.

Present.	Imperf.	Part. past.	
wrége	wrégde	wréged	*be-wray(-ed)*
be-lǽwe	be-lǽwde	be-lǽwed	*accuse(-d)*
fylle	fylde	fylled	*fill(-ed)*
týme	týmde	týmed	*teem(-ed)*
wéne	wénde	wéned	*ween(-ed)*
lǽre	lǽrde	lǽred	*teach*
rǽse	rǽsde	rǽsed	*rush(-ed).*

Some verbs in -gan are contracted; as, þreagan, þreán *to vex, reproach,* tweógan, tweón *to doubt:* pres. þreage or þreá, þreást, þreáð; pl. þreagað, þreáð, &c.; tweóge or tweó, tweóst, tweóð, &c.; imperf. þreáde, tweóde; part. past þreád, tweód.

The second and third persons singular sometimes make -est, -eð, especially when many consonants might otherwise meet; as, nemne (*I*) *name,* nemnest, nemneð; imperf. nemde: some have both forms; as, lǽde, lǽtst, lǽt, or lǽdest, lǽdeð; part. past lǽded or lǽd. Verbs with s, d, and t form the third person in -t; as, rǽse, rǽst; sende, sent; méte, mét: those with ð in ð, as cýðe, cýð; imperf. cýðde or cýdde; p. past cýðed or cýd. Verbs in this and the following classes with a double characteristic, drop one letter and take -e in the imperative; as, dyppe, dype, and the like. To this class belong several transitives, derived from intransitives of the Complex Order; as, bærnan *to burn* (act.), from byrnan *to burn* (neut.); drencan (¹) *to drench,* from drincan *to drink;* fyllan *to fell,* from

---

(¹) Comp. G. tränken, fällen, senken, setzen, from trinken, fallen, sinken, sitzen

feallan *to fall;* a-rǽran *to rear,* from a-rísan *to arise;* sencan *to sink* (act.), from sincan *to sink* (neut.); settan *to set,* from sittan *to sit;* ærnan *to let run,* from yrnan *to run.* Lybban *to live,* and hycgan *to think,* borrow some forms from leofian, and hogian: they are thus conjugated:—

Indic. pres. 1. lybbe   Subj. pres. lybbe
            2. leofast   plur. lybbon
            3. leofað   Imperf. leofode
    plur. { lybbað   plur. leofodon
           { lybbe   Imper. leofa
    Imperf. leofode(-st)
      plur. leofodon   plur. { lybbað
                                  { lybbe
    Infin. pres. lybban   Part. pres. lybbende
      Ger. lybbenne   P.past (ge)leofod.

Hæbban or habban([1]) *to have,* has some forms as if from hafian: it is thus conjugated:—

Ind. pres.1. hæbbe (habbe)   Subj.pres. habbe (hæbbe)
         2. hæfst   (hafast)   plur.   habbon
         3. hæfð   (hafað)   Imperf. hæfde
   plur. { habbað(hafiað)   plur. hæfdon
        { hæbbe (habbe)   Imper. hafa
Imperf.   hæfde(-st)
   plur. hæfdon   plur. { habbað
                                  { habbe
Inf. pres.   hæbban(habban) Part. pres. hæbbende
   Ger. habbenne   P.past(ge-)hæfed, hæfd.

The first person present is sometimes in poetry hafu

([1]) Comp. throughout L. hab-ere, G. hab-en.

or hafo. Nabban (for nehabban) *to have not*, has an Indicative, Subjunctive, and Imperative, following habban.

VI.—*Class III.*

The third Class changes e into ea, é into ó, &c. in the imperfect, forming it in -de or -te, and the part. past in -d or -t by the rules given above. The English synonyms commonly change the vowel in like manner, the German sometimes.

Pres.	Imperf.		Part. past.	
stelle	stealde	(ge-)	steald	*leap*
recce	reahte(²)		reaht	*reck (raught)*
sylle	sealde		seald	*sell (sold)*
secge	{ sægde { sæde		sægd sæd	} *say (said)*
lecge	lede		led	*lay (laid)*
bycge	bóhte		bóht	*buy (bought)*
séce	sóhte		sóht	*seek (sought)*
bringe(³)	bróhte		bróht	*bring (brought)*
wyrce	worhte		worht	*work (wrought)*

Secge makes 3 sing. pres. segð or sagað; imper. sege or saga. The impersonal þincan (G. dünken) *to seem*, must not be confounded with þencan (G. denken) *to think*. Þincan makes 3 sing. pres. þincð (G. dünkt) (*me-*)*thinks*; plur. þincað; imperf. þúhte (G. dünkte) (*me-*)*thought*; part. past (ge-)þúht.

(²) Also rehte, &c.; réce, róhte is another form.
(³) Comp. G. bringe, brachte, ge-bracht.

þencan makes imperf. þóhte (G. dachte) *thought*; part. past (ge-)þóht (G. ge-dacht).

A few transitives also from complex intransitives belong to this class; as, a-cwellan *to kill (quell)*, from a-cwelan *to perish (quail)*; lecgan (¹) *to lay*, from licgan *to lie*; weccan *to awaken*, from wacan *to wake*. Willan(²) *to will*, and nyllan(³) *to will not*, are thus conjugated:

	Indicative.		Subjunctive.
Pres.	1. wille	Pres.	{ wille
	2. wilt		{ willon
	3. wile	Imperf.	{ wolde
pl.	{ willað		{ woldon
	{ wille		Infinitive.
Imperf.	wolde (-st)	Pres.	willan
pl.	woldon	P. pres.	willende

Pres.	1. nelle	Pres.	nelle(nylle)
	2. nelt	pl.	nellon(nyllon)
	3. nele(nyle)	Imperf.	{ nolde
pl.	{ nellað (nyllað)		{ noldon
	{ nelle	Imper.	{ nelle
Imperf.	{ nolde(-st)		{ nellað, &c.
	{ noldon	Infin.	nyllan.

VII.—*Complex Order*.

The Complex Order changes the vowel in the imperfect, as in English and German: the imperfect ends

(¹) Comp. G. legen, wecken, from liegen, wachen.
(²) Βουλ-εσθαι, L. vell-e, vol-ui; G. woll-en, will, &c. woll-te.
(³) L. nolle, for ne velle.

with the characteristic, which however if bb becomes f; if g, h: in the second pers. sing. and in the plural h again becomes g.

The Second Conjugation changes certain vowels in the second and third persons sing. present as in German. The part. past sometimes changes its vowel, as in English and German.

Examples—brecan *to break*, healdan *to hold*, dragan *to draw, drag*.

	Class I.	Class II.	Class III.
		Indicative Mode.	
		Present.	
Sing. 1.	brece(*)	healde	drage
2.	bricst	hyltst	drægst
3.	bricð	hylt(healt)	drægð
Plur.	{ brecað { brece	{ healdað { healde	{ dragað { drage
		Imperfect.	
Sing. 1.	bræc	heóld	dróh
2.	bræce	heólde	dróge
3.	bræc	heóld	dróh
Plur.	brǽcon	heóldon	drógon
		Subjunctive Mode.	
		Present.	
Sing.	brece	healde	drage
Plur.	brecon	healdon	dragon
		Imperfect.	
Sing.	brǽce	heólde	dróge
Plur.	brǽcon	heóldon	drógon.

(*) Comp. G. breche, brichst, bricht; halte, hältst, hält; plur. brechen, halten, &c.

	Class I.	Class II.	Class III.
		Imperative Mode.	
Sing.	brec	heald	drag
Plur.	{ brecað / brece	{ healdað / healde	{ dragað / drage
		Infinitive Mode.	
Pres.	brecan	healdan	dragan
Gen.	tó brecanne	—healdanne	—draganne
P.pres.	brecende	healdende	dragende
P.past.	(ge-)brocen	(ge-)healden	(ge-)dragen

VIII.—*Class I.*

In the First Class e becomes in the second and third persons sing. present, i or y; i remains unchanged, as in German. The imperfect is formed in æ, which in the second pers. sing. and the whole plural becomes ǽ; or in ea: in the part. past i sometimes becomes e; e, o, &c.

First pers. pres.	Third pers.	Imperf.	P. past.
{ sprece(¹) / spece	spricð / spicð	spræc / spæc	(ge-)sprecen / specen
speak		*spake*	*spoken*
trede	trit	træd	treden
tread		*trod*	*trodden*
ete	yt	æt	eten
eat		*ate*	*eaten*
lese	list	læs	lesen
lease, gather			

(¹) Comp. G. spreche, sprach; trete, trat, ge-treten, &c. ge-Läre, -bar, -boren; stehle, stahl, ge-stohlen, &c.

VERBS—COMPLEX ORDER. 49

First pers. pres.	Third pers.	Imperf.	P. past.
bidde	bitt	bæd	beden
bid		*bade*	*bidden*
sitte	sitt	sæt	seten
sit		*sate*	*sitten*
licge	lið	læg	legen
lie		*lay*	*lien, lain*
swefe	swefð	swœf	swefen
sleep			
bere	byrð	bær	boren
bear		*bare*	*born*
stele	styld	stœl	stolen
steal		*stole*	*stolen*
for-gite	for-git	for-geat	for-giten
forget		*forgat*	*forgotten*
gife	gifð	geaf	gifen
give		*gave*	*given*

Niman *to take*, makes third pers. pres. nimð; imperf. nam, name, &c. p. past numen. Cuman (cwuman) *to come* makes third pers. cymð; imperf. ᴚom (cwom), come, &c. p. past cumen.

Wesan *to be* is thus conjugated:

INDICATIVE.

Pres. 1. eom(²)   Imperf. 1. wæs
     2. eart   2. wǽre
     3. is (ys)   3. wæs
  plur. synd (syndon)   plur. wǽron

(²) Comp. εἰμ-ί, ἐστ-ί; L. sum, est, sum-us, sunt, sim, er-am, &c.; G. ist, sind, scyd, scy, war, würe, ge-wesen.

SUBJUNCTIVE.

Pres. sý, (síg, seó)   Imperf. wǽre
plur. sýn   plur. wǽron
Imper. wes   Inf. pres. wesan
plur. { wesað   Ger. tó wesanne
      { wese   Part. pres. wesende
       Part. past (ge-)wesen.

With some of these forms the negative ne is thus combined:

Pres. 1. (ic) neom (*I*) *am not*. 3. nis (nys); imperf. næs, &c.; subj. imperf. nǽre, &c.

Cweðan *to say* is thus conjugated:

Indic. pres. cweðe, cwyst, cwyð; imperf. cwæð, cwǽde, cwæð *(quoth)*, pl. cwǽdon; subj. pres. cweðe, imperf. cwǽde; part. past (ge-)cweden: it is otherwise regular.

IX.—*Class II*.

In the Second Class á becomes ǽ; ea, y; eá, ý; ó, é, in the second and third persons: the imperf. has é, or eó (e or eo).

First pers. pres.	Third person.	Imperf.	Part. past.
læte([1]) *let*	læt	let	(ge-)læten
slǽpe *sleep*	slǽpð	slép / slep-t([2])	slǽpen

([1]) Comp. G. lasse, lässt, liess, ge-lassen; heisse, hiess; wachse, wuchs; laufe, lauft, lief, &c.

([2]) *Slept, lept, swept, wept,* are complex forms become simple: *slep, lep,* &c., as also *bet,* are still in P. use.

VERBS—COMPLEX ORDER.

First pers. pres.	Third person.	Imperf.	Part. past.
háte *command*	hǽt	{ héht(³) / hét }	háten
hange, hó *hang*	héhð	heng *hung*	hangen
wealde *govern, wield*	wylt	weóld	wealden
fealle *fall*	fylð (fealð)	feoll *fell*	feallen *fallen*
weaxe *wax, grow*	wyxð	weox	weaxen *waxen*
beáte *beat*	beáteð	beót (bet)	beáten *beaten*
blóte *sacrifice*	blét	bleót	blóten
hleápe *leap*	hlýpð	hleóp *lep-t*	hleápen
swápe *sweep*	swǽpð (swápeð)	sweóp *swep-t*	swápen
wépe *weep*	wépð	weóp *wep-t*	wépen
cnáwe *know*	cnǽwð	cneów *knew*	cnáwen *known*
heáwe *hew*	heáweð	heów	heówen *hewn*
grówe *grow*	gréwð	greów *grew*	grówen *grown*

(³) Héht is a relic of the reduplication in use in Gothic as in Greek, and of which Latin retains several instances; leólc from lúcan *to play* (O. *lake*), is of like nature.

The imperfects without an accent are of doubtful quantity.

Hátan when meaning *to be called*, has the simple imperfect hátte, but part. past (ge-)háten.

Hó makes pres. plur. hóð, hó; imper. hóh; infin. hangan or hón, and is followed by fangan, fón *to take*.

Cneów and the like often become cnéw &c.

Gangan, gán(¹) *to go*, dón *to do*, and búan *to inhabit, cultivate* (G. bauen, L. colere) are thus conjugated:

INDICATIVE.

Pres. 1. gange, gá(²)	dó	búe
2. gæst	dést	býst
3. gæð	déð	býð
pl. { gáð / gá	{ dóð / dó	
Imperf. geóng, eóde	dyde	búde

SUBJUNCTIVE.

Sing. gá	dó	bú
Pl. gán	dón	bún

IMPERATIVE.

Sing. gang, gá	dó	
Pl { gáð / gá	{ dóð / dó	

(¹) S. and P. gang, gae. The contracted forms are most used; 'eóde is the common imperfect, geong the poetical.

(²) Comp. G. gehe, gleng, ue, that, ge-than.

INFINITIVE.

Pres.   gangan, gán   dón   búan
Ger.   tó dónne
P. pres. gangende   dónde   búende
P. past gangen, gán   (ge-)dón   (ge-)bún.

X.—*Class III.*

In the Third Class, a becomes æ; eá, ý, &c. in the second and third persons: the imperfect has ó.

First pers. pres.	Third person.	Imperf.	Part. past.
scace	scæcð	scóc (sceóc)	(ge-)scacen
shake		*shook*	*shaken*
fare([3])	færð	fór	faren
fare, go			
hlihhe	hlihð	hlóh	hlogen
laugh			
sleá	slýhð	slóh	slegen
slay		*slew*	*slain*
hlade	hlæt	hlód	hladen
lade			*laden*
grafe	græfð	gróf	grafen
grave, dig			*graven*
hebbe	hefð	hóf	hafen
heave		*hove*	
scyppe	scypð	scóp (sceóp)	sceapen
shape, create			*shapen*
wacse	wæxð	wócs	wæscen
wash			*washen*

([3]) G. fahre, fährt, fuhr, ge-fahren; schlage, schlug; hebe, hob, ge-hoben; scheide, schied, ge-schieden, &c.

First pers. pres.	Third pers.	Imperf.	Part. past.
stande *stand*	stent	stód *stood*	standen
gale *enchant*	gæld	gól	galen
spane *allure*	spænd	spón	spanen
sceade *part, shed*	scyt	sceód(')	sceaden

Sleá makes imper. slýh or sléh; infin. sleán: thus also leán *to blame,* and þweán *to wash;* p. past þwegen, þwogen. Stande sometimes has standest, standed.

XI.—*Conjugation III.*

In the Third Conjugation the vowel remains the same in the present; but that of the imperfect is changed in the second person singular, and in the whole plural: the part. past has either the same vowel as these persons, or one near akin.

Examples:—bindan *to bind,* drífan *to drive,* clúfan *to cleave.*

Class I.	Class II.	Class III.
	Indicative Mode.	
	Present.	
Sing. 1. binde	drífe	clúfe
2. bintst	drífst	clúfst
3. bint	drífd	clúfd

(') P. *shod.*

Plur.	{bindađ {binde	{drífađ {drífe	{clúfađ {clúfe

Imperfect.

Sing. 1.	band	dráf	cleáf
2.	bunde	drife	clufe
3.	band	dráf	cleáf
Plur.	bundon	drifon	clufon

Subjunctive Mode.
Present.

Sing.	binde	drífe	clúfe
Plur.	bindon	drífon	clúfon

Imperfect.

Sing.	bunde	drife	clufe
Plur.	bundon	drifon	clufon

Imperative Mode.

Sing.	bind	drif	clúf
Plur.	{bindađ {binde	{drífađ {drífe	{clúfađ {clúfe

Infinitive Mode.

Pres.	bindan	drífan	clúfan
Ger.	bindanne	drífanne	clúfanne
P. pres.	bindende	drífende	clúfende
P. past	(ge-)bunden	(ge-)drifen	(ge-)clofen.

XII.—*Class I.*

In the First Class, i (y), e, eo, become a (o), ea, æ, in the imperfect, and these in the second person and plural are again changed to u: the part. past has u or o.

First pers. pres.	Third pers.	Imperf.	Part. past.
yrne(¹)	yrnð	arn	(ge-)urnen
run		*ran*	*run*
frine / frigne	frinð	fran / frægn	frunen / frugnen
enquire			
singe	singð	sang	sungen
sing		*sang*	*sung*
drince	drincð	dranc	druncen
drink		*drank*	*drunken*
swimme	swimð	swamm	swommen
swim		*swam*	*swum*
climbe	climbð	clomm	clumben
climb		*clomb*	
swelle	swylð	sweoll	swollen
swell			*swollen*
swelge	swylgð	swealh	swolgen
swallow			
melte	mylt	mealt	molten
melt			*molten*
gelde	gylt	geald	golden
pay			
helpe	hylpð	healp	holpen
help			*holpen*
delfe	dylfð	dealf	dolfen
delve			
murne	myrnð	mearn	mornen
mourn			

(¹) G. rinne, rann, ge-ronnen; singe, sang, ge-sungen; trinke, trank; schwelle, schwillt, schwoll, ge-schwollen, &c.

First pers. pres.	Third pers.	Imperf.	P. past.
beorge *save, defend*	byrgð	bearh	borgen
weorpe *throw*	wyrpð	wearp	worpen
steorfe *die, starve*	styrfð	stærf	storfen
berste *burst*	byrst	bærst	borsten *borsten*
þersce *thresh*	þyrscð	þærsc	þorscen
feohte *fight*	fyht	feaht *fought*	fohten *foughten*
{ bregde { brede *braid, draw*	brit	brægd bræd	brogden } broden }

Weorðan(²) *to be, to become,* is thus conjugated:

Indic. pres. sing. 1. weorðe   Subj. pres. weorðe, &c.
             2. wyrst   Imperf.   wurde, &c.
             3. wyrð   Imper.   weorð

       plur. { weorðað / weorðe   plur. { weorðað / weorðe

Imperf. sing. 1. wearð   Infin. pres. weorðan
            2. wurde   Ger.   weorðanne
            3. wearð   Part. pres. weorðende
        plur. wurdon   P. past (ge-)worden

(²) Comp. throughout G. werden.

XIII.—*Class II.*

In the Second Class, í becomes in the imperfect á, and this in the second person, &c. i: the part. past has likewise i.

First pers. pres.	Third pers.	Imperf.	Part. past.
scíne(¹) *shine*	scínđ	scán *shone*	(ge-)scinen
wríte *write*	wrít	wrát *wrote*	writen *written*
a-ríse *arise*	a-ríst	a-rás *arose*	a-risen *arisen*
be-swíce *deceive*	be-swícđ	be-swác	be-swicen
stíge *ascend*	stíhđ	stáh	stigen
a-bíde *abide*	a-bídeđ	a-bád *abode*	a-biden *abiden*
grípe *gripe*	grípđ	gráp	gripen
ríde *ride*	rít	rád *rode*	riden *ridden*
spíwe *spew*	spíwđ	spáw	spiwen *spewn*
wríđe *writhe, wreathe*	wríđ	wráđ	wriđen

(¹) G. scheine, schien, ge-schienen; steige, stieg; greife, griff, ge-griffen, &c.

XIV.—*Class III.*

In the Third Class, eó or ú becomes eá in the imperfect; in the second person &c. u: the part. past has o.

First pers. pres.	Third pers.	Imperf.	Part. past.
reóce([2]) *reek*	rýcđ	reác.	(ge-)rocen
sceóte *shoot*	scýt	sceát *shot*	scoten *shotten*
creópe *creep*	crýpđ	creáp	cropen
ceówe *chew*	cýwđ	ceáw	cowen
leóge *lye*	lýhđ	leáh	logen
fleóge *fly, flee*	flýhđ	fleáh *flew*	flogen *flown*
beóde *bid*		beád *bade*	boden *bidden*
súce *suck*	sýcđ	seác	socen
búge *bow, bend*	býhđ	beáh	bogen *bown*
lúte *lout, bow*	lýt	leát	loten

([2]) G. rieche, roch, ge-rochen; schiesse, schoss, &c.

Ceósan *to choose*, makes third pers. pres. cýst; imperf. ceás *chose*, second pers. cure, plur. curon; p. past coren(¹).

Seóðan *to seethe*, has third pers. sýð; imperf. seáð, sode, &c.; p. past soden *sodden*.(²) Thus also others in -san and -ðan.

Fleóge is contracted to fleó, plur. fleóð, fleó; infin. fleógan, fleón; thus likewise teógan, teón *to draw*, tug: wreón *to cover*, and þeón *to thrive*, have only the contracted forms.

Seón *to see*, makes imperf. seáh or séh, sáwe or sége, &c. imper. seóh or sýh; part. present seónde; part. past (ge-)sewen, or segen.

Ge-feón (-feán) *to rejoice*, has imperf. ge-feáh or -féh, ge-fage or -fege; part. past ge-fagen, -fægen. Beón *to be*, is defective:

Indic. pres. 1. beó(³)   Subj. pres. beó
           2. býst   plur. beón
           3. býð   Imper. beó
    plur. { beóð   plur. { beóð
          { beó   { beó

Infin. beón.   Ger. tó beónne.   Part. pres. beónde.

XV.—*Anomalous Verbs.*

The following verbs are Anomalous, having for their present an old imperfect of the Complex Order, and for their imperfect one formed since after the Simple Order.

(¹) G. kiese, kor, ge-koren.   (²) G. siede, sott. ge-sotten.
(³) G. bin, bist.

VERBS—ANOMALOUS. 61

Pres. 1. 3. A'h, 2. áge, pl. ágon *(owe)*; imperf. áhte *(ought)*; infin. ágan; p. past. ágen: *own, possess.* Likewise combined with ne; náh, náhte, &c.

An, 2. unne, pl. unnon; imperf. úðe; inf. unnan; p. past (ge-)unnen: *grant.*

Can(²) *(can)*; 2. cunne or canst, pl. cunnon; imp. cúðe *(could)*; inf. cunnan; p. past (ge-)cúð: *know, ken, be able.*

Deáh, duge, dugon; imp. dóhte; inf. dúgan: *be good, brave, worth.*

Dear, dearst, durron; subj. durre: imp. dorste *(durst)*; inf. dearan: *dare.*

Ge-man(³), ge-manst, ge-munon: imp. ge-munde; inf ge-munan: *remember.*

Mæg(⁴), miht, magon *(may)*; subj. mæge (mage); imp. mihte (meahte) *(might)*; inf. magan : *be able.*

Mót(⁵), móst, móton; subj. móte; imp. móste: *may, might, must.*

Sceal(⁶) *(shall)*, scealt *(shalt)*, sceolon (sculon); subj. scyle; imp. sceolde *(should)*; inf. sculan: *owe.*

Wát(⁷) *(wot)*, wást, witon; imp. wiste (wisse) *(wist)*; subj. wíte; imper. wíte, wítað; inf. wítan; ger. tó wítanne (*to wit*); p. pres. wítende; p. past witen: *know.* Thus also nýtan *to know not.*

(²) Comp. L. novi *I know* ; G. kenne, kann. kannte, konnte, &c.
(³) Comp. L. defective me-min-i *I remember.*
(⁴) G. mag, möge, mögte, &c.
(⁵) G. muss, musste, &c.
(⁶) G. soll, sollte, &c.
(⁷) Comp. οἶδα *I know* ; G. weiss, wusste, wissen ; L. scio ; as distinguished from can (cnúwe) γινωσκω, L. novi.

G

þearf(¹), þearſt or þurfe, þurfon; subj. þurfe; imp. þorſte; inf. þearfan: *nçed*.

XVI.—*Auxiliaries, &c.*

The A. S. has no future tense, the present serving for both: wille and sceal, like G. will and soll, imply will, duty, and the like, and are not used like *will* and *shall*, to form a simple future; the present of beón has commonly a future power. The perfect and pluperfect are formed as in English, German, &c. by means of the verb *to have*; as, ic hæbbe (ge-)lufod *I have loved*.(²) The participle past being as in the above-named tongues the only true passive form, the passive tenses are formed throughout by the help of the auxiliaries wesan, weorđan, and beón *to be*; as, present ic eom, or weorđe lufod(³) *I am loved*; imperf. ic wæs, or weard lufod; perf. ic eom lufod worden *I have been loved*; pluperf. ic wæs lufod worden *I had been loved*; future, ic beó lufod *I shall be loved*.

Impersonal verbs are like those of other languages; as, hit rinđ *it rains*; hit ge limpđ *it happens*. Some have a passive sense; as, a-lýfđ *it is allowed, lawful* (L. licet); ge-wyrđ *it is agreed, seems good* (L. convenit).

(¹) G. darf, durfte.
(²) The imperfect is often used for the pluperfect.
(³) Comp. G. ich habe, hatte, werde, wurde, ge-liebt; ich bin, war, geliebt worden.

CHAPTER VI.

I.—*Formation of Words. Prefixes.*

As in Greek, Latin, German, &c. this branch of the language must be strictly attended to, if we would learn the origin, gender, and inflection of words: it consists of Derivation, and Composition, in both which the A. S. closely resembles the German. Derivation either modifies the meaning of a word by putting before it a prefix, or changes its part of speech, and inflection, by adding a termination. Composition forms new words by joining one or more together.

The following are the chief prefixes:

un- (on-) (L. *in-*; E. and G. *un-*): un-scyldig (G. un-schuldig) *in-nocent*; un-tigian *to un-tie*.

n- (ne *not*; L. *ne*): n-yllan (for newillan; L. n-olle for ne velle) *to will not, nill*; n-án *none*.

mis- (E. *mis-*; G. *miss-*, *misse-*): mis-truwian (G. mis-trauen) *to mis-trust*; mis-dǽd (G. misse-that) *mis-deed*.

wan ([4]) (wana *wanting*): wan-hál *unhealthy*.

to-([5]) (L. *dis-*; G. *zer-*): to-brecan (L. dis-rumpere, G. zer-brechen) *to break in pieces*; to-drífan (L. dis-pellere, G. zer treiben) *to scatter, drive away*.

[4] Hence O. *wan-hope* (D. wan-hoop) *despair*; *wan-trust* (D. wan-trouw) *mis-trust*.

[5] Hence O. *to-broken, to-torn* &c. The *prefix* to- must be carefully distinguished from the *preposition* tó.

for-(¹) (L. *per-*; F. *for-*; G. *ver-*): for-beódan (G. ver-bieten) *to for-bid*; for-swerian (L. per-jurare) *to for-swear*; for-gán *to for-go*; for-bærnan (G. ver-brennen) *to burn up, consume*; for-gifan (G. ver-geben) *to give away, for-give.*

wiđer- (wiđ *against*; G. *wider-*): wiđer-saca (G. wider-sacher) *adversary.*

and- (ἀντι; G. *ant-*): and-wlíta (G. ant-litz) *countenance.*

ge- (G. *ge-*; L. *com-, con-, co-*): has in general a collective sense; as, ge-bróđra (G. ge-brüder) *brethren*; ge-scý (G. ge-schuhe, F. chaussure) *shoes*; ge-mǽne (G. ge-mein, L. com-mune) *common*; ge-fera (G. gefährte, L. com-es) *companion*; it forms active verbs from neuters, nouns, &c. as, ge-standan *to urge*; ge-þencan (G. ge-denken) *to think of, remember*; ge-strangian *to strengthen*; ge-leánian *to reward*; ge-niđerian *to degrade, condemn*; from standan, þencan, strang, leán (*reward*), niđer; or gives a figurative sense; as, biddan *to ask, beg*, ge-biddan *to pray.* Many words, however, take ge- without any change of meaning; as, seón, ge-seón *to see*; hýran, ge-hýran *to hear, obey*; mearc, ge-mearc *mark, limit*; rúm, ge-rúm *wide, roomy.*

be- (E. and G. *be-*) makes neuter verbs active; as, gán *to go*, be-gán *to commit*, &c. (G. gehen, be-gehen); feran *to go*, be-feran *to travel over* (G. fahren, befahren). It is sometimes privative; as, bycgan *to buy*, be-bycgan *to sell*; be-heáfdian *to be-head:* often in-

---

(¹) Hence O. *for-done, for-spent*, &c. The *prefix* for- must not be confounded with the *preposition* for, which seems not to occur in composition.

tensive; as, reáfian *to rob*, be-reáfian *to be-reave* (G. rauben, be-rauben); be-gyrdan (G. be-gürten) *to be-gird*; or otherwise modifies the sense; as, be-healdan *to be-hold*, be-sprecan (G. be-sprechen) *to be-speak*.

ed- (*again, re-*) : ed-niwian *to re-new*.

sin- (simle *always*, L. semper) : sin-grén *ever-green*.

sam- (L. *semi-*) : sam-cucé(²) *half-quick, half-dead*.

æg- or ge- gives pronouns and adverbs an indeterminate sense; as, æg-hwylc (ge-hwylc) *each, every*, æg-hwider *whithersoever*.

II.—*Nominal Terminations.*

The following are the chief Nominal Terminations, denoting for the most part persons:

-a(³): cemp-a *warrior, champion*; hunt-a *hunter*; bog-a *bow*.

-ere: (E. and G. *-er*; L. *-or*): reáf-ere (G. räub-er) *robb-er*; sǽd-ere (L. sat-or) *sow-er*.

-end (from the part. pres.): Hǽl-end (G. Heil-and) *Saviour, healer*; weald-end *ruler*.

-e: hyrd-e *herd, keeper*; sig e *victory*; riht-wís-e *righteousness*.

-el, -ol, -l (E. *-le*; G. *-el*): byd-el (G. bed-el) *herald*, bead-le; gaf-ol *tribute, gav-el*; set-l (G. sess-el) *seat, sett-le*.

-ing: ædel-ing *prince, young noble*; Wóden-ing *son of Woden*; earm-ing *poor wretch*.

(²) Cuc, cucu, cucen, cwic (-e) are also found.

(³) Answering sometimes to L. *-o*; as, gum-a, L. hom-o *man, groom*; hence brýd-guma G. bräuti-gam, *bride-groom*.

-ling (E. -*ling*; G. -*lein*, -*ling*): cnæp-ling (G. knäb-lein) *little boy;* .leór-ling (G. theuer-ling) *dar-ling.*
-incle (L. -*uncul-us,* -*a*): ráp-incle *little rope.*
-en (E. -*en*; G. -*chen*): mægd-en *maid-en,* from mægd *maid* (G. magd, mäd-chen); cyc-en *chick-en,* from cocc *cock.*
-en (E. -*en*): þeód-en *sovereign;* byrð-en *burth-en.*
-en (E. -*en*; G. -*in*). Feminines from masculines sometimes change the vowel; as, þen, þin-en *slave, female slave;* fox, fyx-en (G. fuchs, füchs-in) *fox, vix-en;* sometimes not; as, þeów, þeów-en *slave.* Some change the vowel, and take -e; others change the vowel only; as, mearh, myr-e *horse, mare;* wulf, wylf (G. wolf, wölf-in) *wolf, she-wolf.*
-estre (E. and D. -*ster*): sang-estre (D. zang-ster) *song-ster,* from sangere *singer;* sæm-estre *seam-ster,* from sæm-ere *seamer, tailor.*(¹)

The following denote a state, action, or the like:
-dóm (E. -*dom;* G. -*thum*): wís-dóm *wis-dom;* cyne-dóm(²) (G. könig-thum) *king-ship.*
-hád (E. -*head, -hood;* G. -*heit*): mæden-hád *maid-en-head;* cild-hád (G. kind-heit) *child-hood.*

(¹) In *songstr-ess, seamstr-ess,* a Latin-French termination has been super-added. Huck-ster, *malt-ster, tap-ster,* and the like, are the true feminines of *hauk-er, malt-er, tapp-er,* &c. *Spin-ster* is yet rightly used.

(²) We have confounded -*dom* and -*ric,* but -*dóm* was properly the *office, rank,* -*ríce the territory:* thus, cyne-dóm, cyne-ríce (G. könig-reich); bisceop-dóm, bisceop-ríce, and the like.

ADJECTIVAL TERMINATIONS.

-scipe (E. *-ship;* G. *-schaft*): hláford-scipe *lord-ship;* freónd-scipe (G. freund-schaft) *friend-ship.*

-lác (E. *-lock*): wíf-lác, *wed-lock.*

-ađ, -ođ: hunt-ađ *hunting;* war-ođ *sea-shore.*

-uđ, -đ (E. *th;* G. *-end*): geóg-uđ (G. jug-end) *youth;* treów-đ *troth, truth.*

-leást (-lýst; from adj. in -leás): gýme-leást *heedlessness.*

-ung, -ing (E. *-ing;* G. *-ung*): hálg-ung (G. heilig-ung) *hallow-ing;* leorn-ing *learn-ing.*

-nes (-nys, -nis: E. *-ness;* G. *-niss*): car-leás-nes *careless-ness;* ge-líc-nes (G. gleich-niss) *like-ness.*

-u, -eo, -o (G. *-e*): hǽt-u (G. hitz-e) *heat;* mænig-eo (G. meng-e) *many, multitude;* brǽd-o (G. breit-e) *breadth.*

-els (E. *-le;* G. *-el*): rǽd-els (G. räths-el) *ridd-le;* sticc-els (G. stach-el) *stick-le, sting.*

-ed: rec-ed *mansion;* eow-ed *flock.*

-m (E. *-om;* G. *-en*): bot-m (G. bod-en) *bott-om.*

-ot, -et, -t: þeow-ot, þeow-t *slavery;* bœrn-et *burning.*

-d, -t (E. *-th, -d, -t;* G. *-t*): ge-byr-d (G. ge-bur-t) *bir-th;* ge-cyn-d *kin-d, nature;* mih-t (G. mach-t) *migh-t.*

-rǽden (rǽd *counsel*): hiw-rǽden *house-hold;* mœg-rǽden *relationship.*

III.—*Adjectival Terminations.*

-e: œđel-e *noble;* fǽg-e *fated, fey.*

-ig (E. *-y,* G. *-ig*): dreór-ig (G. traur-ig) *drear-y:*

-líc (E. -*like*, -*ly*, G. -*lich*): leóf-líc (G. lieb-lich) *love-ly*; wíf-líc (G. weib-lich) *woman-like, woman-ly.*

-isc (E. -*ish*, G. *isch*): cild-isc (G. kind-isch) *child-ish*; Engl-isc (G. engl-isch) *Engl-ish, Anglo-Saxon.*

-sum (E. -*some*, G. -*sam*): lang-sum (G. lang-sam) *tedious, long-some*; wyn-sum (G. wonne-sam) *amiable, win-some.*

-ol (-ul) (L. -*ul-us*): sprec-ol *talkative.*

-en (E. and G. *en*): fleax-en (G. flachs-en) *flax-en*; hæð-en *heath-en.*

-bǽre (beran *to bear*: G. -bar): lust-bǽre (G. lust-bar) *pleasant*; wæstm-bǽre *fruitful.*

-cund (cynn *kind, race*): woruld-cund *worldly.*

-iht (G. -*icht*): þorn-iht (G. dorn-icht) *thorny.*

-weard (adj. and adv.; E. -*ward*): tó-weard *to-ward, to come*; hám-weard *home-ward.*

-feald (E. -*fold*): án-feald *single, one-fold*; twi-feald, *two-fold*; manig-feald *mani-fold.*

-leás (E. -*less*, G. -*los*): syn-leás (G. sünde-los) *sin-less*; ár-leás (G. ehr-los) *void of honour, impious.*

-wís *(wise)*: ge-wís (G. ge-wiss) *certain*; riht-wís *righteous.*

-ern (E. -*ern*): súð-ern *south-ern.*

-tyme: hefig-tyme *troublesome.*

IV.—*Verbal Terminations.*

-ian (-igan, -igean) forms verbs (I. 1.) from nouns, adjectives, and particles; as, cear-ian *to care*, ge-hýrsumian *to obey*, wiðer-ian *to oppose*; from cearu *care*, ge-hýrsum *obedient*, wiðer *against.*

PARTICLES.

C, g, n, or s, sometimes stands before -ian; as, gear-c-ian *to prepare*, syn-g-ian *to sin*, wít-n-ian *to punish*, mǽr-s-ian *to magnify*; from gearu *ready, yare*, syn *sin*, wíte *punishment*, mǽre *great, famous*.

-án is contracted from -angan, -ágan, or -agan, and -ahan; as, gangan, gán *to go*; smeágan, smeán *to consider, enquire*; þreagan, þreán *to vex*; sleahan, sleán (G. schlagen) *to strike, slay*.

-ón is contracted from -angan, or -ógan; as, fangan, fón *to take*; teógan, teón *to draw, tug*.

-ettan: hál-ettan *to hail, greet*, from hál *whole, hale*.

After c and g, e is not seldom inserted; as, rǽc-ean, þicg-ean, for rǽc-an *to reach*, þicg-an *to touch, taste*, &c.

Other verbs in general form the infinitive in -an.

V.—*Particles.*

Adverbs, prepositions, and conjunctions, are either primitive words, that is, not to be further resolved in the language treated of, or are formed from nouns (often obsolete), adjectives, &c. governed by a preposition expressed or understood. Of the former kind are nú *now*, geó (iú), *formerly*, eft *again*, get (iet), *yet*, be *by*, &c. for *for*, tó *to*, ac *but*, gif *if*, &c. Of the latter kind, (to take the cases in order) are the accusatives on-weg (a-weg) *a-way*; on-bæc (under-, ofer-bæc) *a-baçk, back*; (on-)ge-mang *a-mong*; on-gean (a-gen) *a-gain, a-gainst*; ealne-weg *al-way*.

-e (abl. or dat.) forms many adverbs from nouns, adjectives,(¹) &c. ; as, on-riht-e (L. rect-e) (²) a-riht *a-right, rightly*; lang-e (L. long-e) *long;* mid-ealle *altogether;* be-dǽle *partly;* tó-sóðe *in sooth, truly;* of-dúne, a-dún *a-down, down;* tó-gædere (æt-gædere), tó-somne (æt-somne, G. zu-sammen), *to-gether.*

líc-e (E. *-ly;* the same, borrowed from adjectives in -líc): sceort-líc-e *short-ly*, strang-líc-e *strong-ly.*

Other ablatives are the conjunctions for-þý *therefore;* (for-) hwý? *(for) why?* ; datives for-þám *because*, tó-þón-þæt *in order that*, síð-þán (G. seit-dem) *since.*

-um, -on (abl. or dat. plur.): (on) hwíl-um, hwíl on *whilome, whiles*, wundr-um *wondrously*, hwyrft-um *by turns*, sticce-mǽlum(³) *piece-meal*, be lytl-um and lytl-um *by little and little*, furð-um (-on) *even, just*, on-sundr-on *in-sunder, a-sunder.*

-es (genitive): niht-es(⁴) (*νυκτ-ος*, G. nacht-s) *of a night, by night*, will-es *willingly*, néd-es *of necessity, needs*, eall-es *altogether*, nall-es *by no means*, sóð es *of a truth*, tó-gean-es *against*, tó-midd-es *amidst.*

-a, -unga, -inga (perhaps gen. plur.): gear-a *of*

(¹) Those in -h and -u take g and w, as, heáh, heáge; nearu, nearwe: see Adjectives Def., and Indef. I.

(²) L. adverbs in -e were perhaps ablatives, like those in -o, as *ver-o* and the like.

(³) S t i c (II. 1) *piece, bit, (steak)* (G. stück); mǽl (II. 3) (G. mahl) *meal, time of eating, milking cows, &c.*

(⁴) The proper genitives of niht, willa, and néd (neód) are nihte, willan, néde; at an early stage of the language, all nouns formed the gen. in -es or s; comp. the many Gr. and L. genitives in *-ος* &c. and -is.

yóre, son-a *soon, forthwith,* eall-unga *altogether,* hol-inga *in vain,* yrr-inga *angrily.*

-an (an oblique case): níw-an *of late, newly,* for-an *before,* on midd-an, a-midd-an *a-mid,* wið-út-an *without,* búf-an(⁵) (for be-úf-an) *a-bove;* a-bút-an (for on-be-út-an) *a-bout,* &c.

Other adverbial terminations are:—

-der *(motion to—)*: hi-der *hi-ther,* þi-der *thi-ther,* hwi-der *whi-ther.*

-on, -an *(motion from—)*: heon-on *hence,* þan-on *thence,* hwan-on *whence.*

-r, -ra, -e, &c. *(rest in—)*: her *here,* þær (þara) *there* hwær (hwar) *where;* inn-e *within,* út-e *without.*

VI.—*Composition.*(⁶)

The A. S. language, like the Greek, German, &c. abounds in compound words, of which the last part commonly settles the part of speech. Nouns and adjectives are usually compounded together, and with verbs, without change, as in English, &c.; as, fíc-treów *fig-tree,* heáfod-man (G. haupt-mann) *head-man, captain,* heáh-sacerd, *high-priest,* bisceop-ríce *bishop-ric,* stæf-cræft *letter-craft, grammar,* medo-ærn(⁷) *mead-hall,* þeow-boren *slave-born,* stede-fæst *stead-fast,* bealo-full *baleful,* snáw-hwít (G. schnee-weiss) *snow-white,* íren-heard (G. eisen-hart) *as hard as iron,* lif-fæstan

---

(⁵) D. boven; "Oranje boven!"   (⁶) See Rask, pp. 113—117.
(⁷) Or-ern; sealt-ern *salt-ern.*

to quicken, ful-fremman (G. voll-bringen) *to ful-fil,* and the like.

A noun, however, standing first, is often put in the genitive case, especially in local names; as, dómes-dæg *doom's-day,* hilde-byrne *war-corslet;* Engla-land *England, land of the Angles;* Cant-wara-burh *Canterbury, burgh of the Kenters;* Cinges-tún *King's-town, Kingston;* Beorminga-hám *Birming-ham, home of the Beormings;* Oxena-ford *Ox-ford, ford of oxen;* from dóm, hild, Engle, Cant-ware, cing, Beorming, oxa. One or each part is sometimes shortened, &c.; as, frum-cenned *first-born,* œl-beorht *all-bright,* mild-heort *mild-hearted;* from fruma *beginning,* eall, milde, heorte. Prepositions and adverbs commonly stand before verbs, &c. without change, as in English, German, &c.; as, ymb-gang (G. um-gang) *circuit;* þurh-faran (G. durch-fahren) *to go through;* wið-standan (G. wider-stehen) *to with-stand;* tó-cyme *coming to* (L. ad-ventus); fore-rynel *fore-runner;* fore-mihtig (L. præ-potens) *very mighty;* úp-riht (G. auf-recht) *up-right;* úp-stígan(¹) (G. auf-steigen) *to go up;* nider-stígan (G. nieder-steigen) *to go down;* forð-gán (G. fort-gehen) *to go forth;* út-lág *out-law* (L. ex-lex); ofer-cuman *to over-come;* ofer-mód (G. über-muth) *pride;* under-niman (G. unter-nehmen) *to under-take;* fram-ge-wítan *to depart from;* in-lǽdan (G. ein-leiten) *to lead in;* geond-geótan *to pour through, suf-fuse;* on-gean-cyrran *to turn back again;* of-sceótan

---

(¹) Stígan (G. steigen) answers to L. scandere; ad-scendere, de-scendere, &c.

(G. ab-schiessen) *to shoot off;* æfter-fyligend *successor, one who follows after;* mid-síðian *to travel with;* sundor-spræc *conversation apart;* samod-(sam-)-wyrcan *to work together, co-operate.*

The preposition be, bi, usually becomes big in composition; as, big-spel (G. bei-spiel) *example, parable;* big-standan (G. bei-stehen) *to stand by;* it may thus be known from the particle be, which sometimes becomes bi; as, be-standan, bi-standan (G. be-stehen) *to stand on, occupy.*(²) On often becomes an- or a-; as, on-bídan, an-bídan, a-bídan *to a-bide.* Æt and oð in composition often mean *from, away;* as, æt-berstan *to burst away,* oð-yrnan *to run away, escape,* like G. ent-bersten, -rinnen.

Particles are also freely compounded together.

Prepositions, and other particles in composition, are often parted from their verb, as in German; but the same rules can hardly be given in A. S.

In general, þurh, úp, niðer, tó, forð, út, in, on, bi (big) are separable; a-, an-, be-, ge-, ed-, un-, or-, mis-, oð, and-, wið, sam-, for-, to-, are inseparable; æt, of, &c. are rarely separated.

CHAPTER VII.

I.—*Syntax.*

THE A.S. Syntax in general resembles that of Greek and German; but it bears the closest likeness, with some remarkable points of difference from that and other

(²) See Formation of Particles.

tongues, to the Latin, with which it should be compared throughout. The concords agreeing in A. S. with those in Latin, &c. need not be repeated. With regard to the construction of sentences it may be observed, that the verb often stands after both the subject and the object, coming last of all, as for the most part in German; as,

On þǽre tíde þa Gotan wið Rómana-ríce gewinn úp-a-hófon, *at that time the Goths raised up war against the Roman empire.*

Þá Darius ge-seáh þæt he ofer-wunnen beón wolde, þá wolde he hine sylfne on þám ge-feohte for-spillan, *when Darius saw that he should be overcome, then he would lose his life in the fight.*

We sceolon mid biternysse sóðre be-hreowsunge úre mód ge-clǽnsian, *we must with the bitterness of true repentance cleanse our mind.*

Often, however, sentences are in this and other respects framed as in English; and on the whole this part of the grammar will not prove difficult to the student, and may be better learned from reading than from any rules that might be given.

II.—*Syntax of Nouns.*

Nouns of time answering to the question, "how long?" are put in the accusative or ablative; as,

Ealle wucan *all the week.*

Þrý dagas, or þrym dagum *three days.*

Answering to the question "when?" they stand in the ablative, dative with on, or genitive; as,

SYNTAX OF NOUNS. 75

Þý feorðan dógore *on the fourth day.*
On þissum geare *in this year.*
Ussa tída(¹) *in our times.*
Measure, value, age, and the like, are used in the genitive; as,
Twegra elna heáh *two ells high.*
Ynces lang *an inch long.*
Þreora mila brád *three miles broad.*
Sex peninga wyrðe *worth six pence.*
A'nes geares lamb *a lamb of one year.*
The matter to which a measure, &c. is applied, stands in the genitive; as,
Hund mittena hwǽtes *a hundred measures of wheat.*
Hund-teontig punda goldes *a hundred pounds of gold.*
It sometimes remains unchanged; as,
Twegen marc gold(²) *two marks of gold.*
Quality, praise, or blame, stands in the genitive; as,
A'r-wyrðre yldo *of venerable age.*
Fægeres and-wlítan *of fair countenance.*
Two ablatives or datives are used absolutely like the L. double ablative; as,
Ge-togene þý wæpne(³) *the weapon (being) drawn.*
A-fundenum sceápe *the sheep (being) found.*
Two datives, the latter governed by tó, are used like the L. double dative; as,
Þæt he ús tó fultume sý(⁴) *that he may be (for) a help to us.*

(¹) Comp. F. de nos temps. (²) G. zwei mark gold.
(³) L. stricto telo; ove repertâ. (⁴) L. ut nobis auxilio sit.

The means or instrument stands in the ablative or dative, with or without the preposition mid; as,

Hine mid þý heofon-lícan weg-nyste ge-trymmende *strengthening himself with that heavenly viaticum.*

Þý betstan leóđe ge-glenged *adorned with the best lay.*

Heó hí sylfe mid cyne-lícum reáfe ge-frætwode *she adorned herself with royal attire.*

Híg sprecađ niwum tungum *they shall speak with new tongues.*

III.—*Syntax of Adjectives.*

Adjectives in general, especially those denoting want, desire, knowledge, remembrance, and the like, have a genitive case of the noun which defines them, and often stand after it; as,

Feos wana *wanting money.*
Freónda leás *lacking friends.*
Hrægles þearfa *devoid of raiment.*
Earn ætes georn *an eagle eager for food.*
Ac ic heora eom swíđe gifre *but I am very greedy of them.*
Bóca gleáw *skilful in books.*
Un-wís God-cundan Naman *ignorant of the Divine Name.*
Hí næron his ge-myndige *they were not mindful of him.*
Módes blíđe *blithe of mood.*
Sídes wérig *weary of travel.*
Mægenes strang *strong of might.*

I'sig feðera *icy of wings.*
They sometimes take an ablative; as,
Wintrum geong *young in years.*
Blind bám eágum *blind of both eyes.*
Adjectives denoting pleasure, profit, injury, and the like, govern a dative; as,
Þeáh he him leóf wǽre *though he were dear to them.*
Eallum and-feng *acceptable to all.*
Þæt he mynster-lícum cumum ge-þensum wǽre *that he might be serviceable to the monastic guests.*
Rinca ge-hwylcum un-nyt *useless to every man.*
Derigend-líc býð þe *it will be hurtful to thee.*
Full *full,* wyrðe *worthy,* scyldig *guilty,* have an ablative, dative, or genitive; as,
Full Hálgum Gáste *full of the Holy Ghost.*
Full deádra bána *full of dead bones.*
Se wyrhta is wyrðe his metes *the workman is worthy of his meat.*
Se býð dóme scyldig *he shall be guilty of the judgment.*
He is deáðes scyldig *he is guilty of death.*
Ge-líc *like,* has a dative or genitive; as,
Híg synd ge-líce þám cildum(¹) *they are like the children.*
Nán man nis his ge-líca *no man is like him.*
The word which determines a comparative stands before it in the ablative neuter; as,
Þrym mundum hýrra *three hands higher.*

(¹) Thus L. similes pueris; ejus similis.

Micle má *much more.*

Þý weorðra *so much the worthier.*

Comparatives require either þonne or þe *than,* with a nominative, or an ablative or genitive without; as,

Ge synd sélran þonne manega spearwan, or ge synd beteran manigum spearwum *ye are better than many sparrows.*

O'ðer-healf gear læs þe þrittig wintra *a year and a half less than thirty years.*

Se is his mára *he is greater than him.*

Superlatives take a genitive; as,

Ealra wyrta mǽst *greatest of all herbs.*

*** For the Syntax of Pronouns see Chapter IV.

IV.—*Syntax of Verbs.*

Verbs, as in other tongues, agree in number with their subject; after ælc þára (þǽra) þe *each of them that, every one that,* however, the singular is used, agreeing with ælc and not with þára; as,

Ælc þára þe tó me cymð (lit. *each of them that cometh*—) *every one that cometh to me.*

Swá ge-býrað ælcum þára þe winð *so it befitteth every one that contendeth.*

With a noun of multitude the verb may be either singular or plural; as,

Þá com micel mænigeo and tó him éfston *then came a great multitude and hastened to him.*

Transitive verbs in general, as in other tongues, govern the direct object in the accusative case; as,

Lufa þínne nextan *love thy neighbour.*

Seó sǽ ge-tácnađ þás and-weardan woruld *the sea betokeneth this present world.*

A'xian *to ask,* takes a double accusative ; as,

Nán ne dorste hine nán þing máre áxian *no one durst ask him anything more.*

Verbs of naming have an accusative of the object named, and a nominative of the name; as,

Þone un-ge-met líce eargan þú miht hátan hara *the immoderately timid thou mayest call hare.*

Rǽdan *to rule,* a-bregdan *to draw (a weapon),* and to-bregdan *to cast off (sleep,)* govern the ablative ; as,

Þenden hí þý ríce rǽdan móston *while they might rule the realm.*

A'n of þám þý sweorde a-brǽd *one of them drew his sword.*

Mid-þý heó þá þý slǽpe to-brǽd *when she then had cast off sleep.*

Verbs of bidding, forbidding, serving, following, obeying, consenting to, opposing, pleasing, trusting, injuring, profiting, escaping from ; likewise for-swerian *to forswear,* cídan *to chide,* árian *to honour, spare,* beorgan *to save, defend,* déman *to judge,* oleccan *to flatter,* *stillan([1]) *to still,* fylstan *to succour,* efen-lǽcan *to imitate,* ge-nea-lǽcan *to approach,* and heorcnian *to hearken to,* govern the dative; as,

Un-clǽnum gástum be-být *he commandeth the unclean spirits.*

Ne for-beóde ge him *forbid him not.*

([1]) The verbs marked thus * sometimes govern the accusative.

Ne mæg nán man twám hláf-ordum þeowian *no man can serve two lords.*

Heó him þenode *she served him.*

Þa sceáp him fyligeað *the sheep follow him.*

Þá se wer hýrde his waldende *then the man obeyed his ruler.*

Gif þú þonne Dryhtne ge-hýrsumast *if thou then obeyest the Lord.*

Þes ne ge-þwǽrede heora ge-þeahte *this (man) agreed not to their counsel.*

Ge þafiað eówera fædera weorcum *ye consent to your fathers' works.*

Him ne wið-stent nán þing *no thing withstandeth him.*

Nemne him wyrd for-stóde *unless fate had opposed him.*

Eallum his wordum wið-cwǽdon and wið-wunnon *(they) contradicted and opposed all his words.*

Pilatus wolde þám folce ge-cweman *Pilate would please the people.*

Heó on-gan his wordum truwian *she began to trust his words.*

Ne derode Iobe náht þæs deófles costnung, ac fremode *the devil's temptation hurt Job no whit, but profited him.*

Hú heó þám feónd-lícum gástum oð-fleón mage *how she may escape from the hostile spirits.*

Sið-þán hí feóndum oð-faren hæfdon *when they had escaped from the enemies.*

Ac he sige-wæpnum for-sworen hæfde *but he had forsworn the weapons of victory.*

Gif þín bróðer syngað cíd him *if thy brother sinneth chide him.*

Þú nelt árian þǽre stówe *thou wilt not spare the lace.*

Beorh þínum feore *save thy life.*

Démað him be eówre ǽ *judge him by your law.*

He wolde him oleccan mid his hearpan *he would flatter them with his harp.*

Ýðum stilde *he stilled the waves.*

Him fylston wel gistas síne *his guests succoured him well.*

Uton for-þý ge-efen-lǽcan þisum men *let us therefore imitate this man.*

Þám deáðe ge-nea-lǽcende *drawing nigh to death.*

Ypolitus heora wordum heorcnade *Hippolytus hearkened to their words.*

Verbs of motion, and likewise on-drædan *to dread*, often have a redundant dative of the subject; as,

Gá þe forð(¹) *go forth.*

He him hám-weard ferde *he journeyed homeward.*

Him þá Scyld ge-wát *then Scyld departed.*

He him on-drǽt(²) monigne feónd *he dreads many a foe.*

Wealdan *to wield, govern,* *on-fón *to receive,* *miltsian *to pity,* hlystan *to listen to,* helpan *to help,* *gelýfan *to believe,* wið-sacan *to deny,* ge-feón *to rejoice at,* *hrínan *to touch,* with its compounds; likewise

---

(¹) Hence " hie thee home," and the like.   (²) O. " I fear me."

wesan *to be,* when implying possession, govern the dative or genitive; as,

Ætla weóld Hunum *Attila ruled the Huns.*

Þe on þám dagum ge-weóld cyne-dómes *who in those days ruled the kingdom.*

On-fóh þissum fulle *receive this cup.*

Þá on-fengon híg þæs feos *then took they the money.*

He miltsađ úrum gyltum *he hath compassion on our sins.*

Ge-miltsa mín *have pity on me.*

Hwý hlyste ge him? *why listen ye to him?*

Hlyste he gódes rǽdes *let him listen to good counsel.*

He him helpan ne mæg *he cannot help him.*

Ge-help þú earmra manna *help thou poor men.*

For-þám-þe þú ne ge-lýfdest mínum wordum *because thou believedst not my words.*

We ne sculon þæs ge-lýfan *we must not believe that.*

Iulianus his Cristen-dóme wiđ-sóc *Julian denied his Christianity.*

Þry-wa þú wiđ-sæcst mín *thrice thou shalt deny me.*

Secg weorce ge-féh *the warrior rejoiced in the work.*

Cwen weorces ge-feáh *the queen was glad of the work.*

Ne him hrínan ne mehte fær-grípe flódes *nor might the sudden gripe of the flood touch him.*

SYNTAX OF VERBS. 83

þá æt-hrán he hyra eágena *then touched he their eyes.*

þá him wæs manna þearf(¹) *since he had need of men.*

þa þing þe þæs Caseres synd *the things that are the Cæsar's.*

Verbs of desiring, needing, tempting, wondering at, using, enjoying, *remembering, *forgetting, caring for, ceasing from; together with cepan *to take, keep,* &c., wénan *to hope for,* *neósian *to visit.* on-byrian *to taste,* éhtian or éhtan *to persecute,* oð-sacan *to deny,* earnian *to earn, deserve,* gilpan *to boast of,* fægnian *to rejoice at,* *on-drædan *to dread;* likewise bídian (bídan) *to bide, wait for,* with its compounds, govern the genitive; as,

We ge-wilniað friðes wið eów *we desire peace with you.*

Þæs ic wilnige and wisce *that I desire and wish.*

Þæt mæden gyrnde deáðes *the maiden yearned for death.*

Ne be-þurfon læces þa þe hále synd *they need not a leech that are whole.*

U're man-dryhten mægenes be-hófað *our liege lord requires strength.*

Hwý fandige ge mín? *why tempt ye me?*

For-þón ic his cost node *therefore I tempted him.*

We wundriað þæs wlítan þære sunnan *we wonder at the beauty of the sun.*

(¹) L. illi hominum opus erat

Eówre fýnd wafiað eówer *your foes shall be amazed at you.*

Brúc þisses beáges, and þisses hrægles neót *enjoy this ring, and use this dress.*

Ne ge-mune ic nánra his synna *I will remember none of his sins.*

Ne ge ne ge-þencað þæra fíf hláfa? *and do ye not remember the five loaves?*

Þú hæfst þára wæpna for-giten *thou hast forgotten the weapons.*

Hí þæs ne gýmdon *they cared not for that.*

Feores hí ne róhton *for life they recked not.*

Héddon here-reáfes *they heeded the war-spoil.*

Ge-swíc þínes wópes *cease thy weeping.*

Sceolde æðeling ealdres linnan(¹) *the noble must part from life.*

Hí nánre bricge ne cepton *they kept to no bridge.*

He nolde nánes fleámes cepan *he would not take to flight.*

Ne þearf ic ænigre áre wénan *I may not hope for any honour.*

Ge-wát þá neósian heán húses *(he) then departed to visit the lofty mansion.*

On-byrige metes(²) *let him taste meat.*

Paulus ehte Cristenra manna *Paul persecuted Christian men.*

Hwá oð-sæcð þæs? *who denies that?*

Seó þeód þe his earnað *the people that deserveth it.*

(¹) Linnan sometimes has a dative.
(²) We say also " taste of—."

SYNTAX OF VERBS.

Hú ne gilpst þú þonne heora fægeres?(³) *boastest thou not then of their fairness?*

Ne sceal he fægnian þæs folces worda *he must not rejoice at the people's words.*

Híg on-dredon þǽra Israhela tó-cymes *they dreaded the coming of the Israelites.*

Se hýr-man his ed-leánes an-bídað *the hireling awaiteth his reward.*

Verbs of granting, likewise tilian *to till, get,* forwyrnan *to deny,* þancian *to thank,* stýrian (stýran) *to chastise,* have a dative of the person or near object, and a genitive of the thing or far object; as,

Se hálga him þæs ge-úðe *the saint granted him that.*

Þá þúhte me hefig-tyme þe þæs tó tiðienne *then it seemed to me troublesome to grant thee that.*

Þá Metod on-láh Medum and Persum aldordómes *when the Lord bestowed the supremacy on the Medes and Persians.*

Þá Noe on-gan him ætes tilian *then Noah began to get him food.*

Þe him ne for-wyrnde cyne-líces weorðscipes *who denied him not kingly honour.*

Apollonius hire þæs þancode *Apollonius thanked her for that.*

He him þæs þinges stýrede *he chastised him for that thing.*

Verbs of depriving, likewise teón &c. *to accuse,*

(³) neuter adjective used and declined as a noun.

have an accusative of the near object, and an ablative or genitive of the far object; as,

Nelle ic þa rincas rihte be-næman *I will not deprive the warriors of their right.*

Heó hit ne mæg his ge-wittes be-reáfian *she cannot bereave it of its understanding.*

Dyrnum ge-þingum be-togen *charged with secret practices.*

Hwý týhð ús úre hláf-ord swá micles falses? *why doth our lord accuse us of so great deceit?*

Biddan *to ask for,* has an accusative of the near, and a genitive of the far object; as

Gif his sunu hine bitt hláfes *if his son asketh him for bread.*

Some impersonal verbs govern the person affected in the accusative or dative: hit is often left out; as,

Hyngrað hine (¹) *he is hungry.*

Seó swefen þe hine mætte *the dream that he dreamed.*

Hire ge-býrað *it becometh her.*

Hit lícode Herode *it pleased Herod.*

Him þúhte *it seemed to him* (lit. *him thought*).

Ne ge-wearð unc wið ænne pening? *did we not agree for a penny?*

Others have beside a genitive of the far object, after rules for other verbs; as,

Þone weligan lyst an-wealdes *the rich lusteth for power.*

Nænne mon þæs ne tweóð *no man doubts of that.*

(¹) Comp. G. es hungert ihn; es ge bührt ihr; ihm dünkte.

þe nánre be-hreowsunge ne be-hófað *thou needest no repentance.*

Him þæs ne sceamode *of that they were not ashamed.*

V.—*Syntax of Prepositions.*

Prepositions, as in German, &c., require various oblique cases of the nouns before which they are placed; thus,

geond *through, throughout*   ymb(-e)(³) ⎱ ⎰ *round,*
þurh(²) *through*   ymb-útan ⎰ ⎱ *about.*
wið-æftan *behind*

govern the accusative; as,

Gá geond wegas and hegas *go through the ways and hedges.*

Þurh his micle ge-þyld *through his great patience.*

Wið-æftan þá burh *behind the town.*

Ymb þæs cyninges slege *about the slaying of the king.*

Ymb-útan þone weall *around the wall.*

The following govern the dative

be (bi, big) (⁴) *of, about, by*   in-tó *into*
of *off, from, of*   ǽr *ere, before*
fram *from, by*   feor *far from*
æt *at, to*   un-feor(⁵) *near*
tó *to*   neah (nean) *nigh*

(²) G. durch.   (³) Comp. ἀμφι, L. amb-, G. um.
(⁴) Comp. ἐ-πι, G. bei; ἀπ-ο, L. ab, D. af, G. ab-; L. ad; G. zu, &c.
(⁵) Lit. *un-far;* G. un-fern.

ge-hende *near, handy* tó-middes ⎫
æfter *after* on-middan ⎭ *amid*
búfan ⎫ *above* binnan(²) ⎫
on-úfan ⎭ wið- ⎫ -innan ⎫ *within,*
be-æftan (bæftan) ⎫ *abaft,* on- ⎭ *inside*
be-hindan ⎭ *behind* æt- ⎫
be-heonan *on this side* tó- ⎭ -foran *before*
bútan (¹) *without, outside* tó-weard *toward*
be-twynan *between* tó-eácan *besides.*
tó-emnes *along*

Be þám heáh-fædere *concerning the patriarch.*
Be mínes fæder leáfe *by my father's leave.*
Far of þínum lande *depart from thy country.*
Of ánre úp-flóran *off an upper floor.*
Æt þám burnan(³) *at the brook.*
Fram cild-háde *from childhood.*
Gá tó þínum húse *go to thy house.*
Þá híg in-tó þǽre byrgene eódon *then they went into the tomb.*
Ǽr sunnan setl-gange *before the setting of the sun.*
He wæs him feor *he was far from him.*
Un-feor þám húse *near the house.*
Neah þám forda *nigh the ford.*
Ge-hende þǽre ceastre *near the town.*
Æfter þám ge-feohte *after the fight.*
Búfan þǽre heofenan *above the heaven.*
Bæftan þǽre mænigeo *behind the multitude.*
Be-heonan þǽre strǽte *on this side the street.*

(¹) D. buiten, O. bout, but.   (²) G. binnen, S. ben.
(³) S. burn.

Bútan þǽre wíc-stówe *outside the camp.*
Bútan ælcum an-ginne *without any beginning.*
Bútan wífum and cildum *besides women & children.*
Be-twynan þám twám mynstrum(⁴) *between the two monasteries.*
Tó-middes þám wæterum *amid the waters.*
On-middan þám treowe *in the midst of the tree.*
Binnan þám ge-telde *within the tent.*
Æt-foran his þrym-setle *before his glory-seat.*
Tó-weard þám háligdóme(⁵) *toward the sanctuary.*
Tó-eácan þám fodre *over and above the fodder.*
Tó sometimes has a genitive ; as,
Tó middes dæges *at mid-day:* likewise in several compound prepositions above and below.
And-lang *along* (like G. ent-lang) governs the genitive; as,
And-lang þæs wéstenes *along the desert.*
The following govern the accusative or dative; the former usually, as in Latin, &c., when motion to, the latter when motion from, or rest in, a place, is signified : but this rule is not strictly followed in A. S.

fore (⁶) ⎱ *before*	on *on, in, into*
be-foran ⎰	in *in, into*
on-bútan *about, around*	(on-)ge-mang *a-mong*
oð *unto, till*	be-tweox(⁷) *betwixt, among*
úppon *upon*	úton ⎱ *outside,*
innon *within*	wiðútan ⎰ *without*

(⁴) Hence *minster;* G. münster; all from L. monasterium.
(⁵) Hence O. halidom : " by my halidom !"
(⁶) Comp. προ, L. pro, G. (be-)vor; G. an ; ἐν, L. and G. in ; ὑπερ, L. super, G. über, D. over ; G. unter, gegen, &c.
(⁷) Like be-twynan from twá ; comp. G. zwi-schen from zwei.

ofer *over*   tó-geanes ⎫ *against,*
under *under*   on-gean   ⎭ *toward*
                    be-geondan *beyond.*

Fore Healf-denes hilde-wísan *before Healfdene's war-chiefs.*

Þá he þá be-foran þone graman cyning ge-lǽd wæs *when he then was led before the cruel king.*

Ic eóm a-send be-foran hine *I am sent before him.*

Be-foran eallum folce *before all the people*

On-bútan þæt cealf *around the calf.*

On-bútan þám weofode *about the altar.*

Oð Rin þá eá *unto the river Rhine.*

Oð Daniele þám witegan *till Daniel the prophet.*

On þá ealdan wísan *in the old wise.*

He sylf oð-fleáh on Asiam *he himself escaped into Asia.*

On þám heán munte *on the high mount.*

Heó hine in þæt mynster on-feng *she received him into the monastery.*

In ge-limp-lícre tíde *at a fitting time.*

Ic eów sende swá sceáp ge-mang wulfas *I send you as sheep among wolves.*

On-ge-mang óðrum mannum *among other men.*

Be-tweox his magas *among his kin's-folk.*

Be-tweox þǽre ealdan ǽ and þǽre niwan *betwixt the old law and the new.*

Þá feoll he úppon hine *then fell he upon him.*

Úppon ánum beáme *upon a beam.*

Heó be-seáh innon þá byrgene *she looked into the tomb.*

Innon þǽre healle *within the hall.*

Hí comon ofer þá sǽ *they came over the sea.*

Micel man-cwealm be-com ofer þǽre Romaniscre leóde *a great plague came upon the Roman people.*

Under þǽre fæstnesse *under the firmament.*

Wið-útan his dóm-ern *outside his judgment-hall.*

Wið-útan þám díce *without the ditch.*

Tó-geanes his fýnd he gǽð *he goeth against his foes.*

Hí þá ferdon tó-geanes þám hǽðenum *they then marched against the heathen.*

Feohtende on-gean hine *fighting against him.*

Þá com him þær on-gean *then came there to meet him.*

Be-geondan Iordanem *beyond Jordan.*

Be-geondan þám mere *beyond the lake.*

For *for*, and mid([1]) *with*, govern the accusative, ablative, or dative; as,

For eall Cristen folc ge-biddan *to pray for all Christian people.*

For þý máne *for that crime.*

For hwylcum intingan? *for what cause?*

Mid þá fore-sprecenan fæmnan([2]) *with the fore-said damsel.*

Mid þý áðe *with the oath.*

Mid his ágenum life *with his own life.*

Wið *against, with*, &c. governs the accusative, dative, or genitive; as,

Wið þá reádan sǽ *by the Red Sea.*

Wið þín folc *toward thy people.*

Þa assan wið hí læswodon *the asses were grazing with them.*

([1]) Comp. G. für; μετα, G. mid.   ([2]) L. femina.

A'na wið eallum *alone against all.*

Eáge wið eágan, tóð wið téð *eye for eye, tooth for tooth.*

Wið þæs holtes(¹) *toward the wood.*

He éfste wið þæs heres *he hastened against the army.*

A preposition sometimes stands after its case; as,

Hí him mid sǽton *they sate with him.*

Him bi twegen beámas stódon *by him stood two trees.*

It is sometimes parted from it altogether, and placed either next before the verb, or last of all; as,

Þe he man-cyn mid a-lýsde *with which he redeemed mankind*

Þá ge-nea-lǽhte him án man tó *then drew nigh to him a man.*

Ymb-útan is sometimes divided; as,

Ymb han-cred útan *about cock-crow.*

Wið and weard are sometimes used, the one before, the other after an accusative or genitive; as,

Wið heofonas weard(²) *toward the heavens.*

Wið Petres weard *toward Peter.*

VI.—*Syntax of Conjunctions.*

The following conjunctions require the verb to be in the indicative mode:

and (³) *and.*   eác *eke, also.*

(¹) P. holt, G. holz.   (²) Comp. the use of L. ad—versus.
(³) Comp. G. und, auch, so, da, dann, denn, da—da, &c.

SYNTAX OF CONJUNCTIONS. 93

ac *but*
swá, swá-swá *so, as*
swá—swú *so—as*
þá }
þonne } *then*
þá }
þá-þá } *when, as*
(for-)hwý *why?*
mid-þý(-þe) (⁴) } *when,*
mid-þám(-þe) } *while*
þenden *while*
síð-þán *since*

oððe— }
óðer-twega — } oððe { *either*
óðer-þára — } { *—or*
ge— } ge { *as well—as*
ǽgðer-ge, } ge { *both—and*
náðer-ne—ne *neither—nor*
swá-þeáh } *yet,*
(þeáh-)hwæðere } *nevertheless*
ná-læs—ac *not only—but*
(for-)þý(-þe) } *for, because,*
for-þám(-þe) } *therefore.*

The following require the subjunctive, though in general, as in Latin, in subordinate prepositions only:

þæt, þæt-te (⁵) *that*
þeáh(-þe) *though*
swylce *as if*
þonne } *when*
hwænne }
hwær } *where*
hwar }
þý-læs(-þe) *lest*
tó-þón-þæt *in order that*
á-þý—þe *so much the—as*

oð(-þæt) *until*
þá-hwíle(-þe)(⁶) *(the) while*
ǽr } *ere,*
ǽr-þám(-þe) } *before*
hwæðer(-þe)(⁷) } *whether*
sam—sam } *(—or)*
gif (⁸) *if*
nemne }
nymðe } *unless*
hú, hú-meta *how.*

(⁴) The particle þe is added or not at pleasure to several conjunctions.

(⁵) G. dass, D. dat; G. doch, wann, wenn, &c.

(⁶) Hwíl is a noun, (II. 3.) *while, time*; G. weile.

(⁷) Answering to πότερον—ἤ, L. utrum—an; like these hwæðer is properly a neuter pronoun.

(⁸) The conjunction gif has no more to do with the verb gifan than S. gin has with *given*, or O. an with unnan.

Hwæt dó ic þæt ic éce lif áge? *what shall I do that I may possess eternal life?*

Ic wát þæt hit býð sáwl and líc-homa *I know that it is soul and body.*

Þeáh hwylc of deáðe a-ríse *though one arise from death.*

Þeáh-þe ic sceal ealle wucan fæstan *though I shall fast all the week.*

Swylce þú hí ge-sceópe *as if thou hadst created them.*

Þý-læs þú þinne fót æt stáne æt-sporne *lest thou dash thy foot against a stone.*

Tó-þón-þæt he his ríce ge-brǽdde *in order that he might extend his empire.*

Á'-þý un-weorðra þe hine manige men for-seón *so much the unworthier because many men despise him.*

Oð-þæt þú cume tó þám fyrmestan *till thou come to the first.*

Oð-þæt se A-lýsend com *until the Redeemer came.*

Þá-hwíle-þe ge leóht habban *while ye have light.*

Þá-hwíle-þe he on life býð *while he is a-live.*

Ǽr-þám-þe se hana tuwa cráwe *before the cock crow twice.*

Ǽr-þám-þe ge hine biddað *before ye ask him.*

Þonne þú þe ge-bidde *when thou prayest.*

Þonne he hám cymð *when he cometh home.*

Sege ús hwænne þás þing ge-weorðon *tell us when these things shall come to pass.*

Ge nyton hwænne seó tíd is *ye know not when the time is.*

Ic axige hwær seó offrung síg *I ask where the offering is.*

Hwar synd þa nigene? *where are the nine?*

Sceáwa hwæðer hit síg þínes suna þe ne síg *look whether it be thy son's or be not.*

Sam hit sý sumor sam winter *whether it be summer or winter.*

Gif wén sý *if there be hope.*

Gif we secgað, of heofone—*if we say, of heaven*—

Nemne him wyrd for-stóde *unless fate had opposed him.*

Þú sædest þæt þú·ne mihte wítan hú-meta he his weólde *thou saidst that thou couldst not know how he ruled it.*

Hú Boetius hine singende ge-bæd *how Boëtius singing prayed.*

Bútan for *but* has an indicative, for *unless* a subjunctive; as,

Bútan ic wát *but I know.*

Bútan we gán *unless we go.*

Hú ne with an indicative, and hwæðer with a subjunctive, are used to make prepositions interrogative; as,

Hú ne dóð mán-fulle swá? *do not the wicked so?*

Hwæðer ge nú sécan gold on treowum *do ye now seek gold on trees?*

Cwyst þú, or segst þú? *sayest thou?* cweðe ge *say ye?* &c. serve the same purpose with an indicative; as,

Segst þú mæg se blinda þone blindan lǽdan? *may the blind lead the blind?*

Cweðe ge hæbbe ge sufol? *have ye meat?*

Uton (-an) with an infinitive, expresses a wish or intention; as,

Uton gán *let us go*.

The negative ne *not* stands (like L. non, ne, F. ne) before the verb; as,

Ne for-læt he eów *he will not forsake you*.

Two([1]) or more negatives are often used, ne being usually prefixed to each word capable of taking it; as,

Ne wép þú ná *weep not*.

Þá næs nán cræft þæt ic ne cúðe *then there was no art that I knew not*.

Se-þe nis náðer ne ge boren ne ge-sceapen fram nánum óðrum *who is neither born nor created by any other*.

Bútan *but, only* takes ne before it; as,

We nabbað búton([2]) fíf hláfas *we have but five loaves*.

VII.—*Syntax of Interjections*.

Wá *wo* takes a dative; as,

Wá þám men!([3]) *wo to the man!* where sý (beó) *be*, or býð *shall be* is understood.

[1] The doctrine, therefore, that "two negatives make an affirmative," is as foreign to the true spirit of the English as it would be to that of the Greek language.

[2] Comp. F. nous n'avons que.

[3] L. væ homini! G. weh dem manne!

SYNTAX OF INTERJECTIONS.

Wá is me(⁴)! *wo is me!*

On the other interjections, of which the following are he chief, nothing need be added:

lá! *O, oh, lo!*
ea-lá! *oh, halloo, alas!*
efne! *behold!*
wá-lá-wá (wei-lá-wei) *well-a-way!*
hwæt! *lo! indeed!*

Leóf(⁵) is used as an expletive; as,

Gea(⁶), leóf, ic hæbbe *yea marry have I.*

(⁴) Οὐαί μοι ἐστι.
(⁵) Analogous to our P. and familiar use of the word *dear*
(⁶) G. and D. ja.

CHAPTER VIII.

Prose Extracts.

N B. Some words that have already occurred are not explained in lie notes to this and the next chapter.

I.—S. *Matthew*, xii. 1—13.

⁎ The Gospels([1]), and parts of the Old Testament, were rendered into A. S. by one or more ecclesiastics named Ælfric, in the 9th or 10th century; the former from the Vulgate, the latter from some other early Latin translation. The sense therefore, differs now and then from that of the original, and of our authorised version.

1. Se Hǽlend([2]) fór on reste-dæg(") ofer æceras([4]); sóđ-líce his leorning-cnihtas([5]) hyngrede, and híg ongunnon([6]) pluccian([7]) þa ear and etan.

2. Sóđ-líce þá þa sundor-hálgan([8]) þæt ge-sáwon, hí

([1]) The extracts from the Gospels are from Mr. Thorpe's edition, the only one founded on a collation of the best MSS.

([2]) Hǽlend (11. 2.) *Saviour, healer* (G. Heiland), from *bǽlan to heal:* the Name Jesus is thus rendered throughout the A. S. Gospels.

([3]) *Day of rest, sabbath:* rest II. 3 ; G. rast.

([4]) Æcer (II. 2.) (*corn*) *field ;* ἀγρος, L. ager, G. acker: hence *acre.*

([5]) *Disciples:* cniht (II. 2.) *youth, servant;* hence *knight:* G. knecht *servant ;* comp. L. puer.

([6]) On-ginnan (III. 1.) *to be-gin.*   ([7]) I. 1. *to pluck ;* G. pflücken.

([8]) Sundor-hálga (I. 2.) *Pharisee,* lit. *separate saint.*

cwǽdon tó him: Nú þine leorning-cnihtas dóð þæt him a-lýfed(¹) nis reste-dagum tó dónne.

3. And he cwæð tó him: Ne rǽdde(²) ge hwæt Dauid dyde þá hine hyngrede, and þa þe mid him wǽron,

4. Hú he in-eóde on Godes hús, and æt þa offring-hláfas(³) þe nǽron him a-lýfede tó etanne, búton þám sacer.lum(⁴) ánum?

5. Oððe ne rǽdde ge on þǽre ǽ, þæt þa sacerdas on reste-dagum on þám temple(⁵) ge-wemmað(⁶) þ ne reste-dæg, and synd búton leahtre(⁷)?

6. Ic secge sóð-líce eów þæt þes(⁸) is mǽrra(⁹) þonne þæt templ.

7. Gif ge sóð líce wiston hwæt is: Ic wille mild-heortnesse and ná on-sægdnesse(¹⁰), ne ge-niðrode ge næfre un-scyldige.

8. Sóð-líce mannes sunu is eác reste-dæges hláf-ord(¹¹).

9. Þá se Hǽlend þanon fór, he com in-tó heora ge-somnunge(¹²):

10. Þá wæs þær án man se hæfde for-scruncene(¹³

(¹) A-lýfan (I. 2.) *to allow*; G. *er-lauben.*   (²) Rǽdan (I. 2.) *to read.*
(³) *Loaves of offering, show-bread*; offring II. 3. hláf II. 2.
(⁴) Sacerd (II. 2.) *priest* L. *sacerdos.*   (⁵) Templ (III. 1.) *temple.*
(⁶) Ge-wemman (I. 2.) *to pollute, profane.*
(⁷) Leahter (II. 2) *crime, sin*   (⁸) *This man.*
(⁹) Mǽre (I.) *great, famous.*
(¹⁰) On-sægdnes (II. 3.) *sacrifice*; on-secgan *to offer.*
(¹¹) II. 2. *lord*; said to be from hláf *bread, loaf,* and ord *beginning, origin*; that is, *giver of bread.*   (¹²) *Assembly, synagogue*; G. ver-sammlung.
(¹³) For-scrincan (III. 1.) *to shrink up, wither away*: mark the intensive force of for-.

hand. And híg ácsodon hine, þus cweðende: Is hit a-lýfed tó hǽlanne on reste-dagum? þæt híg wrégdon(¹) hine.

11. He sǽde him sóð-líce: Hwylc man is of eów, þe hæbbe án sceáp, and gif hit a-fylð reste-dagum on pyt(²), hú ne nimð he þæt, and hefð hit úp?

12. Witod-líce(³) micle má man is sceápe betera(⁴); witod-líce hit is a-lýfed on reste-dagum wel tó dónne.

13. Þá cwæð he tó þám men: A-þena(⁵) þíne hand. And he hí a-þenede; and heó wæs hál ge-worden swá seó óðer.

II.—*S. Mark,* vi. 32.

32. And on scip(⁶) stígende, híg fóron on-sundron on wéste(⁷) stówe(⁸).

33. And ge-sáwon híg farende, and híg ge-cneowon manega, and gangende of þám burgum(⁹), þider urnon and him be-foran comon.

34. And þá se Hǽlend þanon eóde, he ge-seáh micele mænigeo, and he ge-miltsode him, for-þám-þe híg

---

(¹) Wrégan (I. 2.) *to accuse, be-wray.*

(²) II. 2. *pit, hole;* D. put, L. put-eus.

(³) *Verily, truly, for, but, therefore;* a common expletive: from witian (I. 1.) *to decide.*   (⁴) Vulgate: " Quantò magis melior."

(⁵) A-þenian (I. 1.) *to stretch out.*

(⁶) Comp. σκαφη, G. schiff, D. schip; hence also *skiff.*

(⁷) Wéste (I.) *waste, desert;* G. wüst, D. woest.

(⁸) Hence *stow* in local names, and *to stow, be-stow.*

(⁹) Burh (p. 19—20), G. burg (πυργος) *a (fortified) town, burgh.*

wǽron swa-swá scép(¹) þe nǽnne hyrde nabbað; and he on-gan híg fela lǽran(²).

35. And þá hit micel ylding(³) wæs, his leorning-cnihtas him tó comon and cwǽdon:

36. Þeós stów is wéste, and tíma is forð-a-gán(⁴); for-lǽt þás mænigeo, þæt híg faron on ge-hende túnas(⁵), and him mete bycgon þæt híg eton(⁶).

37. Þá cwæð he: Sylle(⁷) ge him etan. Þá cwǽdon híg: Uton gán, and mid twám hundred penigum(⁸) hláfas bycgan, and we him etan syllað.

38. Þá cwæð he. Hú fela hláfa(⁹) habbe ge? gáð and lóciað(¹⁰). And þá híg wiston híg cwǽdon: Fíf hláfas and twegen fixas.

39. And þá be-beád(¹¹) se Hǽlend þæt þæt folc sǽte ofer þæt gréne hig(¹²).

40. And híg þá sǽton, hundredum(¹³) and fíftigum.

41. And fíf hláfum and twám fixum on fangenum(¹⁴), he on heofon locoðe, and híg bletsode, and þa hláfas bræc, and sealde his leorning-cnihtum þæt híg tó-foran him a-setton; and twegen fixas him eallum dǽlde(¹⁵).

(¹) Two accusatives as with L. doceo.
(²) *Lateness, delay*; from eald.   (³) For sceáp · see p. 5.
(⁴) *Gone forth*; "*far passed.*"
(⁵) Tún (II. 2.) *village, town*: originally *enclosure, farm*: comp. G. zaun *hedge*; D. tuin *garden*.   (⁶) Comp. ἰδεῖν, L. edere.
(⁷) Syllan (I. 3.) *to give, sell*.   (⁸) Penig (pening) (II. 2.) G. pfennig.
(⁹) Geṅ: see p. 32.   (¹⁰) Lócian (I. 1.) *to look*.
(¹¹) Be-beódan (III. 3.) *to command*.
(¹²) Ll. 1. *hay*; G. heu. Vulg. "super viride fœnum."
(¹³) *By hundreds, &c.*   (¹⁴) Abl. or dat. absolute, p. 75.
(¹⁵) Dǽlan (I. 2.) *to deal, divide, distribute*; G. theilen, D. deelen.

42. And híg æton þá ealle, and ge-fyllede wurdon.

43. And híg namon þǽra hláfa and fixa láfa(¹), twelf wilian(²) fulle.

44. Sóð-líce fíf þúsend manna þǽra etendra wǽron.

45. Þá sona he nýdde(³) his leornīng-cnihtas on scip stígan, þæt híg him be-foran fóron ofer þone múðan(⁴) tó Bethsaida, oð he þæt folc for-lete(⁵).

46. And þá he híg for-let, he ferde(⁶) on þone munt(⁷), and hine ána þar(⁸) ge-bæd(⁹).

47. And þá æfen(¹⁰) wæs, þæt scip wæs on middre sǽ, and he ána wæs on lande.

48. And he ge-seáh híg on réwette(¹¹) swincende(¹²); him wæs wiðer-weard(¹³) wind(¹⁴): and on niht, ymbe þá feorðan wæccan(¹⁵), he com tó him ofer þá sǽ gangende, and wolde híg for-búgan(¹⁶).

49. Þa híg hine ge-sáwon ofer þá sǽ gangende, híg wéndon þæt hit un-fǽle(¹⁷) gást(¹⁸) wǽre, and híg clyp-edon,

(¹) Láf (II. 3.) *leaving, remnant*; lǽfan (I. 2.) *to leave*; λειπειν.

(²) Wilia (I. 2.) *basket.* (³) Nýdan (I. 2.) *to compel*; from neód.

(⁴) Múða (I. 2.) *mouth of a river*; here *lake*; Vulg. " fretum."

(⁵) For-lætan (II. 2.) *to forsake, abandon*, (G. ver-lassen, D. ver-laaten), *send away.* (⁶) Feran (I. 2.) *to go.*

(⁷) II. 2. *mount:* we have " *a* mountain."

(⁸) Þar=þær, þara. (⁹) Ge-biddan (II. 1. reflect,) *to pray.*

(¹⁰) Æfen (II. 2.) *even*, G. abend: -ung (II. 3.) *evening.*

(¹¹) Réwet (II. 2.) *rowing*; rówan (II. 2.) *to row*; D. roeijen.

(¹²) Swincan (III. 1.) *to labour*; O. *swink.*

(¹³) *Adverse, way-ward*; G. wider-würtig.

(¹⁴) II. 2. G. & D. wind; L. vent-us.

(¹⁵) Wæcce (I. 3.) *watch.* (¹⁶) III. 3. *avoid, pass by.*

(¹⁷) *Unclean*; fǽle *pure, faithful*; fǽl-s-ian *to purify.*

(¹⁸) Comp. G. geist, D. geest, S. ghaist.

50. Híg ealle hine ge-sáwon, and wurdon ge-dréfede([1]). And sona he spræc tó him, and cwæð: Gelýfað; ic hit eom ([2]); nelle ge ([3]) eów on-drædan.

51. And he on scip tó him eóde; and se wind geswác ([4]); and híg þæs þe má ([5]) be-tweox him wundredon.

52. Ne on-geaton ([6]) híg be þám hláfum; sóð·líce heora heorte wæs a-blend ([7]).

53. And þá híg ofer seglodon, híg comon tó Genesaret and þar wícedon ([8]).

54. And þá híg of scipe eódon, sona híg hine ge-cneówon;

55. And eal þæt ríce be-farende ([9]), híg on sæccingum ([10]) bæron þa un-truman ([11]), þar híg hine ge-hýrdon.

56. And swá-hwar-swá he on wíc ([12]) oððe on túnas eóde, on stræton ([13]) híg þa un-truman ledon, and hine bædon þæt híg huru ([14]) his reáfes fnæd ([15]) æt-hrinon ([16]). And swá fela swá hine æt-hrinon, híg wurdon hále.

([1]) Drefan (I. 2.) *to trouble, offend.*
([2]) Comp. G. *ich bin es*
([3]) L. *nolite.*
([4]) Ge-swícan (III. 2.) *to cease.*
([5]) *So much the more;* G. *des-to mehr.*
([6]) On-gitan (II. 1.) *to understand.*
([7]) A-blendan (I. 2.) *to blind;* blind *blind.*
([8]) Wícian (I. 1.) *to dwell:* see wíc below.
([9]) Be-faran=be-feran, p. 55. ([10]) Sæccing (II. 3.) *sacking, bed.*
([11]) *Diseased, infirm;* trum *firm.*
([12]) Wíc (II. 1.) *dwelling, village;* L. vic-us: hence *wich* and *wick* in local names; D. wijk. ([13]) Strǽt (II. 3.) *street;* G. strasse, D. straat.
([14]) *At least, at all events.* ([15]) *Hem.*
([16]) Æt-hrínan (III. 3.) *to touch.*

III.—*S. Luke,* xx. 9—25.

9. He on-gan þá þis big-spel(¹) tó þám folce cweðan: Sum man plantode(²) him wín-geard(³), and hine gesette(⁴) mid tilium( ), and he wæs him feor manegum tídum(⁶).

10. Þá on tíde he sende his þeów tó þám tilium, þæt híg him sealdon of þæs wín-geardes wæstme; þá swungon(⁷) híg þone and ídelne(⁸) hine for-leton.

11. Þá sende he óðerne þeów; þá beóton híg þone, and mid teónum(⁹) ge-wǽcende(¹⁰) hine for-leton ídelne.

12. Þá sende he þryddan; þá wurpon híg út þone ge-wundodne(¹¹).

13. Þá cwæð þæs wín geardes hláf-ord: Hwæt dó ic? ic a-sende minne leófan sunu; wénunga(¹²) hine híg for-wandiað(¹³) þonne híg hine ge seóð.

(¹) *Parable·* see p. 73. Spel (II. 1.) *story, tale;* hence *spell.*
(²) Plantian (1. 1.) *to plant.*
(³) *Vine-yard;* D. wijn-gaard: geard or eard (II. 2.) *yard, (garden), inclosure, dwelling, country.*
(⁴) Ge-settan (I. 2.) *to furnish, people:* perhaps a mis-translation of Vu'g. "locavit;" we read "*let it forth.*"
(⁵) Tilia (I. 2.) *tiller, husbandman.*
(⁶) Tíd (II. 3.) *time, tide, season;* G. zeit, D. tijd. *For a long time, many seasons,* Vulg. "multis temporibus."
(⁷) Swingan (III. 1) *to beat, swinge.*
(⁸) I'del (I.) *empty, idle, vain;* G. eitel, D. ijdel.
(⁹) Teóna (I. 2.) *injury, wrong.*
(¹⁰) Ge-wǽcan (I. 2.) *to weaken, injure:* wác (G. weich) *weak.*
(¹¹) Wundian (I. 1.) *to wound:* wund (II. 2.) *wound.*
(¹²) *Perhaps:* wénan *to ween, hope, expect;* G. wähnen *to fancy,* &c.
(¹³) For-wandian (I. 1.) *to respect, reverence.*

14. Þá hine þa tilian ge-sáwon, híg þóhton be-tweox him, and cwǽdon: Her is se yrfe-weard(¹); cumađ, uton hine of-sleán(²), þæt seó ǽht(³) úre sý.

15. And híg hine of þám wín-gearde a-wurpon(⁴) of-slegene. Hwæt dẹ́đ þæs wín-geardes hláford?

16. He cymđ and for-spilđ þa tilian, and sylđ þone wín-geard ọ́đrum. Híg cwǽdon þá hig þis ge-hýrdon· þæt ne gḗ-weorđe.

17. Þá be-heóld he híg, and cwæđ: Hwæt is þæt a-writen is, Þone stán(⁵) þe þa wyrhtan a-wurpon, þes is ge-worden on þǽre hyrnan(⁶) heáfod(⁷)?

18. Ælc þe fylđ ofer þone stán býđ for-brytt(⁸); ofer þone þe he fylđ, he to-cwyst(⁹).

19. Þá sóhton þǽra sacerda ealdras(¹⁰) and þa bóceras(¹¹) hyra handa on þǽre tíde on hine wurpan(¹²); and híg on-dredon him þæt folc: sóđ-líce híg on-geton þæt he þis big-spel tó him cwæđ.

(¹) Heir; yrfe (I. 3.) *inheritance* (G. erb-schaft) · weard (II. 2.) *keeper, ward-en, &c.*

(²) Sleán (II. 3.) *to strike, beat, slay;* of-sleán *to kill outright.* of- in composition often strengthens the sense or makes it bad.

(³) Æ'ht (II. 3.) *possession;* from ágan.

(⁴) A-weorpan (III. 1.) *to cast out, reject.*

(⁵) Comp. G. stein, D. steen, S. stane.

(⁶) Hyrne (I. 3.) *corner.*

(⁷) Heáfod (III. 1.) *head;* G. haupt, D. hoofd.

(⁸) For-bryttan (I. 2.) *to break, shatter:* Vulg. "conquassabitur."

(⁹) To-cwysan (I. 2.) *to crush, squeeze to pieces;* G. quetschen. With *s-queeze*, comp. bar, *s-par*; melt, *s-melt*; tumble, *s-tumble*, &c. &c.

(¹⁰) *Chief(s of the) priests.*

(¹¹) Bócere (II. 2.) *book man, learned man, scribe, lawyer.*

(¹²) Or weorpan; see p. 5.

20. Þá sendon híg mid searwum(¹) þa þe híg riht-wíse leton(²), þæt híg hine ge-scyldigodon(³), and þæt híg hine ge-sealdon þám ealdron(⁴) tó dóme(⁵), and tó þæs déman(⁶) an-wealde(⁷) tó for-démanne(⁸).

21. Þá ácsodon híg hine, and cwædon: Láreow, we witon þæt þú rihte spricst and lærst, and for nánum men ne wandast(⁹), ac Godes weg on sóð-fæstnisse lærst:

22. Is hit riht þæt man þám Casere(¹⁰) gafol(¹¹) sylle, þe(¹²) ná?

23. Þá cwæð he tó him þá he heora fácen(¹³) on-get(¹⁴): Hwý fandige(¹⁵) ge mín?

24. Y'wað(¹⁶) me ánne pening. Hwæs an-lícnesse(¹⁷)

(¹) Searu (III. 1.) *ambush, stratagem*.

(²) *Who might feign themselves righteous men.*

(³) Ge-scyldigan (-ian, see p. 41) (I. 1.) *to accuse*; G. be-schuldigen. Scyld (II. 3.) (G. schuld) *debt, guilt*.

(⁴) *Deliver him to the chief priests:* Vulg. " traderent illum principatui."

(⁵) Dóm (II. 2.) *doom, judgment, power, &c.*

(⁶) Déma (I. 2.) *judge, doomer, deemer;* hence *deemster* (démestre) properly feminine; see p. 66.

(⁷) An-weald (II. 2.) *power*; G. ge-walt, fem. another exception to the general rule.

(⁸) Déman (I. 2.) *to judge*, for-déman *to condemn*: comp. κρινειν, κατα-κρινειν; G. urtheilen, ver-urtheilen.

(⁹) The for in for-wandian, is the preposition, not the prefix; the latter is inseparable: see p. 73.

(¹⁰) Casere (II. 2.) *Cæsar, Emperor*; G. kaiser.

(¹¹) Tribute, *gavel*; F. gabelle.

(¹²) *Or*; seldom used independently, but often affixed to other conjunctions: see p. 93.   (¹³) III. 1. *deceit, fraud.*

(¹⁴) For on-geat; see p. 5.   (¹⁵) Fandian (1. 1.) *to tempt.*

(¹⁶) Y'wian (eówian) (I. 1.) *to show.*

(¹⁷) An-lícnes (II. 3.) *likeness, image.*

hæfð he, and ofer-ge-writ(¹)? Þá cwǽdon híg: Þæs Caseres.

25. Þá cwæð he tó him: A-gifað(²) þám Casere þa þing þe þæs Caseres synd, and Gode þa þing þa Godes synd.

IV.—S. John vii. 14—28.

14. Þá hit wæs mid-dæg þæs freols-dæges(³), þá eóde se Hǽlend in-tó þám temple, and lǽrde.

15. And þa Iudeas wundredon and cwǽdon: Hú-meta can þes stafas, þonne he ne leornode(⁴)?

16. Se Hǽlend him and-swarode(⁵) and cwæð: Mín lár nis ná mín, ac þæs þe me sende.

17. Gif hwá(⁶) wile his willan dón, he ge-cnǽwð be þǽre láre hwæðer heó síg of Gode, hwæðer-þe ic be me sylfum spece.

18. Se-þe be him sylfum spicð sécð his ágen wuldor(⁷); se-þe sécð þæs wuldor þe hine sende, se is sóðfæst(⁸), and nis nán un-riht-wísnes on him.

19. Hú ne sealde Moises eów ǽ, and eówer nán ne healt þá ǽ? Hwý séce ge me tó of sleánne?

(¹) III. 1. *super-scription.*
(²) A-gifan (II. 1.) *to render, restore, give back.*
(³) Freols (II. 2.) *feast, festival.*
(⁴) Leornian (I. 1.) *to learn;* G. *lernen.*
(⁵) And-swarian (I. 1.) *to answer,* governing the dative.
(⁶) *If any one;* comp. L. *si quis.* (⁷) Wuldor (-er) (II. 2.) *glory.*
(⁸) *Sooth-fast, truthful, just;* fæst forms the second part of several compound adjectives.

20. Þá and-swarode seó mænio and cwæð: Deófol þe sticað on(¹); hwá sécð þe-tó of-sleánne?

21. Þá and-swarode se Hǽlend, and cwæð tó him: án weorc ic worhte, and ealle ge wundriað.

22. For-þý Moises eów sealde ymb-snidennesse(²); (næs(³) ná for-þýg-þe heó of Moises sý, ac of fæd- eron(⁴);)

23. And on reste-dæge ge ymb-sn'ðað man þæt Moises ǽ ne sý to-worpen(⁵); and ge belgað(⁶) wið me for þám-þe ic ge-hǽlde ǽnne man on reste-dæg.

24. Ne déme ge be an-sýne(⁷), ac démað rihtne dóm.

25. Sume cwǽdon, þa þe wǽron of Ierusalem: Hú nis þes se þe híg sécað tó of-sleánne?

26 And nú he spicð open-líce(⁸), and híg ne cweðað nán þing tó him. Cweðe we(⁹) hwæðer þa ealdras on-giton þæt þes is Crist?

27. Ac we witon hwanon þes is: þonne Crist cymð, þonne nát nán man hwanon he býð.

28. Se Hǽlend clypode and lǽrde on þám temple, and cwæð: Me ge cunnon(¹⁰), and ge witon hwanon ic

(¹) On-stician (I. 1.) *to prick, urge on.*

(²) Ymb-snidennes (II. 3.) *circum-cision;* ymb-sníðan (III. 2.) *to cir-cum-cise;* part. p. -sniden.

(³) Næs (nas) *not;* usually joined with ná.

(⁴) For fæderum; see p. 12.

(⁵) To-weorpan (III. 1.) *to over-throw, cast down, destroy;* L. dis-jicere, G. zer-werfen.   (⁶) Belgan (III. 1.) *to be angry.*

(⁷) An-sýn (II. 3.) *countenance, appearance.*

(⁸) Open (II.) *open;* G. offen, D. open.   (⁹) See pp. 95—6.

(¹⁰) Observe the distinction between cunnan and wítan (p. 61, note 7); *me ye* know, *and ye* wot *whence I am.*

eom: and ic ne com tram mə sylfum, ac se is sóđ þe me
ende, þone ge ne cunnon.

V.—*Genesis*, ch. xlv.(¹)

1. Þá ne mihte Iosep hine leng dyrnan(²), ac he dræ-
ealle þa Egiptiscan út, þæt nán fremde(³) man be-twyx
him nære;

2. And he weóp, and clypode hlúdre(⁴) stefne, and
þa Egiptiscan ge-hýrdon, and eal Pharaones hired(⁵);

3. And he cwæđ tó his ge-bróđrum: Ic eom Iosep;
lyfađ úre fæder nú git? Þá ne mihton his ge-bróđru
him for ege(⁶) ge-and-wyrdan(⁷).

4. Þá grétte(⁸) he híg ár-wurđ-líce(⁹), and cwæđ:
Ic eom Iosep eówer bróđor, þe ge sealdon on Egipta-
land(¹⁰).

5. Ne on-dræde ge eów nán þing, ne eów ne of-
þince(¹¹) þæt ge me sealdon on þis ríce; sóđ-líce for
eówre þearfe me sende God on Egipta-land.

(¹) This and the following chapter are taken with some alterations from
Thwaites's Heptateuchus.
(²) *To hide* (I. 2.); dyrne (I.) *dark*.
(³) Fremed, fremd (I.) *strange, foreign*; G. fremd.
(⁴) Hlúd (I.) *loud*; G. laut, D. luid.   (⁵) II. 1. *household*.
(⁶) II. 1. *awe, fear*.
(⁷) And-wyrdan (I. 2.) *to answer*; and-wyrd (II. 3.) *answer*; G. ant-
wort-en. Ge- is used before no other prefixes but and- and ed-, as should
have been stated p. 41, note 2.   (⁸) Grétan (I. 2.) *to greet, salute*.
(⁹) Á'r-wurð-líc (II.) *honorable*; G. ehr-würd-ig.
(¹⁰) *Land of the Egyptians*: comp. Engla-land, &c. p. 72.
(¹¹) (Hit) of-þincð it *repenteth*: L. pœnitet· see p. 86-7.

6. Nu twá gear wæs(¹) hunger ofer ealle eorðan, and git sceolon(²) fífe on þám man ne mæg náðer ne erian(³) ne ripan(⁴).

7. And God me sende tó-þám-þæt ge beón ge-healdene, and þæt ge habbon þæt ge magon big-lybban(⁵).

8. Þæt næs ná eówres þances(⁶) ac þurh God þe ic þurh his willan(⁷) hider a-send wæs, se dyde me swylce ic Pharaones fæder wære, and his hiredes hláf-ord, and he sette me tó ealdre ofer Egipta-land.

9. Faraþ hræd-líce(⁸) tó mínum fæder, and secgað him þæt God me sette tó hláf-orde eallum Egiptum; beódað him þæt he fare tó me,

10. And wunige(⁹) on Gessen-lande(¹⁰), and heó me ge-hende, he and his suna, and his bearna bearn, and eówre sceáp, and eówre hrýðer-heorda(¹¹) and eal þæt ge ágon.

11. And ic eów féde. Git synd fíf hunger-gear bæftan(¹²) : dóð þus þæt ge ne for-wurðon(¹³).

12. Nú ge ge-seóð hú hit mid me is, and ge ge-hýrað hwæt ic tó eów sprece.

(¹) *Has been*: see p. 62, note 2. (²) *Shall be, are to come.*
(³) *To ear, plough*; L. arare. (⁴) I. 2. *to reap.* (⁵) See p. 73.
(⁶) *Of your own accord*: see p. 70. Vulg. has "vestro consilio."
(⁷) *Through whose will*: see p. 31.
(⁸) *Quickly*;=hraðe: see p. 25.
(⁹) Wunian *to dwell*; G. wohnen. (¹⁰) *Land of Goshen.*
(¹¹) Hrýðer (III. 1.) *ox, rother-beast*; G rind, D. rund: mark the n dropped and the vowel lengthened: see p. 2. Heord (II. 3.) *herd*; G. herde.
(¹²) *Behind, to come.*
(¹³) For-weorðan (III. 1.) *to perish*; observe the force of the prefix

EXTRACTS—GENESIS.

12. Cýdað mínum fæder eal mín wuldor, and ealle þa þing þe ge ge-sáwon on Egipta-lande: eístað and lædað hine tó me.

14. And he clypte(¹) heóra ælcne, and cyste(²) híg,

15. And weóp: æfter þisón híg ne dorston sprecan wið hine.

16. Þá spræc man ofer-eal(³), and wið-mærsode(⁴) þæt Iosepes bródru comon tó Pharaone, and Pharao wæs glæd, and eal his hired;

17. And he beád Iosepe þæt he bude his bródrum and þus cwǽde: Sýmað(⁵) eówre assan, and farað tó Chanaan-lande.

18. And nimað þær eówerne fæder, and eówere mægða(⁶), and cumað tó me, and ic eów sylle ealle Egipta gód.

19. Beód him eác þæt híg nimon wænas(⁷) tó hyra cilda fare(⁸) and tó hyra ge-mæccena(⁹), and beód him eác þæt híg nimon hyra fæder, and éfston hider swá híg hraðost magon.

20. And ne for-læte ge nán þing(¹⁰) of eówrum yddisce(¹¹), for-þám ealle Egipta spéda(¹²) beóð eówre.

21. Israeles suna dydon swá him be-boden wæs, and

(¹) Clyppan (I. 2.) *to embrace, clip.*
(²) Cyssan (I. 2.) *to kiss;* G. küssen.   (³) *Everywhere;* G. über-all.
(⁴) Wíd-mærsian *to noise, spread abroad;* from wíd and mǽre.
(⁵) Sýman (I. 2.) *to load.*   (⁶) Mægð (II. 3.) *family, household, tribe.*
(⁷) Wægn, wæn (II. 2.) *wagon, wain;* G. wagen.
(⁸) Far (II. 3.) *going, journey;* hence *fare.*
(⁹) Ge-mœcca, -e (I. 2, 3.) *husband, wife, companion, mate;* O. *make.*
(¹⁰) Vulg. " Nec dimittatis quicquam."
(¹¹) Yddisc *food,* from etan; hence P. eddish, ashes, &c. *feed for cattle, after-grass, stubble.*   (¹²) Spéd

Iosep him sealde wænas eal-swá Pharao him beád, and
fór-mete(¹),
22. And sealde hyra ælcum twá scrúd(²); and he
sealde Beniamine fíf scrúd, and þreo hundred sylfringa(³).
23. And he sende his fæder tyn assan þe wǽron ge-
sýmed mid feó, and mid hrægle(⁴), and mid Egipta
welon(⁵), and tyne þe bǽron hwǽte and hláf.
24. Witod-líce he let þa his ge-bródru faran, and
cwæð tó him: Ne for-lǽte ge nán þing(⁶) be wege, ac
beóð swíðe ge-sóme(⁷).
25. Híg foron of Egipta-lande, and comon tó Chanaan-lande tó Iacobe hyra fæder,
26. And cwǽdon tó him: Iosep lyfað þín sunu, and
wealt ealles Egipta-landes. Þá Iacob þæt ge-hýrde þá
þúhte him swylce he of heftgum slǽpe a-wacode,
27. And þeáh he him ne ge-lýfde, híg rehton(⁸) him
hyra færeld(⁹) be ende-byrdnesse(¹⁰) and þá he ge-seáh
þa wænas, and ealle þa þing þe him ge-sende wǽron,
his gást wearð ge-ed-cwicod(¹¹),

(¹) " *Provision for the way;*" fór (II. 3.) *journey;* mete (II. 2.) *meat.*

(²) Vulg. "*stolas;*" "*changes of raiment:*" scrúd (II. 1.) *garment, shroud.*

(³) Sylfring (II. 2.) "*piece of silver.*"

(⁴) Hrægl (II. 2.) *raiment, garment;* hence *night-rail.*

(⁵) Wela (I. 2.) *weal, wealth:* pl. *riches, prosperity.*

(⁶) Perhaps repeated by mistake from v. 5. Vulg. has here " Ne irascamini:" we " *see that ye fall not out.*"

(⁷) Mild, gentle. (⁸) Reccan (II. 2.) *to relate.*

(⁹) *Going, journey,* or perhaps, *how they had fared.*

(¹⁰) *In order, succession:* Vulg. "Illi econtra referebant omnem ordinem rei."

(¹¹) Ge-ed-cwician *to make alive again, quicken,* cwic, cuc, &c. *quick, living.*

28. And he cwæð: Ge-noh ic hæbbe gif Iosep mín sunu gyt leofað; ic fare and ge-seó hine ǽr-þám-þe ic swelte(¹).

VI.—*Exodus,* ch. xxiii.(²)

1. Ne under-fóh(³) leáse(⁴) ge-witnesse(⁵).
2. Ne fylig(⁶) þú þám folce þe yfel wille dón, ne be-foran manegon sóðes ne wanda(⁷).
3. Ne miltsa(⁸) þú þearfan(⁹) on dóme.
4. Gif þú ge-méte þínes feóndes oxan oððe assan, lǽd hine tó him.
5. Gif þú ge-seó his assan licgan under byrðene(¹⁰), ne gá þú þanon, ac hefe hine úp mid him.
6. Ne þú ne wanda on þearfan dóme.
7. Fleóh(¹¹) leásunga(¹²); un-scyldigne and riht-wísne ne of-sléh þú.

(¹) Sweltan (III. 1.) *to die.*
(²) This chapter is imperfect in several places, and the 30th verse is wanting.
(³) Under-fangan, -fón (II. 2.) *to undertake, receive.*
(⁴) Leás (I.) *false, lying.*   (⁵) *Witness, testimony.*   (⁶) See p. 42.
(⁷) Wandian *to fear,* &c. : *shrink not, decline not from the truth through fear.*   (⁸) Miltsian *to pity;* from milde.   (⁹) þearf (I.) *poor.*
(¹⁰) Byrðen (II. 3.) *burthen;* G. bürde: from beran.
(¹¹) Fleógan, fleón (II. 2.) *to flee, fly;* G. fliehen, fliegen.
(¹²) Either sing, or plur. Nouns in -ung sometimes form the oblique cases singular in -a. Leásung *leasing, lying,* from leás.

8. Ne nim þú lac(¹) þa a-blendad. gleáwne(²), and a-wendað(³) riht-wísra word.

9. Ne beó þú æl-þeódigum(⁴) gram(⁵), for-þám ge wǽron æl-þeódie on Egipta-lande.

10. Sáw(⁶) six ger(⁷) þín land, and gadera(⁸) his wœstmas,

11. And læt hit restan on þám seofoðan, þæt þearfan eton þær-of, and wild-deór(⁹) : dó swá on þínum wín-carde, and on þínum ele-beámon(¹⁰).

12. Wyrc six dagas, and ge-swíc(¹¹) on þám seofoðan, þæt þín oxa and þín assa híg ge-reston, and þæt þínre wylne sunu sý ge-hyrt(¹²), and se útan-cumena(¹³).

13. Healdað ealle þa þing þe ic eów sæde, and ne swerie ge þurh útan-cumenra goda naman.

14. Þrywa on gere ge-wurðiað(¹⁴) mínne freols.

15. Þú ytst þeorf-symbel(¹⁵); seofon dagas ge etað

(¹) *Gifts,* here neuter II. 1., but see p. 9.

(²) Gleáw (I.) *skilful, clever ;* G. klug.

(³) A-wendan (I. 2.) *to turn away, sub-vert, per-vert ;* G. ab-wenden: the prefix a- sometimes has the force of of-.

(⁴) Æl-þeódig (II.) *foreign, strange;* æl- is here=ἀλλ-ος, L. al-ius, al-ienus ; and not to be confounded with æl for eal, in æl-mihtig, æl-beorht and the like. (⁵) *Angry, cruel.* Vulg." molestus."

(⁶) Sáwan (II. 2.) *to sow;* G. säben.   (⁷) =gear, see p. 5.

(⁸) Gaderian *to gather.*   (⁹) *Wild beasts.*

(¹⁰) *Olive-trees ;* ele *oil,* beám *beam, tree ;* G. baum, D. boom, whence *broom.*   (¹¹) Ge-swícan (III. 2.) *to cense.*

(¹²) Ge-hyrtan (I. 2.) *to encourage, hearten, strengthen,* from heorte.

(¹³) *Stranger, one come from without ;* ít-on, see p. 71.

(¹⁴) Ge-weorðian (wurðian) *to honour, celebrate ;* G. würdigen.

(¹⁵) *Feast of unleavened bread.*

þeorf, swá ic þe be-beád, on þæs monðes tíd níwra(¹) wæstma, þá þú út-fóre of Egipta-lande : ne cymst þú bútan ælmyssan (²) on míne ge-sýhðe.

16. Heald þá symbel-tíde þæs monðes frum-sceatta(³) þines weorces þe þú on lande sǽwst, and on geres útgange (⁴), þonne þú ge-gaderast þine wæstmas tógædre.

17. Þrywa on gere æle wæpned-man (⁵) æt-ýwð (⁶) beforan Dryhtne (⁷).

18. Ne offra þú þínre on-sægdnesse blód (⁸) úppan beorman (⁹), ne se rysel (¹⁰) ne be-lýfð (¹¹) oð morgen (¹²).

19. Bring þine frum-sceattas tó Godes húse.

20. Nú ic sende mínne engel þæt he þe lǽde in-tó þǽre stówe þe ic ge-gearwode (¹³).

21. Gým (¹⁴) his, and ge-hýr his stemne (¹⁵), for-þám

(¹) Níwe (I.) *new; νεος,* L. novus, G. neu, D. nieuw.

(²) Ælmysse (1. 3.) *alms;* (S. awmous;) *gift* would here have been better.

(³) *First fruits;* fruma *beginning,* sceat (II. 2.) *coin, value, profit, &c.* hence *shot, scot :* G. schatz *treasure.*

(⁴) Ut-gang (II. 2.) *out-going, end ;* G. aus-gang.

(⁵) Lit. *weaponed-man ;* the common use of this word for *male* is a strong proof of the warlike habits of our A. S. forefathers.

(⁶) Æt-ýwan (-ian, -eówian)(I. 2.) *to appear, show, &c.*

(⁷) Dryhten (II. 2.) *Lord, chief ;* dryht (II. 3.) *troop, band.*

(⁸) Blód (II. 1.) *blood ;* G. blut, D. bloed.

(⁹) Beorme (I. 3.) *barm, leaven, leavened bread.* (¹⁰) II. 2. *fat.*

(¹¹) Be-lýfan (III. 2.) *to remain ;* G. b-leiben, D. b-lijven.

(¹²) Morgen, mergen, merigen (II. 2.) *morn, morrow ;* G. and D. morgen.

(¹³) Gearwian *to prepare, make yare or ready.*

(¹⁴) Gýman (I. 2.) *to take care of, care for, heed, attend to.*

(¹⁵) Stemn = stefn *voice ;* G. stimme, D. stem

he ne for-gifð þonne ge syngiað, and mín nama is on him.

22. Ic beó þínra feónda feónd,

23. And þe in ge-lǽde tó Amorrea lande.

24. Ne ge-eáð-méd(¹) þú hira godas, ac to-brec hira an-lícnessa.

25. Þeówiað Dryhtne : ic ge-bletsie eów, and dó ælce un-trumnesse fram eów,

26. And ge-íce(²) eówer dagas,

27. And a-flýme(³) þíne fýnd be-foran þe ;

28. And ic a-sende hyrnetta(⁴), þe aflýmað Efeum(⁵) and Chananeum,

29. Twelf monðum ǽr þú in-fare.

*　　*　　*　　*　　*　　*

31. Ic sette þíne ge-mǽro(⁶) fram þǽre Reádan(⁷) Sǽ oð Palastinas Sǽ, and fram þám wéstene oð þæt flód.

32. Nafa þú náne sibbe(⁸) wið hira godas,

33. Þý-læs híg þe be-swícon(⁹).

(¹) Eáð-médan (eád-) (I. 2.) *to humble one-self, worship, " bow down to:"* from eáð and mýd.

(²) Ge-ícan (I. 2.) *to increase, lengthen, eke out ;* from eác.

(³) A-flýman (I. 2.) *to put to flight, from fleám flight.*

(⁴) Hyrnet *hornet.* (⁵) *The Hivite ;* Vulg. " Hevæum."

(⁶) Ge-mǽre (III. 1.) *boundary ;* P. *meer.*

(⁷) Reád (I.) *red ;* G. roth, D. rood.

(⁸) Sib (II. 3.) *peace.* (⁹) Be-swícan (III. 2.) *to deceive.*

VII.—*Saxon Chronicle*(¹).

⁎ The Saxon Chronicle is a series of annals of A. S. affairs, from the earliest times to A.D. 1154, compiled by Monks.

Brytene(²) ig-land(³) is eahta hund mila lang and twá hund mila brád; and her syndon on þám ig-lande fíf ge-þeóda(⁴), Englisc, and Bryt-Wylisc(⁵), and Scytt-isc(⁶), and Pyhtisc(⁷), and Bóc-leden(⁸). Æ'rost wǽron búgend(⁹) þisses landes Bryttas(¹⁰) þa comon of Armorica(¹¹), and ge-sǽton(¹²) súðan-weard Brytene ǽrost.

A.D. 449. Her(¹³) Martianus and Valentinianus onfengon ríce(¹⁴), and rícsodon seofon winter. On heora dagum Hengest(¹⁵) and Horsa fram Wyrtgeorne(¹⁶) ge-laðode(¹⁷) Brytta cyninge tó fultume, ge-sóhton(¹⁸) Brytene on þám stede(¹⁹) þe is ge-nemned Yp-winesfleót(²⁰), ǽrost Bryttum tó fultume, ac hí eft(²¹) on hí(²²)

(¹) Taken with some slight changes from the edition of Dr. Ingram, President of Trinity College, Oxford. (²) II. 2. *Britain*.

(³) Ig-land, ea-land, (II. 1.) e, *iland*; G. ei-land, D. ey-land : *island* has arisen from a confusion with *isle*, (L. insula, G. insel, F. isle, île) with which it has no connexion. (⁴) Ge-þeód (II. 3.) *nation*.

(⁵) Lit. *British-Welsh*. (⁶) *Scottish*.
(⁷) *Pictish*. (⁸) *Book-Latin, Roman*.
(⁹) For búend (II. 2.) *inhabitant*: see p. 15.
(¹⁰) Brytte (II. 2.) *Briton*. (¹¹) A various reading has Armenia.
(¹²) Ge-sittan (II. 1.) *to occupy, settle in*.
(¹³) Here and below means *this year*. (¹⁴) The Roman *Empire*.
(¹⁵) II. 2. Not *Hengist* as commonly spelt; *horse*, G. hengst. Horsa too meant the same. (¹⁶) *Vortigern*. (¹⁷) Laðian (I. 1.) *to invite*, G. laden.
(¹⁸) Sécan is here *to go to* ; comp. the use of L. petere.
(¹⁹) II. 2. *Place, stead*; G. statt, stütte.
(²⁰) *Ebb's-et* in the Isle of Thanet; fleót *stream, creek*; *fleet* is common in locname.asl (²¹) *Again, afterwards*. (²²) *Against them*; in eo

118   ANGLO-SAXON GUIDE.

fuhton. Se cing hét hí feohtan on-gean Pyhtas, and hí swá dydon, and sige(¹) hæfdon swá-hwær-swá hí comon. Hí þá sendon tó Angle(²) and héton heom sendan máre fultum, and heom secgan Bryt-Walena(³) náhtnesse(⁴), and þæs landes cysta(⁵). Hí þá sendon heom máre fultum: þá comon þa men of þrym mægdum Germanie(⁶):—of Eald-Seaxum(⁷), of Englum(⁸), of Iótum(⁹). Of Iótum comon Cánt ware(¹⁰), and Wiht-ware, þæt is seó mæd(¹¹) þe nú eardad(¹²) on Wiht(¹³), and þæt cyn on West-Seaxum(¹⁴) þe man git hát Iótena-cyn. Of Eald-Seaxum comon East-Seaxan(¹⁵), and Súd-Seaxan(¹⁶), and West-Seaxan. Of

(¹) II. 2. *victory*; G. sieg.

(²) Engle, Angle (Ongle) (II. 2.) *country of the Angles*, the present Sleswig.

(³) Bryt-Wala (I. 2.) lit. *British-Welshman*: the Anglo-Saxons called all not of Gothic race Walan or Wealas, equivalent to *strangers* or *foreigners*, and the Germans still keep up the same idea, calling the French and Italians *Wälschen*, and anything strange or outlandish *wälsch*.

(⁴) Náhtnes (II. 3.) *goodness for nought, cowardice.*

(⁵) Cyst (II. 3.) *choice, excellence*; pl. cysta *good things, abundance.*

(⁶) Gen. of Germania; see p. 13.

(⁷) Seaxa (I. 2.) *Saxon*: the Old-Saxon dialect nearly resembled the A. S.

(⁸) See p. 19.

(⁹) Ióta, Iúta (I. 2); the Jutes occupied the present Jutland, which was bounded to the south by Angle; the Old-Saxons' land, now Holstein, lay still further southward.   (¹⁰) *Dwellers in Kent*: see p. 20.

(¹¹) = mægð, p. 5.   (¹²) Eardian *to dwell*, from eard.

(¹³) Or Wiht-land *Isle of Wight.*

(¹⁴) The West-Saxons occupied Berks, Hants, Wilts, Dorset, and parts of Somerset and Devon.

(¹⁵) The East-Saxons occupied Essex, as the name implies, Middlesex, and part of Herts.

(¹⁶) The South-Saxons had Sussex, named after them, and Surrey.

EXTRACTS—SAXON CHRONICLE.   119

Angle comon (se á síd-þán stód wéstig(¹) be-twyx
Iótum and Seaxum) Eást-Engle(²), Middel-Engle(³),
Mearce(⁴), and ealle Norð-Ymbra(⁵).   *   *   *
A.D. 596. Her Gregorius Papa sende tó Brytene
Augustinum, mid wel monegum(⁶) munucum(⁷) þa
Godes word sceoldon bodian(⁸) Angel-cynne.   *   *
A.D. 806. Her se mona a-þýstrode(⁹) on kalendis
Septembris(¹⁰). Eád-wulf Norðan-Hymbra cyning
wæs of his ríce a-drifen, and Heard-byrht bisceop on
Hagustealdes-e (¹¹) forð-ferde (¹²).   Eác on þissum
ylcan geare pridie nonas Iunii (¹³) róde-tácn (¹⁴) wearð
at-eówed (¹⁵) on þam monað, ánes Wódnes-dæges (¹⁶),

(¹) *Waste, desert.*
(²) East Anglia comprised Norfolk, Suffolk, and Cambridge.
(³) The Middle Angles had Salop, Worcester, Warwick, Gloucester, &c.
(⁴) Mercia included the remaining midland counties, together with Chester, Derby, Nottingham, and Lincoln.
(⁵) Northumbria consisted of York, Lancaster, and the other northern counties: as these were united or divided into two kingdoms, Saxon England formed either a heptarchy or an octarchy.
(⁶) *Very many, a good number.*
(⁷) Munuc (II. 2.) *monk*; G. mönch, L. monachus.
(⁸) *To announce, proclaim, preach*; hence *to bode*: boda *messenger*; G. bote, D. boode.
(⁹) A-þýstrian *to become dark, be eclipsed*, from þýstru (p. 10.); þýster *dark*; G. düster.
(¹⁰) *Sept.* 1.: the Roman name for the day of the month was used sometimes, but not always: see p. 36.   (¹¹) *Hexham.*
(¹²) *Went forth, departed, died.*   (¹³) *June* 4.
(¹⁴) *Sign of the Cross*; ród (II. 3.) *rood, Cross*; tácen *token, sign*; G. zeichen, D. teeken.   (¹⁵) At- for æt-; see p. 4.
(¹⁶) "*Of a Wednesday*," as we still say.

ANGLO-SAXON GUIDE.

innan þære daginge(¹); and eft on þissum geare
tertio kalendas Septembris(²) án wundor-lic trendel(³)
weard æt-eowed a-bútan þære sunnan.
    And þý ylcan geare (A.D. 853.) sende Æðel-wulf
cyning Ælf-red his sunu tó Rome, (þá wæs þonne
Leo(⁴) Papa on Rome) and he hine tó cyninge ge-
hálgode, and hine him tó bisceop-suna ge-nam(⁵).
    A.D. 871. þá feng Ælfred Æðel-wulf-ing(⁶) tó(⁷)
West-Seaxna ríce; and þæs ymb æhne monað(⁸) ge-
feaht Ælf-red cyning wið ealne þone here(⁹) lytle
werode(¹⁰) æt Wil-túne(¹¹) and hine lange on dæg
ge-flýmde(¹²), and þa Deniscan áhton wæl-stówe(¹³)
ge-weald. And þæs geares wurdon nigon folc-ge-
feoht(¹⁴) ge-fohten wið þone here on þám cyne-rice
be súdan Temese, bútan þám þe him Ælf-red, and
ealdor-men(¹⁵), and cyninges þegnas oft ráda(¹⁶) on-
ridon þe man ná ne rimde(¹⁷). And þæs geares

(¹) Daging (see p. 67.) *dawn*; dagian *to dawn*, O. *daw*.
(²) *Aug.* 29.   (³) *Round, circle*: hence *to trundle*.   (⁴) Leo IV.
(⁵) *Stood sponsor to him at Confirmation*; an ancient custom of the Churches; see the 3rd rubric after Confirmation, and thereon Wheatley, &c.
(⁶) *Son of Æthelwulf*; see p. 65.
(⁷) Feng tó "*took to*," as is still said.   (⁸) *One month after that*.
(⁹) The Danish host of plunderers was called emphatically "*se here*" *the army*; G. das heer: see p. 9.
(¹⁰) Abl. *with a little band*: werod II. 1.   (¹¹) Wil-tún *Wilton*.
(¹²) Ge-flýman = a-flýman above.
(¹³) Wæl-stów *slaughter-place, battle-field*; G. wahl-platz.
(¹⁴) *Great battles, battles of nations*.
(¹⁵) Ealdor-man (III. 2.) *senator, chief*; hence *alderman*.
(¹⁶) Rúd (II. 3.) *road, in-road, raid, foray*; from rídan.
(¹⁷) Ríman *to count, number*; hence *to rime*; G. reimen, D. rijmen.

wǽron of-slegene higon eorlas (¹), and án cyning, and þý geare namon West-seaxan frið (²) wið þone here.

A.D. 901. Her forð-ferde Ælf-red Æðel-wulfing six nihtum (³) ǽr Ealra Háligra Mæssan (⁴), se wæs cyning ofer eal Angel-cyn bútan þám dǽle þe under Dena on-wealde wæs. And he heóld þæt ríce óðer-healf (⁵) gear læs þe þryttig wintra (⁶).

VIII.—*Apollonius.* (⁷)

*** Translated from the Gesta Romanorum, a monkish collection of tales, by whom is not known. This story is the original of the play called "Pericles Prince of Tyre."

Sóð-líce mid-þý-þe þæs cynges dóhtor ge-seáh þæt Apollonius on eallum gódum cræftum swá wel wæs ge-togen (⁸), þá ge-feoll hyre mód on his lufe. Þá æfter þæs beórscipes (⁹) ge-endunge, cwæð þæt

(¹) Eorl *earl.*
(²) Namon frið *made peace*: frið (II. 2.) *peace;* G. friede.
(³) The Anglo-Saxons reckoned time by *nights:* of this our *se'n-night* (seven-night) and *fo'rt'night* (fourteen-night) are relics.
(⁴) *All Hallows' Mass, Feast of All Saints:* mæsse I. 3.
(⁵) See p. 36.   (⁶) See p. 35, note 5.
(⁷) From Mr. Thorpe's edition, pp. 17—19, 23—25.
(⁸) Teógan, (túgan), teón *to draw &c., educate:* comp. G. er-ziehen; L. e-ducare from ducere.
(⁹) Beór-scipe (II. 2.) *feast, banquet;* beór (II. 1.) *beer.*

mæden tó þám cynge: Leófa fæder, þú lýfdest me lytle ǽr þæt ic móste gifan Apollonio swá-hwæt-swá ic wolde of þínum gold-horde(¹). Arces-trates se cyng cwæð tó hyre: Gif him swá-hwæt-swá þú wile. Heó þá swíðe(²) blíðe(³) út-eóde and cwæð: Láreow Apolloni, ic gife þe be mínes fæder leáfe twá hund punda(⁴) goldes, and feower hund punda ge-wihte(⁵) seolfres, and þone mǽstan dǽl(⁶) deór-wyrðan(⁷) reáfes, and twentig þeówa manna. And heó þá þus cwæð tó þám þeówum mannum: Berað þás þing mid eów þe ic be-hét(⁸) Apollonio mínum láreowe, and lecgað innon búre(⁹) be-foran mínum freóndum. Þis wearð þá þus ge-dón æfter þǽre cwene(¹⁰) hǽse(¹¹), and ealle þa men hyre gife heredon þe híg ge-sáwon. Þá sóð líce ge-endode se ge-beórscipe, and þa men ealle a-rison, and grétton þone cyng and þá cwene, and bǽdon híg ge-sunde(¹²) beón and hám ge-wendon. Eác-swylce(¹³) Apollonius

(¹) Hord (II. 2.) *hoard, treasure.*

(²) Swíð (1.) *strong, powerful;* swíðe *greatly, v ry;* comp. L. (validc) va!de, F. fort.   (³) Blíðe *blithe;* D. blijde.

(⁴) Pund (II. 1.) *pound.*   (⁵) Ge-wiht (II. 3.) *weight;* G. ge-wicht.

(⁶) *A very great deal.*

(⁷) *Precious;* deór *dear;* G. theuer, D. duur.

(⁸) Be-hátan (II. 2.) *to promise;* G. ver-heissen.

(⁹) Búr (II. 2.) *chamber, bower.*

(¹⁰) Cwen (II. 3.) *queen;* quean is likewise from cwen, which meant originally *woman;* γυνη.

(¹¹) Hǽs (II. 3.) *command,* he-hest; G, ge-heiss.

(¹²) Ge-sund *sound, whole;* bade them *fare-well;* L. valere eos jusse-runt.   (¹³) *So in like manner.*

cwæð: þú góda cyning and earmra ge-miltsigend, and þú cwen láre lufigend, beó ge ge-sunde. He be-seáh(¹) eác tó þám þeówum mannum þe þæt mæden him for-gifen(²) hæfde, and heom cwæð tó: Nimað þás þing mid eów þe me seó cwen for-geaf, and gán we sécan úre gæst-hús(³) þæt we magon ús ge-restan.

Þá a-dred þæt mæden þæt heó næfre eft Apollonium ne ge-sáwe swá hraðe swá heó wolde, and eóde þá tó hyre fæder and cwæð: Þú góda cyning, lícað þe wel þæt Apollonius þe þurh ús tó-dæg ge-gódod(⁴) is, þus heonon fare, and cuman yfele men and be-reáfian hine? Se cyng cwæð: Wel þú cwæde: hát him findan hwar he hine mæge wurð lícost(⁵) ge-restan. Þá dyde þæt mæden swá hyre be-boden wæs, and Apollonius on-feng þære wununge(⁶) þe him be-tǽht(⁷) wæs, and þar-in-eóde, Gode þancigende þe him ne for-wyrnde cyne-líces wurðscipes and frófre.

Ac þæt mæden hæfde un-stille niht mid þǽre lufe on-ǽled(⁸) þára worda and sanga þe heó ge-hýrde æt Apollonige(⁹), and ná leng heó ne ge-bád þonne hit dæg was, ac eóde sona swá hit leóht(¹⁰) wæs, and

---

(¹) Be-seón (III.3.) *to look, look at.*

(²) For-gifan (II. 1.) *to give away, present, forgive.*

(³) *Inn, guest-house;* G. gast-haus.

(⁴) Ge-gódian, *to endow, enrich;* G. be-gütern.

(⁵) Wurð-líc (II.) *honourable.*   (⁶) *Dwelling, habitation;* G. wohnung.

(⁷) Be-tǽcan (I. 2.) *to commit, assign;* hence *betake.*

(⁸) On-ǽlan (I. 2.) *to inflame.*

(⁹) Abl. or dat. formed A. S.-wise from Apollonius; the g inserted as p. 41.

(¹⁰) *Light;* G. licht.

ge-sæt be-foran hyre fæder bedde. þá cwæð se cyng: Leófe dóhtor, for-hwý eart þú þus ǽr-wacol(¹)? Þæt mæden cwæð: Me a-wehton(²) þa ge-cneordnessa(³) þe ic girstan-dæg(⁴) ge-hýrde; nú bidde ic þe for-þám þæt þú be-fæste(⁵) me úrum cuman Apollonige tó láre(⁶). Þá wearð se cyng þearle(⁷) ge-blissod(⁸), and hét feccan Apollonium and him tó cwæð: Mín dóhtor gyrnð þæt heó móte leornian æt þe þa ge-sǽligan(⁹) láre þe þú canst, and gif þú wilt þisum þingum ge-hýrsum beón, ic swerige þe þurh mínes .ícos mægna(¹⁰) þæt swá-hwæt-swá þú on sǽ for-lure, ic þe þæt on land ge-staðelige(¹¹). Þá-þá Apollonius þæt ge-hýrde, he on-feng þám mædenne tó láre, and hyre tǽhte swá wel swá he sylf ge-leornode.

* * * * *

Þá wæs hyre ge-cýd þe þar ealdor(¹²) wæs, þæt þar wǽre cumen sum cyngc(¹³) mid his aðume(¹⁴), and mid his dóhtor, mid miclum gifum. Mid-þám-þe heó

(¹) *Early-wakeful;* comp. L. vigil.

(²) A-weccan (I. 2.) *to awake* (act.) G. er-wecken: the neut. is wacian (I. 1.) or wacan (II. 3.); G. wachen.   (³) *Studies, accomplishments.*

(⁴) *Yesterday;* G. gestern; comp. L. hestern-us.

(⁵) Be-fæstan (I. 2.) *to commit, intrust.*   (⁶) *For instruction.*

(⁷) Þearl (I.) *strong;* þearle *very, greatly;* comp. swíðe above.

(⁸) Blissian *to rejoice;* bliss (II. 3.) *bliss, joy.*

(⁹) Ge-sǽlig (I.) *happy, blessed;* G. selig: hence *silly,* O. sely.

(¹⁰) Mægen (III. 1.) *power.*

(¹¹) Ge-staðelian *to establish, make good,* from staðol *station;* whence staðol-fæst *stead-fast,* &c.

(¹²) Here used for *chief priestess.*

(¹³) See p. 5.   (¹⁴) Aðum *son-in-law.*

þæt ge-hýrde, heó hí sylfe mid cyne-lícum reáfe ge-frætwode(¹), and mid purpran ge-scrýdde, and hyre heáfod mid golde and mid gimmon(²) ge-glengde(³), and mid miclum fæmnena(⁴) heápe(⁵) ymb-trymmed(⁶), com tó-geanes þám cynge(⁷). Heó wæs sóðlíce þearle wlítig(⁸), and for þære(⁹) miclan lufe þáre clǽnnesse hí sǽdon ealle þæt þar nǽre nán Dianan(¹⁰) swá ge-cweme(¹¹) swá heó.

Mid-þám-þe Apollonius þæt ge-seáh, he mid his aðume, and mid his dóhtor tó hyre urnon, and feollon ealle tó hyre fótum, and wéndon þæt heó Diana wǽre seó gyden(¹²) for hyre miclan beorhtnesse and wlíte. Þæt háli(¹³) ern(¹⁴) wearð þá ge-openod, and þa lác wǽron in-ge-bróhte; and Apollonius on-gan þá sprecan and cweðan: Ic fram cild-háde wæs Apollonius ge-nemned, on Tirum ge-boren. Mid-þám-þe

---

(¹) Ge-frætwian *to adorn;* frætu (III. 1.) *ornament, fret.*

(²) Gim (II. 2.) *gem.*   (³) Ge-glengan (I. 2.) *to adorn.*

(⁴) Fœmne *damsel;* L. femina.

(⁵) Heáp (II. 2.) *troop, heap;* G. haufe, D. hoop.

(⁶) Ymb-trymmian *to surround,* trymmian *to strengthen,* hence *to trim,* guard, *a garment,* &c.

(⁷) *To meet the king;* comp. G. dem könige ent-gegen.

(⁸) *Beautiful;* wlíte (II. 2.) *beauty.*

(⁹) = þǽre; at p. 5, l. 1, it should have been stated that ǽ is sometimes changed to á, as well á to ǽ.   (¹⁰) Dat. of Diana.

(¹¹) *Pleasing, agreeable,* from cwuman (cuman) *to come;* comp. G. bequem *con-venient.*

(¹²) Feminine of god; see p. 66, and comp. G. gott, gött-in.

(¹³) = hálig, see p. 5.

(¹⁴) Ern, ærn (II. 1.) *house, room;* see p. 71, n. 7.

ic be-com tó fullon and-gite(¹) þá næs nán cræft þe wǽre fram cyngum be-gán(²) oððe fram æðelum mannum þæt ic ne cúðe: ic a-rǽdde(³) Antiochus rǽdels(⁴) þæs cynges tó-þón-þæt ic his dóhtor underfenge me tó ge-mæccan, ac he sylfa wæs mid þám fúlestan horwe(⁵) þar-tó ge-þeód(⁶), and me þá syrwode(⁷) tó of-sleánne. Mid-þám-þe ic þæt for-fleáh(⁸), þá wearð ic on sǽ for-liden(⁹), and com tó Cyrenense(¹⁰). Þá under-fengc me Arcestrates se cyngc mid swá micelre lufe, þæt ic æt nyhstan(¹¹) ge-earnode(¹²) þæt he geaf me his á-cennedan(¹³) dóhtor tó ge-mæccan. Seó fór þá mid me tó on-fónne mínon cyne-ríce, and þás míne dóhtor þe ic be-foran þe, Diana, ge-and-weard(¹⁴) hæbbe, a-cende on sǽ, and hyre gást a-let(¹⁵). Ic þá hí mid cyne-lícum reáfe ge-scrýdde, and mid golde and ge-write(¹⁶) on ciste(¹⁷) a-legde(¹⁸), þæt se-þe hí funde hí wurð-líce

(¹) And-git (II. 1.) *understanding*.
(²) Be-gán *to exercise, cultivate, attend to.*
(³) A-rǽdan *to read, guess;* G. er-rathen *to guess.*
(⁴) II. 2. *riddle;* G. räthsel. (⁵) Horu (III. 1.) *pollution.*
(⁶) Ge-þeódan (I. 2.) *to join.*
(⁷) Syrwian *to plot;* searu (III. 1.) *ambush, stratagem.*
(⁸) For-fleón *to escape, flee from.*
(⁹) *Shipwrecked;* líðan (III. 2.) *to sail,* for-líðan *to sail with ill success, suffer shipwreck.* (¹⁰) *Cyrene.* (¹¹) *At last.*
(¹²) *Earned, deserved, obtained.*
(¹³) A'-cenned = án-cenned *only begotten.* (¹⁴) *Present.*
(¹⁵) A-lǽtan = of-lǽtan *to let forth, give up.*
(¹⁶) Ge-writ (III. 1.) *writing, writ, inscription.*
(¹⁷) Cist (II. 3.) *chest, coffin;* P. kist, G. kiste.
(¹⁸) Usually -lede; from -lecgan.

be-byrigde (¹), and þás míne dóhtor be-fæste þám mán-fullestan (²) mannan to fédanne (³). Fór me (⁴) þá tó Egipta-lande feower-tyne gear on heófe (⁵): þá ic on-gean (⁶) com, þá sædon hí me þæt mín dóhtor wǽre forð-faren (⁷); and me wæs mín sár (⁸) eal ge-ed-níwad.

Mid-þám-þe he þás þingc eal a-reht hæfde, Arcestrate sóð-líce his wíf úp-a-rás, and hine ymb-clypte (⁹). Þá niste ná Apollonius ne ne ge-lýfde þæt heó his ge-mæcca (¹⁰) wǽre, ac sceáf (¹¹) hí fram him. Heó þá micelre stefne clypode, and cwæð mid wópe: Ic eom Arcestrate þín ge-mæcca, Arcestrates dóhtor þæs cynges, and þú eart Apollonius mín láreow þe me lǽrdest! Þú eart se for-lidena man þe ic lufode, ná for gálnesse (¹²) ac for wis-dóme! Hwar is mín dóhtor? He be-wende hine þá tó Thasian (¹³) and cwæð: Þis heó is; and híg weópon þá ealle, and eác blissodon. And þæt word sprang geond eal þæt land þæt Apollonius se mǽra cyngc hæfde funden his wíf; and þá wearð or-mǽte (¹⁴) bliss, and þa or-

---

(¹) (Be-) byrigan *to bury.*

(²) Mán-full *wicked;* mán (II. 1.) *wickedness, sin, crime;* mán-swara *a man-sworn, perjured man;* G. mein-eid, *false oath.*

(³) *To feed, nourish, bring up.* (⁴) See p. 81.

(⁵) Heáf, heóf (II. 2.) *sigh, groan, grief.* (⁶) *Again, back again.*

(⁷) Forð-faran = forð-feran. (⁸) *Pain, grief, sore.*

(⁹) Ymb-clyppan *to embruce, clip round.*

(¹⁰) Ge-mæcca *mute* serves for both genders; thus correct n. 9, p. 111.

(¹¹) Scúfan (III. 3.) *to shove, push;* G. schieben, D. schuiven.

(¹²) *Lust.*

(¹³) The A. S. dative, like Dianan above and Antiochian below.

(¹⁴) *Measureless, immense;* from or- and metan *to mete, measure;* see Additions, &c.

gana(¹) wǽron ge-togene(²), and þa býman(³) ge-bláwene(⁴), and þar weard blíðe ge-beórscipe ge-gearwod be-twux þám cynge and þám folce. And heó ge-sette hyre gyngran(⁵) þe hyre folgode tó sacerde, and mid blisse and heófe ealre þáre mægðe on Efesum, heó fór mid hyre were(⁶), and mid hyre aðume, and mid hyre dóhtor tó Antiochian, þar Apollonio wæs þæt cyne-ríce ge-healden(⁷). Fór(⁸) þá síð-þán tó Tiıum(⁹) and ge-sette þar Athenagoras his aðum tó cynge; fór þá sóð líce þanon tó Tharsum mid his wife, and mid his dóhtor, and mid cyne-lícre fyrde(¹⁰), and hét sona ge-læccan(¹¹) Stranguilionem and Dionisiaden, and lǽdan be-foran him þar he sæt on his þrym-setle(¹²).

(¹) L. organum, commonly used in the plural, as *organs* formerly was.

(²) Lit. *drawn*; from some peculiar way either of playing the instrument or of blowing the bellows. (³) Býme *trumpet*.

(⁴) Bláwan (II. 2.) *ta blow*; G. blähen.

(⁵) Gyngre (*female*) *disciple, follower*, lit. *younger*; G. jünger is used in the same sense.

(⁶) Wer (fir) II. 2. *man, husband*; L. vir; aior was the Scythian (Herod. iv. 110), and the Celtic dialects have a similar word.

(⁷) *Had been kept for A.* (⁸) *He, Apollonius went.*

(⁹) Copied probably from the L. "(ad) Tyrum" (as also Tharsum below); tó seems properly to have always governed the dative.

(¹⁰) Fyrd (II. 3.) *army, array, march, &c.*; G. fahrt *journey, &c.*

(¹¹) I. 2. *to seize, catch.*

(¹²) *Glory-seat, throne;* þrym II. 2., setl III. 1.

IX.—*Boëthius.* Cap. xvii.(¹)

⁎ King Ælfred translated Boëthius de Consolatione Philosophiæ, interweaving much original matter of his own: the following is his expansion of 3 or 4 lines, lib. II. prosa 7.

Hú þæt Mód(²) sæde þæt him næfre seó mægð and seó gitsung(³) for-wel(⁴) ne lícode(⁵), bútan tó láðe(⁶) he tilade(⁷).

Þá se Wís-dóm þá þis leóð(⁸) a-sungen hæfde, þá ge-swígode(⁹) he, and þá and-sworede þæt Mód and þus cwæð: Ea-lá Ge-scead-wísnes(¹⁰)! hwæt(¹¹) þú wást þæt me næfre seó gitsung and seó ge-mægð þisses eorð-lícan an-wealdes for-wel ne lícode, ne ic ealles for-swíðe ne gyrnde þisses eorð-lícan ríces. Búton lá ic wilnode þeáh and-weorces(¹²) tó þám weorce

(¹) From Mr. Cardale's edition, slightly altered.

(²) II. 1. neuter, while G. muth is masculine: another exception to the general rule, pp. 8, 9.

(³) II. 3. *desire, covetousness;* gitsian *to covet.*

(⁴) *Very well, too well;* for- is sometimes intensive; for-nean *well nigh,* for-swíðe *too much, excessively.* (⁵) See p. 86.

(⁶) *Unwillingly;* see p. 70: láð (1.) *hateful, loathsome.*

(⁷) Tilian (teolian) *to toil, till, &c.*: see p. 42.

(⁸) III. 1. *song, lay;* G. lied.

(⁹) Swígian *to be silent;* G. schweigen.

(¹⁰) *Reason, discretion;* sceadan (p. 54.) *to divide, discriminate, &c.;* G. scheiden.

(¹¹) Hwæt, and lá (below) are often used as expletives.

(¹²) And-weorc (II. 1.) *matter, material, substance.*

þe me be-boden wæs tó wyrcanne; þæt wæs þæt ic un-fracod-líce (¹) and ge-rísen-líce (²) mihte steóran (³) and reccan (⁴) þone an-weald þe me be-fæst wæs. Hwæt þú wást þæt nán mon ne mæg nǽnne cræft cýðan (⁵), ne nánne an-weald reccan ne steóran, búton tólum (⁶) and and-weorce : þæt býð ælces cræftes and-weorc, þæt mon þone cræft búton (⁷) wyrcan ne mæg. Þæt býð þonne cyninges and-weorc and his tól mid tó rícsianne (⁸), þæt he hæbbe his land ful-mannod (⁹) : he sceal hæbban ge-bed-men (¹⁰), and fyrd-men (¹¹), and weorc-men. Hwæt þú wást þætte bútan þissum tólum nán cyning his cræft ne mæg cýðan. Þæt is eác his and-weorc þæt he hæbban sceal tó þám tólum, þám þrym ge-ferscipum (¹²) bi-wiste (¹³); þæt is þonne heora bi-wist, land tó búgienne (¹⁴), and gifta (¹⁵), and wæpna (¹⁶), and mete, and ealo (¹⁷), and cláðas (¹⁸), and ge-hwæt

(¹) Fracod (I.) *vile, shameful.*
(²) Ge-rísen-líc (II.) *fit, proper;* hit ge-ríst *it is fit, becoming,*=L. decet.
(³) Or stýran (I. 2,) *to steer, guide, govern;* G. steuern, D. stuuren.
(⁴) I. 3 *reckon for, give an account of.*
(⁵) *To make known, show forth, practise.*
(⁶) Tól (II. 1.) *tool.*   (⁷) Þæt—búton *without which.*
(⁸) *To rule with:* rícsian, (ríxian); L.. reg-ere, rex-i.
(⁹) Mannian *to man.*   (¹⁰) *Prayer-men, clergy.*
(¹¹) *Army-men, soldiers.*
(¹²) Ge-ferscipe (II. 2) *company;* ge-fera *companion,* O. fere.
(¹³) Bi-wist (II. 3) *provision, food:* wist *feast,* &c.
(¹⁴) Búgian=búan.
(¹⁵) Gift (II. 3.) *gift;* plur. gifta usually means *marriage.*
(¹⁶) Wæpen (III. 1.) *weapon;* D. wapen.   (¹⁷) Ealo (-u) (III. 3. *ale.*
(¹⁸) Cláð (II. 2.) *cloth, garment;* G. kleid.

þæs þe þa þreo ge-ferscipas be-hófiað: ne mæg he bútan þissum þás tól ge-healdan, ne bútan þissum tólum nán þára þinga wyrcan þe him be-boden is tó wyrcanne. For-þý ic wilnode and-weorces þone an-weald mid tó ge-reccenne, þæt míne cræftas and an-weald ne wurden for-gitene and for-holene (¹); for-þám ælc cræft and ælc an-weald býð sona for-ealdod(²) and for-swígod(³), gif he býð bútan Wís-dóme; for-þám-þe hwæt-swá(⁴) þurh dysige(⁵) ge-dón býð, ne mæg hit nán mon næfre tó cræfte ge-reccan. Þæt is nú hraðost tó secganne þæt ic wilnode weorð-ful-líce(⁶) tó lybbanne þá-hwíle-þe ic lyfode, and æfter mínum life þám monnum tó læfanne þe æfter me wǽren mín ge-mynd(⁷) on gódum weorcum.

Cap. xxxiv. 10.

*** A free translation of part of prosa ii. lib. III.

Þá cwæð ic: Ne mæg ic náne cwice wuht on-gitan þára þe wíte(⁸) hwæt hit(⁹) wille eððe hwæt hit nille, þe un-ge-néd(¹⁰) lyste for-weorðan. For-þám ælc wuht wolde beón hál and lybban þára þe me cwice

---

(¹) For-helan (II. 2.) *to hide*; G. ver-hehlen.
(²) For-ealdian *to wear out, perish from old age*.
(³) For-swígian *to pass in silence*; G. ver-schweigen; here and above mark the force of for-.
(⁴) Usually swá-hwæt-swá.
(⁵) *Folly*; dysig *foolish, absurd*; hence *dizzy*.
(⁶) *Worthily, honorably*.   (⁷) II. 1. *memory, mind*.
(⁸) Wíte singular agreeing with wuht and not with þára þe; see p. 78.
(⁹) Hit neut. while wuht is fem.   (¹⁰) Nédan=nýdan.

þincð, bútan ic nát be treówum, and be wyrtum([1]), and be swylcum ge-sceaftum([2]) swylce([3]) náne sáwle nabbað. Þá smearcode([4]) he and cwæð: Ne þearft þú nó([5]) be þám([6]) ge-sceaftum tweógan([7]), þe má þe([8]) be þám óðrum. Hú ne miht þú ge-seón þæt ælc wyrt and ælc wudu([9]) wile weaxan on þám lande sélost([10]) þe him betst ge-rist, and him ge-cynde([11]) býð and ge-wune-líc([12]), and þær þær hit ge-fret([13]), þæt hit hraðost weaxan mæg, and latost wealcwigan([14])? Sumra wyrta oððe sumes wuda eard býð on dúnum([15]), sumra on merscum([16]), sumra on mórum ([17]), sumra on cludum ([18]), sumra on barum([19]) sondum([20]). Nim þonne swá wudu swa

([1]) Wyrt (II. 3.) *herb, wort.*
([2]) Ge-sceaft (II. 3.) *creation, creature.*
([3]) Swylc—swylc answers to L. talis—qualis.
([4]) Smearcian *to smirk, smile.* ([5]) Nó=ná.
([6]) See p. 30.
([7]) Tweógan, tweón (III. 3. See p. 60.) *to doubt,* from twá; comp. δοια-ζειν, L. du-bitare, G. zwei-feln, from δοια (δυο), duo, zwei.
([8]) *Any more than.* ([9], III. 2. *wood;* D. woud.
([10]) *Best:* sél *good, excellent.*
([11]) *Kind, kindly, natural:* ge-cynd (II. 3.) *nature, kind.*
([12]) *Common, usual;* G. ge-wöhnlich.
([13]) *Where it takes root, draws nourishment,* lit. *bites:* fretan (II. 1.) (G. fressen) *to eat, devour, fret.*
([14]) *Fade;* G. ver-welken, P. welk.
([15]) Dún (II. 3.) *down, hill, mountain;* hence *don* in local names: G. düne, D. duin, F. dune is a sand-*hill* near the sea.
([16]) Mersc (II. 2.) *marsh;* P. mesh.
([17]) Mór (II. 2.) *moor;* D. moer. ([18]) Clud (II. 2.) *rock, cliff*
([19]) Bær (II.) *bare;* G. bar. ([20]) Sand, sond (II. 2.) *sand*

wyrt, swá-hwæđer-swá þú wile of þǽre stówe þe his eard and æđelo(¹) býđ on tó weaxanne, and sete on un-cyndre(²) stówe him, þonne ne ge-gréwđ hit þær náuht, ac for-searađ(³); for-þám ælces landes ge-cynd is, þæt hit him ge-líce wyrta and ge-lícne wudu tydrige(⁴); and hit swa déđ, friđađ(⁵), and fyrđrađ(⁶) swíđe georne(⁷), swá longe swá heora ge-cynd býđ, þæt hí grówan móton. Hwæt wénst þú for-hwý ælc sǽd(⁸) grówe innon þá eorđan, and tó ciđum(⁹) and tó wyrt-rumum(¹⁰) weorđe on þǽre eorđan, búton for-þý þe hí teóhhiađ(¹¹) þæt se stemn(¹²) and se helm(¹³) móte þý fæstor and þý leng standan? Hwý ne miht þú on-gitan, þeáh þú hit ge-seón ne mæge, þæt eal se dæl, se þe þæs treówes on twelf monđum ge-weaxeđ, þæt he on-ginnđ of þám wyrt-rumum, and swá úp-weardes gréwđ ođ þone stemn, and síđ-þán and-lang þæs piđan(¹⁴), and and-lang þǽre rinde(¹⁵) ođ þone helm, and síđ-þán æfter(¹⁶) þám bogum(¹⁷), ođ-þæt hit

(¹) *Nature.* (²) Un-cynde (I.) *un-kind, unnatural.*
(³) For-searian *to fade, become sear.*
(⁴) Tydrian *to produce, bring forth,* from tudor, tudr (II. 2.) *offspring, progeny.*
(⁵) Friðian *to make flourish, grow well;* friðII. 2. *peace,* G. friede.
(⁶) Fyrðrian *to further, forward, assist,* from forð.
(⁷) *Willingly, readily, earnestly;* G. gerne.
(⁸) Sǽd (II. 1.) *seed;* G. saat, D. zaad.
(⁹) Ciðð (II. 2.) *shoot, sprout.* (¹⁰) Wyrt-ruma *root.*
(¹¹) Teóhhian *to resolve, endeavour.* (¹²) *Stem, trunk.*
(¹³) *Crown, head, top, helm-et.* (¹⁴) Piða *pith;* D. pit.
(¹⁵) Rind (II. 3.) *rind, bark;* G. rinde.
(¹⁶) *Along;* like L. secundum. (¹⁷) Bch (II. 2.) *bough.*

út-a-springð (¹) on leáfum (²), and on blostmum (³), and on blædum (⁴)? Hwý ne miht þú on-gitan þætte ælc wuht cwices býð innan-weard hnescost (⁵), and útan-weard heardost? Hwæt þú miht ge-seón hú þæt treów býð útan ge-scyrped (⁶), and be-wæfed (⁷) mid þǽre rinde wið þone winter, and wið þa stearc-an (⁸) stormas, and eác wið þǽre sunnan hǽto on sumera (⁹). Hwá mæg þæt he ne wundrige swylcra ge-sceafta úres Sceoppendes (¹⁰), and huru (¹¹) þæs Sceopp-endes? And þeáh we his nú wundrien, hwylc úre mæg a-reccan (¹²) medem-líce (¹³) úres Sceoppendes willan, and an-weald, hú his ge-sceafta weaxað and eft waniað (¹⁴) þonne þæs tíma (¹⁵) cymð, and of heora sǽde weorðað eft ge-ed-níwade (¹⁶), swylce hí þonne wurdon tó ed-sceafte (¹⁷)?

(¹) U t-a-springan (III. 1.) *to spring, shoot out.*
(²) Leáf (II. 1.) *leaf;* G. lauh.
(³) Blostm (II. 2.) *blossom;* D. bloessem.
(⁴) Blæd (II. 3.) *fruit, branch;* G. blatt, D. blad *leaf, blade.*
(⁵) Hnesc (I.) *soft, tender, nesh.*
(⁶) Ge-scyrpan (I. 2.) *to scarf, cover;* sceorp (II. 1.) *scarf.*
(⁷) Be-wæfan (I. 2.) *to clothe;* wæfels *garment.*
(⁸) Stearc (I.) *stark, strong, violent;* G. stark.   (⁹) See p. 15.
(¹⁰) Sceoppend or Scyppend (p. 5.) *Creator;* scyppan *to create;* G. schaffen, schöpfen, D. scheppen.
(¹¹) *At least, at all events.*   (¹²) *Reckon, tell up.*
(¹³) Fitly, *worthily;* medeme *middling, moderate, meet.*
(¹⁴) Wanian *to wane,* from wana *want.*
(¹⁵) *The season for that.*   (¹⁶) See p. 42.
(¹⁷) Ed-sceaft (II. 3.) *new creation: as if they then became newly created.*

CHAPTER IX.

Verse Extracts.

I.—*Narrative Verse.*

Anglo-Saxon Poetry is of various kinds, distinguished by rime, by alliteration, or by both; the commonest however only, termed Narrative Verse, will be here described. Its chief characteristic is *Alliteration*[1], or the correspondence of the first letters of a certain number of the most important words in each line of a couplet, two called *sub-letters* riming thus together in the first line, and answering to a third called the *chief letter* in the second. The first line has often but one sub-letter and never more than two; the second never more than one chief letter. The length of the lines varies much, each however must contain at least two emphatic or root syllables, with one or more unemphatic, that is prefixes, terminations, &c.: few lines have less than four syllables, two emphatic, and two unemphatic, and some

---

[1] Alliteration is found in the Latin poetry of the middle ages, sometimes combined with line and final rime, and syllabic metre; it was used more or less in England along with other kinds of rime till a late period, and is still usual in the Scandinavian tongues. The Vision of Piers Plouhman (1350) is a long and regular specimen of English alliterative poetry, on the above rules. For a full account of the A.S. versification, see Rask's Grammar, pp. 136—68.

have as many as eight or nine, or even more. For example(¹):

Hú *l*omp(²) eów on	How befell it you on *your*
*l*áde (³)	voyage
*l*eófa Beó-wulf,	dear Beówulf,
þá þú *f*æringa	when thou suddenly
*f*eor ge-hogodest	far off determinedst
*s*æcce (⁴) *s*écean	warfare to seek
ofer *s*ealt wæter,	over *the* salt water,
*h*ilde (⁵) tó *H*eorote (⁶)?	battle at Heorot?
Ac þú *H*róð-gáre	Hast thou then Hróthgár
wið cúðne *w*ean (⁷)	against *his* known plague
*w*ihte ge-béttest (⁸),	ought booted,
mærum þeódne (⁹)?	*the* famous prince?

Here the first couplet has in the first line two sub-letters, the *l* in *l*omp and *l*áde, answering to the chief letter, the *l* in *l*eófa in the second. The third line has but one sub-letter, the *f* in *f*æringa which rimes with

(¹) Beówulf, ed. Kemble l. 3969—79.
(²) Limpan (III. 1.) *to happen.*
(³) Ládu (III. 3.) líðan *to travel, journey, chiefly by sea.*
(⁴) Sæc (II. 3.) hence *sack* of a town.
(⁵) Hild (II. 3.) *battle, war.*
(⁶) The palace of Hróthgár prince of a Danish tribe.
(⁷) Wea *evil, misfortune.*
(⁸) Bétan *to profit, improve, do good to;* bót (II. 3.) *boot, profit.*
(⁹) Though quantity and number of syllables seem no essential part of A. S. versification, many lines will bear a more or less regular scanning; thus most short lines consist either of two trochees, like the 2nd, 5th, and 11th above, or of a dactyl and spondee like the 10th: the 3rd, and 6th, also might be called imperfect adonics.

that in *f*eor in the fourth. The third and fourth couplets have each two sub-letters like the first; the fourth again but one, wið being here not emphatic. The last line depends for its alliteration on the first of the next period; the couplet joining two lines by alliteration only, is often thus broken by the sense.

When the chief letter is a vowel or diphthong, the sub-letters must likewise be vowels or diphthongs, but need not be the same; as,

U'tan ymbe *æ*ðelne	Without round *the* noble
*e*nglas stódon.	angels stood.
*E*orðan *æ*'ht-ge-streón,	Earth's possessions,
*æ*pplede gold.	appled(¹) gold.

In the first example the sub letters *ú* and *æ* in the first line answer to the chief letter *e* in the second; in the other *eo*, *æ*', and *æ* rime together.

When the chief letter is double, the sub letters are usually double likewise; as,

*Fr*ægn *fr*om-líce (²)	*He* asked prudently
*fr*uman and ende.	*the* beginning and end.
*Sc*eán *sc*ír (³) werod,	Shone *the* bright host,
*sc*yldas lixton.	shields gleamed.

The following prefixes and prepositions in composition are not reckoned as part of the alliteration, which

---

(¹) Hence *d-appled*, as asphodel (O. affndil) has become *d-affodil*; *dappled-gray* is O. *apple-gray*, G. *apfel-grau*, D. *appel-graauw*: comp. F. *grispommelé*. (²) From *brave, pious &c.* G. fromm.

(³) *Clear, sheer*; G. schier.

N 2

falls only on the first root-letter of the word before which they stand: viz. a-, be-(bi-), ge-, to-, for-, æt, oð, of, geond, þurh; as,

A-*rǽ*dde and a-rehte	*That he* should read and relate
hwæt seó *rún*(¹) bude.	what the rune bade.

þonne be-*h*ófað	When it behoveth
se-þe *h*er wunað.	him that here dwelleth.

Þá ge-*w*orhte he þurh his *w*ís-dóm	Then wrought he through his wisdom
tyn engla *w*erod.	ten legions of angels.

To-*sw*eóp hine and to-*sw*ende	*He* swept and dashed it away
þurh his *sw*íðan miht.	through his strong might.

Þý-læs þú for-*w*eorðe	Lest thou perish
mid þissum *w*ær-logan (²)	with these false ones.

Se-þe æt-*f*eohtan *f*rum-gárum (³)—	Who to fight with *the* patriarchs—

(¹) Rún (II. 3.) *a secret, mystery, letter, hieroglyph;* here the hand-*writing on the wall:* hence *to round, whisper;* G. raunen.

(²) Wær-loga *a breaker of faith;* hence *war-lock:* wær (II. 3.) *a promise, compact,* loga *a lyer,* from leógan *to lye.*

(³) Gár (II. 2.) *a* (missile) *weapon, spear* (= L. telum), *chief;* it forms part of many proper names, as Gár-mund, Eád-gár *Edgar, &c.*

þá hie *g*ielp-scea*d*an (¹)	Since them *those* braggart-rebels
of-*g*ifen hæfdon.	had given up.

Si*d*-þán hie *fe*óndum	After they *the* foes
o*d*-*f*aren hæfdon.	had escaped.

Geond-*f*olen *fý*re	Filled through with fire
and *fæ*r-cyle (²).	and intense cold.

*W*ylm (³) þurh-*w*ódon (⁴)	*They the* flame had passed through
swá him *w*iht ne sceód—	so that them no whit hurt—

Big (bi), on, ofer, ymb, sometimes rime and sometimes do not; as,

And *b*egen þa *b*eornas	And both the warriors
þe him *b*ig-stódon.	who stood by him.
Big-*st*anda*d* me *st*range ge-neátas (⁵)	Stand by me strong comrades
þa ne willa*d* me æt þám *st*rí*d*e (⁶) ge-swícan.	who will not fail me at the strife.

(¹) Gilp (II. 2.) *boast;* scea*ð*a *enemy, robber, &c.*

(²) Fær (II. 2.) *stratagem;* in composition it implies *suddenness, danger,* or the like; fær-líc *dangerous;* G. ge fahr *danger,* ge-fähr-lich *dangerous.* Cyle II. 2.; hence *chill;* G. kühle.

(³) Wylm (II. 2.) *heat, boiling* (= L. æstus); welan, weallan *to boil;* G. wallen.   (⁴) Wadan (II. 3.) *to go;* L. vadere.

(⁵) Ge-neát; G. ge-noss, D. ge-noot.

(⁶) Stí*ð* (II. 2.) G. streit, D. strijd.

Þæt we þær *eá*gum	What we there with *our* eyes
*o*n-lóciað.	look upon.
On-*h*ycgað nú	Think now on
*h*álige mihte.	*the* holy might.

And þurh *o*fer-metto	And through pride
sóhton óðer land.	*they* sought another land.
Uton ofer-*h*ycgan	Let us despise
*h*elm (¹) þone miclan.	the great Supreme.

*E*orðan *y*mb-hwyrft	Earth's circuit
and *ú*p-rodor (²).	and *the* upper sky.
*H*eofon ymb-*h*weorfest,	*Thou* compassest heaven,
and þurh þíne *h*álige miht—	and through thy holy might—

And-, un-, ed-, in, tó, &c. are deemed emphatic and therefore rime; as,

Him þá *A*dam	Him then Adam
*a*nd-swarode.	answered.

*U*n-lytel dǽl	No little part
*e*orðan ge-sceafta.	of earth's creatures.

(¹) Helm is the *top* of anything; see p. 133, n. 13.
(²) Rodor (ll. 2.) *heaven, sky.*

Ne hí *e*d-cerres(¹)   Nor they for return
æfre móton wénan.   ever could hope.

Hæfde þá se *a*ðeling   Had then the noble
*i*n-ge-þancum(²)—   fervently—

Him þæt *t*ácen wearð   To him that *a* token was
þær he *t*ó-starode (³).   where he stared.

II.—*Metres of Boëthius*(⁴).

*** The following is King Ælfred's translation of Boëthius, Lib. III. metr. I.

Se-þe wille wyrcan   He that will work
wæstm-bǽre lond,   fruitful land,
a-teó of þám æcere   let him pluck off the field
ǽrest sona   first straightway
fearn(⁵), and þornas(⁶),   fern, and thorns,
and fyrsas, swá-same(⁷)   and furzes, as also weeds,
   weód(⁸),

(¹) Cer, cyr (II. 2.) *turn;* hence *char* a *turn* of work; cyrran *to turn, re-turn;* G. kehren.

(²) Adverb formed from the dative plural; see p. 70. Comp. G. ein-ge-denk *mindful, thoughtful.*

(³) Starian; G. starren, D. staaren.

(⁴) Chiefly from the Rev. S. Fox's edition.

(⁵) P. vearn, G. farn-kraut.   (⁶) Þorn; G. dorn.

(⁷) Same is connected with our *same.*

(⁸) Weód (II. 1.) D. wied.

þa þe willað   that will
wel-hwær(¹) derian   everywhere hurt
clǽnum hwǽte,   *the* clean wheat,
þý-læs he ciða-leás(²)   lest it germ-less
licge on þǽm lande.   lie on the land.
Is leóda(³) ge-hwǽm   Is to all people
þeós óðru bysen   this other example
efn be-héfe(⁴);   even *as* needful;
þæt is þætte þinceð(⁵)   that is that seemeth
þegna ge-hwylcum   to every man
huniges(⁶) beó-breád   honey's bee-bread
healfe þý swétre,   half the sweeter,
gif he hwene(⁷) ǽr   if he a little ere
huniges teare(⁸),   *the* honey's drop,
bitres on-byrgað.   *something* bitter tasteth.
Býð eác swá-same   Is eke in like wise
monna ǽg-hwylc   every man
micle þý fægenra   much the gladder
líðes(⁹) wedres(¹⁰),   of fair weather,
gif hine lytle ǽr   if him a little ere
stormas ge-stondað(¹¹), storms assail,

(¹) Wel prefixed is intensive; wel-oft *very often*, wel-hraðe *very soon*.

(²) Cið *shoot, growth of any kind*; hence *kid*, used either of a child or a young animal: comp. the uses of *imp, scion, sprig*, &c.

(³) Leóde *people, persons*; G. leute, D. lieden.

(⁴) Be-hófian *to need, be-hove*.   (⁵) See Additions, &c.

(⁶) G. honig.   (⁷) Hwene, hwon *a little*, S. *a wheen*.

(⁸) Tear (II. 2.) *tear*; G. zäbre.

(⁹) Líðe *tender, mild, lithe*; G. linde: observe the n dropped and the vowel lengthened, and see p. 2, and Additions, &c.

(¹⁰) Weder (II. 1.) G. wetter, D. weder.

(¹¹) Observe the force of ge-; see p. 64.

and se stearca(¹) wind nordan and eástan.	and the violent wind from north and east.
Nænigum þúhte dæg on þonce (²),	To none would seem *the* day delightful,
gif seó dimme niht ǽr ofer eldum (³) egesan (⁴) ne bróhte.	if the dim night before over men terror had not brought.
Swá þincđ ánra ge-hwǽm eorđ-búendra	So seemeth to every one of *the* earth-dwellers
seó sóđe ge-sǽlđ (⁵) simle þe betere, and þý wynsumre, þe he wíta má, heardra hǽnđa (⁶), her a-dreógeđ (⁷).	the true happiness ever the better, and the winsomer, as he more plagues, *and* hard afflictions, here suffereth.
þú meaht eác micle þý éđ	Thou mayst eke much the easier
on mód-sefan sóđe ge-sǽlđa sweótolor ge-cnáwan, and tó heora cýđđe (⁸) be-cuman síđ-þán, gif þú úp-a-týhst	in *thy* mind true happinesses clearlier know, and to their country come afterwards, if thou pluckest up

(¹) Stearc *stark, strong*; G. stark, D. sterk.
(²) Þonc (þanc) (II. 2.) *thank*; G. dank: comp. L. gratiæ and gratus.
(³) Eld, yld (II. 2.) *man, human being.*
(⁴) Egesa = ege *awe, dread.*   (⁵) II. 3. from sél, sǽl *good.*
(⁶) Hǽnđu (hýnđu) III. 3.; heán *abject, miserable.*
(⁷) (A-)dreógan (III. 3.) *to suffer;* S. dree.
(⁸) Cýđđu (III. 3.) also *acquaintance, knowledge,* hence *kith.*

ǽrest sona,. | first forthwith,
and þú a-wyrt-walast | and thou rootest
of ge-wit-locan(¹) | out of *thy* understanding
leáse ge-sǽlða, | false happinesses,
swá swá londes-ceorl(²) | as *the* husbandman
of his æcere list(³) | off his field gathers
yfel weód monig. | many *an* evil weed.
Sið þán ic þe secge | Afterwards I say to thee
þæt þú sweótole meaht | that thou clearly mayst
sóðe ge-sǽlða | true happinesses
sona on-cnáwan(⁴), | soon recognise,
and þú æfre ne recst | and thou never wilt reck
ǽniges þinges | for anything
ofer þa áne,. | above them alone,
gif þú hí ealles on-gitst. | if thou them quite understandest.

(¹) (Ge-) wit (II. 1.) *wit*, loca *fold, locker, place shut or locked up*.
(²) Ceorl *man* (free not noble) *husband, churl*; S. carl; G. kerl.
(³) Lesan (II. 1.) *to gather, pick;* hence *lease, to glean*. G. lesen *together read;* comp. L. legere.
(⁴) Comp. G. er-kennen.

III.—Cædmon (¹).

⁎ Cædmon, the Anglo-Saxon Milton, author of the Metrical Paraphrase of parts of the Holy Scriptures, from which the following extracts are taken, was first a herdsman, afterwards a monk in the Abbey of Streoneshalh or Whitby, then ruled by S. Hild: he flourished in the 7th century. For an account of him from Ælfred's version of Beda's Ecclesiastical History, see Mr. Thorpe's preface to his edition of Cædmon, and his Analecta Anglo-Saxonica, pp. 54-8.

Part of Book I. Canto II.

Her ǽrest ge-sceóp	Here first shaped
éce Dryhten,	*the* eternal Lord,
Helm (²) eal-wihta,	Chief of all creatures,
heofon and eorđan,	heaven and earth,
rodor a-rǽrde,	*the* firmament reared,
and þis rúme (³) land	and this spacious land
ge-stađelode	established
strangum mihtum,	by *his* strong powers,
Freá (⁴) œl-mihtig.	*the* Lord almighty.
Folde wæs þá gyt	*The* earth was then yet
græse un-gréne;	with grass not green;

(¹) From Mr. Thorpe's edition, more literally translated.
(²) See p. 133. n. 13.   (³) Rúm *wide, roomy*
(⁴) G. frau (*noble*) *woman, lady* is connected with freá.

gár-secg(¹) þeahte, ocean covered,
sweart(²) sin-nihte, swart in eternal night,
síde(³) and wíde, far and wide,
wonne(⁴) wegas. *the* dusky ways.
þa wæs wuldor-torht Then was *the* glory-bright
heofon-weardes gást heaven's Guardian's spirit
ofer holm(⁵) boren over *the* deep born
miclum spédum(⁶): with great speed:
Metod(⁷) engla héht, *the* Creator of angels bade,
lifes Brytta(⁸), life's Distributor,
leóht forð-cuman light come forth
ofer rúmne grund(⁹). over *the* wide abyss.
Raðe wæs ge-fylled Quickly was fulfilled
heáh-cyninges hǽs; *the* high King's behest;
him wæs hálig leóht for him was holy light
ofer wéstenne, over *the* waste,
swá se Wyrhta be-beád. as the Maker commanded.
þá ge-sundrode Then sundered
sigora(¹⁰) Waldend *the* Ruler of triumphs
ofer lago flóde over *the* water-flood
leóht wið þeóstrum(¹¹), light from darkness,

(¹) An obscure mythological word; gár (II. 2.) *weapon*, secg *man, warrior*.
(²) *Black, swart, swarthy*; G. schwarz, D. zwart.
(³) Síd *wide*.   (⁴) Won, wan *wan, dark*.
(⁵) Holm means also an *island* in the sea; Steep-*holm*, Born-*holm*, &c.
(⁶) Spéd (II. 3.) *success, prosperity, speed*; D. spoed.
(⁷) From metan *to mete, measure*: He who "measured the waters, and meted out heaven." (⁸) Bryttan *to distribute*.
) II. 2. *ground, bottom, depth*; G. grund.
(⁹) Sigor (II. 2.) = sige *victory*.   (¹¹) þeóstru = þýstru.

sceade(¹) wið scíman(²);   shade from brightness;
sceóp þá bám, naman,   created then for both,
                            names,
lifes Brytta.   life's Distributor.
Leóht wæs ǽrest   Light was first
þurh Dryhtnes word   through *the* Lord's word
dæg ge-nemned;   day named;
wlíte-beorhte ge-sceaft!   beauty-bright creation!
Wel lícode   Well pleased
Freán æt frymðe(³)   *the* Lord at *the* beginning
forð-bǽre(⁴) tíd.   *the* teeming time.

Part of Book I. Canto XVI.

þá tó Euan God   Then to Eve God
yrringa(⁵) spræc: angrily spake:
Wend(⁶) þe from wynne(⁷);   Turn thee from joy;
þú scealt wæpned-men   thou shalt to man
wesan on ge-wealde;   be in subjection;
mid weres egsan   with fear of *thy* husband
hearde ge-nearwad(⁸),   hardly straitened,
heán, þrowian(⁹)   abject, suffer *for*
þínra dǽda ge-dwild(¹⁰)—   thy deeds' error—

(¹) For sceadwe; sceadu (-o) (II. 2.) G. schatte.
(²) Scíma *light, skimmer*.   (³) Frymð (II. 2.)
(⁴) Lit. *forth-bearing*.
(⁵) See p. 70—1; from yrre (II. 2.) *ire, anger;* L. ira.
(⁶) Wendan *to turn, wend, go;* G. wenden.
(⁷) Wyn (II. 3.) *pleasure;* G. wonne.
(⁸) Ge-nearwian, from nearu *to make narrow, afflict, oppress.*
(⁹) Hence *throe*.   (¹⁰) II. 3. dwelian *to err.*

deáðes bídan;   death abide;
ánd þurh wóp(¹) and heáf,   and through weeping and moan,
on woruld cennan(²),   into *the* world bear,
þurh sár(³) micel,   through much pain,
sunu and dóhtor.   son and daughter.
A-beád eác Adame   Announced eke to Adam
éce Dryhten,   *the* eternal Lord,
lifes Leóht-fruma,   Author of life's light,
láð ærende(⁴):   *the* dire errand:
Þú sceaıt óðerne   Thou shalt *an*other
éðel(⁵) sécean,   country seek,
wyn-leásran wíc,   *a* joylesser dwelling,
and on wræc(⁶) hweorf-an(⁷),   and into exile go,
nacod(⁸), níed-wædla(⁹),   naked, *a* needy beggar,
neorxna-wanges(¹⁰)   of Paradise's
dúgeðum be-dǽled: blessings deprived:
þe is ge-dál witod(¹¹)   to thee is *a* parting decreed
líces(¹²) and sáwle.   of body and soul.

(¹) II. 2. hence *whoop*.
(²) I. 2. comp. γενειν, L. genere; hence *to kindle*.
(³) II. 1. *sore*. (⁴) III. 1. from ar *messenger*.
(⁵) II. 2. *native country, home*. (⁶) II. 3.
(⁷) III. 1. *to turn, return, go*.
(⁸) G. nackt. (⁹) Níed = neód.
(¹⁰) Neorxna-wang (II. 2.) a word of doubtful etymology; wang is *plain, field*. (¹¹) Witian *to decide, decree*; hence witod-líce.
(¹²) Líc (II. 1.) *corpse, dead body*; G. leich, D. lijk: hence *lich-gate* to a Churchyard, *like-wake watching a corpse*, &c.

Hwæt! þú láđ-líce	Lo! thou foully
wróhte(¹) on-stealdest;	crime didst commit;
for-þón þú winnan(²) scealt,	therefore thou shalt labour,
and on eorđan þe	and on earth to thee
þine and-lifne(³)	thy livelihood
selfa ge-rǽcan(⁴),	*th*yself obtain,
wegan(⁵) swátig(⁶) hleor(⁷),	wear a sweaty face,
þinne hláf etan,	thy bread eat,
þenden þú her leofast,	while thou here livest,
uđ-þæt þe tó heortan	until thee at heart
hearde grípeđ(⁸)	hardly gripeth
adl(⁹) un-líđe,	ungentle ailment,
þe þú on æple(¹⁰) ǽr	which thou in *the* apple erst
selfa for-swulge(¹¹);	*th*yself swallowedst down;
for-þón þú sweltan scealt.	therefore thou shalt die.
Hwæt! we nú ge-hýrađ	Lo! we now hear

(¹) Wróht (IN. 3.); wrégan *to accuse;* comp. L. crimen.

(²) Winnan (III. 1.) *to battle, struggle, toil,* also *to win;* ge-winn *labour,* &c.   (³) And-lifn II. 3.

(⁴) I. 2. lit. *reach;* G. reichen, D. reiken.

(⁵) II. 1. *to wag, move, bear;* hence wæg *wey (weight),* wǽg *wave,* wægn *wagon.*

(⁶) Swát (II. 2.) *sweat;* G. schweiss, D. zweet.

(⁷) II. 1. *jaw, cheek;* hence *countenance, complexion,* O. lere.

(⁸) Grípan (III. 2.) G. greifen, D. grijpen.

(⁹) II. 3. *ail, disease.*

(¹⁰) Æpl, æppel (II. 2.) G. apfel, D. appel.

(¹¹) For-swelgan (III. 1.) *to devour;* G. ver-schwelgen.

hwær ús hearm-stafas(¹)	where to us sorrow
wræðe(²) on-wócon(³),	in wrath up-sprang
and woruld-yrmðo(⁴).	and worldly misery.
Híe þá wuldres Weard	Them then glory's Keeper
wǽdum(⁵) gyrede,	with weeds provided,
Scyppend ússer,	our Creator,
hét heora sceome(⁶) þecc-an,	bade their shame hide,
Freá, frum-hrægle;	*the* Lord, with *the* first garment;
hét híe from-hweorfan	bade them depart from
neorxna-wange	Paradise
on nearore lif.	into *a* narrower life.
Him on laste(⁷) be-leác(⁸)	Behind them locked up
líðra and wynna	of comforts and joys
hyht-fulne(⁹) hám,	*the* hopeful home,
hálig engel,	*a* holy angel,
be Freán hǽse,	by *his* Lord's behest,
fýrene(¹⁰) sweorde.	with fiery sword.
Ne mæg þær inwit-ful(¹¹)	May not there guileful
ǽnig ge-feran,	any journey,

(¹) Hearm (II. 2.) *grief, harm, calamity;* G. harm. Stafas (plur. of stæf) forms the second part of several poetical compounds; as, ende-stafas *end,* ár-stafas *honour,* &c. (²) Wræð II. 3.
(³) On-wacan (II. 3.) *to awake, arise, be born.*
(⁴) III. 3. from earm *poor.*
(⁵) Wǽd (III. 1.) *weed, garment.*
(⁶) Sceamu (III. 3.) G. scham.
(⁷) Last (II. 2.) *footstep.* (⁸) Be-lúcan III. 3.
(⁹) Hyht (II. 3.) *hope.* (¹⁰) Fýren *of fire.*
(¹¹) Inwit (II. 1.) *deceit, treachery.*

wom-scyldig(¹) mon;	stain-guilty man,
ac se weard hafað	but the keeper hath
miht and strengðo(²),	might and strength,
se þæt mǽre lif	who that exalted life
dúgeðum(³) deóre,	to *the* good dear,
Dryhtne healded.	for *the* Lord holdeth.
Nó hwædre Æl-mihtig	Not however *the* Almighty
ealra wolde	of all would
Adam and Euan	Adam and Eve
árna(⁴) of-teón,	means deprive,
Fæder æt Frymðe,	*the* Father from *the* beginning,
þeáh he him from-swice(⁵);	though he from them had withdrawn;
ac he him tó frófre let	but he to them for solace let
hwæðre forð-wesan	nevertheless continue forth
hyrstedne(⁶) hróf(⁷)	*the* adorned roof
hálgum tunglum(⁸),	with holy stars,
and him grund-welan(⁹)	and them earth-riches
ginne sealde;	ample gave;

(¹) Wom (II. 2.) *spot, defilement.*
(²) Strengðo (-u) (III. 3.) = strengð II. 3.
(³) Duguð (II. 3.) *virtue, benefit, nobility, chief men;* from dugan.
(⁴) A'r (II. 3.) *honour, wealth,* &c.; nouns of this class sometimes have a simple or weak genitive plural.
(⁵) Swícan (III. 2.) *to cease, depart from.*
(⁶) Hyrst (II. 3.) *ornament.*   (⁷) II. 2. D. roef.
(⁸) Tungel (III. 1.) *heavenly body.*
(⁹) Wela *weal, wealth.*

hét þám sin-híwum(¹)   bade the pairs
saés and eorðan   of sea and earth
tuddor teóndra(²),   producing offspring,
teóhha(³) ge-hwylces   of every substance
tó woruld-nytte(⁴)   to worldly use
wæstmas fédan(⁵).   fruits bring forth.
Ge-saéton þá æfter synne *They* occupied then aftei
                                                      their sin

sorg-fulre land,   *a* sorrowfuller land,
eard and éðel   *a* dwelling and home
un-spédigran(⁶)   more barren
fremena(⁷) ge-hwylcre   of every good thing
þonne se frum-stól(⁸) wæs than the first seat was
þe híe æfter dæde   which they after *that* deed
of-a-drifen wurdon.   were driven from.

(¹) Sin-híwa *mate, partner*.   (²) Teón *to draw, pro-duce*.
(³) Teób (teóg) III. 1. *stuff, material;* G. **zeug**.
(⁴) Nyt (II. 3.) G. nutz, D. nut.
(⁵) Comp. L. fet-us, &c.   (⁶) Spédig *wealthy*.
(⁷) Freme (I. 3.) *advantage, benefit*.
(⁸) Stól (II. 2.) G. stuhl, D. stoel; hence *stool*.

IV.—*Beówulf*(¹).

*** The celebrated poem from which the following extracts are taken, relates the exploits of the hero Beówulf, King of the Weder-Geáts or Angles, about the middle of the 5th century. The author is unknown, and no mention of Britain occurs; the present text is supposed to date from the 7th century.

Part of Canto V. (²)

Strǽt(³) wæs stán-fáh,	*The* street was variegated with stones,
stíg(⁴) wísode(⁵)	*the* path guided
gumum æt-gædere;	*the* men together;
gúđ-byrne(⁶) scán,	*the* war-corslet shone,
heard, hond-locen(⁷);	hard, hand-locked;
hring-íren(⁸) scír	*the* ring-iron bright
song in seɛrwum(⁹),	sang in *their* trappings,
þá híe tó sele(¹⁰) furđum,	when they to *the* hall forward,

(¹) From Mr. Kemble's edition; the translation has been adapted to read line by line.   . (²) Line 637—676.

(³) II. 3. L. strata (via) G. strasse, D. straat.

(⁴) II. 3. G. steig, hence stígan *to go, mount.*

(⁵) Wísian *to show, direct,* governing the dative; G. weisen.

(⁶) Gúđ II. 3.; byrne (I. 3.) O. birnie.

(⁷) *Clasped, closed by the hand.*

(⁸) Hring (II. 2.) G. ring; íren (ísen) (III. 1.) G. eisen. The corslet was of *ring* or *chain* mail.

(⁹) Searu (III. 1.) *equipment,* chiefly for war.

(¹⁰) II. 2. L. aula, G. saal, F. salle.

in hyra grýre-geatwum(¹), in their terrible harness,
gangan cwomon. proceeded to go.
Setton sǽ-méđe(²) *The* sea-weary *men* set
síde scyldas, *their* wide shields,
rondas(³) regn-hearde(⁴), *their* very hard bucklers,
wiđ þæs recedes weal. by the house wall.
Bugon þá tó bence, *They* turned then to *a* bench,

byrnan hringdon, *their* corslets laid in a ring,

gúđ-searo gumena; *the* war-trapping of men:
gáras stódon *their* javelins stood
sǽ-manna searo sea-men's arms
samod æt-gædere, all together,
æsc-holt(⁵) úfan græg(⁶): ash-wood above gray:
wæs se íren-þreát the iron-crowd was
wæpnum ge-wurđad. by *the* weapons honoured.
þá þær wlonc hæleđ(⁷) Then there *a* proud warrior

oret-mecgas(⁸) *the* sons of battle
æfter hæleđum frægn: after *the* heroes asked:
Hwanon ferigeađ ge Whence bear ye

(¹) Grýre (II. 2.) *horror;* comp. G. es grauet, O. it grews. Geatwe (ge-tawe) (I. 3.) = searu. (²) G. müde.
(³) Rand (rond) *edge* (G. rand), *shield.*
(⁴) Regen- is an intensive prefix.
(⁵) Æsc (II. 3.) G. esche; holt (II. 1.) *holt;* G. holz, D. hout.
(⁶) G. grau. (⁷) II. 2. G. held.
(⁸) Mecg (mæg) *kins-man, son, man,* connected with mǽg, and maga, and all with Mac-.

… EXTRACTS—BEOWULF.

fætte scyldas,	*your* thick shields,
græge syrcan ([1]),	gray shirts,
and grim-helmas ([2]),	and visor-helms,
here-sceafta ([3]) heáp?	*your* war-shafts' heap?
Ic eom Hróđ-gáres	I am Hróthgár's
ar and om-biht ([4]) :	messenger and servant:
ne seáh ic el-þeódige	never saw I foreign
þus manige men	thus many men
módig-lícran :	haughtier :
wén ([5]) is þæt ge for wlenco ([6]),	I ween that ye for pride,
nalles for wræc-síđum ([7])	not for exile
ac for hyge-þrymmum ([8]),	but for magnanimity,
Hróđ-gár sóhton.	have sought Hróthgár.

Part of Canto XXII. ([9])

Beó-wulf mađelode ([10]),	Beówulf harangued,
bearn Ecg-þeówes :	son of Ecgtheów :
Ge-þenc nú se mǽra	Consider now *thou* the famous
maga Healf-denes,	son of Healfdene,

([1]) Syrce (I. 3.) S. sark; *gray shirts of iron chain-mail.*
([2]) Grime (II. 2.) *mask, part of the helmet covering the face.*
([3]) Sceaft (II. 2.) G. schaft.
([4]) Om- (am-) bihtu *office;* G. amt.
([5]) (II. 3.) *hope, expectation:* wén is *there is reason to suppose.*
([6]) Wlenco (III. 3.) from wlanc *proud.*
([7]) Wræc (II. 3.) *exile,* &c.; síð *journey.*
([8]) Hyge (II. 2.) *mind,* hycgan (hogian) *to think;* þrym (II. 2.) *glory.*
([9]) Line 2945—2998.   ([10]) Mešel (II. 1.) *discourse, speech.*

snottra (¹) fengel,	prudent chief,
nú ic eom sídes fús,	now I am ready to depart,
gold-wine (²) gumena,	patron of men,
hwæt wit geó sprácon;	what we two erst spake;
gif ic æt þearfe	if I at thy need
þínre sceolde	should
aldre linnan,	from life cease,
þæt þú me á wǽre	that thou to me ever wouldst be
forð-ge-witenum,	departed,
on fæder stæle (³).	in *a* father's stead.
Wæs þú mund-bora (⁴)	Be thou *a* protector
mínum mago þegnum,	to my kindred thanes,
hond-ge-sellum (⁵),	*my* near comrades,
gif mec hild nime.	if me battle should take.
Swylce þú þa mádmas (⁶)	Likewise do thou the treasures
þe þú me sealdest,	that thou gavest me,
Hróð-gár leófa,	Hróthgár dear,
Hige-láce on-send:	to Higelác send:

(¹) Snotor *prudent*; definite form, *se* being understood.

(²) Gold- implies *splendour, munificence*; wine (ll. 2.) *friend* forms part of many proper names: Trum-wine, Eád-wine, Edwin, &c.

(³) Stæl (ll. 2.) hence *stall*; G. stelle.

(⁴) Mund (ll. 3) *protection*; forming part of several proper names; as O's-mund, Sigemund (G. Siegmund) Sigismund, &c.: bora (from beran) *one who bears*; the second part of several compounds.

(⁵) Lit. *hand-comrades*; ge-sel (ll. 2.) G. ge-selle.

(⁶) Múððum, máðm, mádm *treasure, gift.*

mæg þonne on þám golde on-gitan	may then by the gold understand
Geáta dryhten,	*the* lord of the Geáts,
ge-seón sunu Hreðles	Hrethl's son see
þonne he on þæt sinc staraeð,	when he at the treasure stareth,
þæt ic gum-cystum (¹) gódne funde	that I in *his* munificence found *a* good
beága (²) bryttan;	distributor of rings;
breác þonne móste.	*I* enjoyed *it* while *I* might.
And þú Hun-ferð læt	And do thou let Hun-ferth
ealde láfe (³),	*the* old bequest,
wræt-líc (⁴) wǽg-sweord (⁵),	*the* ornamented wave-sword,
wíd-cúðne man,	*the* wide-known man,
heard-ecg (⁶) habban.	*the* hard edged have.
Ic me mid Hruntinge (⁷)	I me with Hrunting
dóm ge-wyrce,	glory will work,
oððe mec deáð nimeð.	or me death shall take.
Æfter þǽm wordum	After those words

(¹) Cyst (II. 3.) *choice, excellence, the best of a thing*; from ceósan.

(²) Beáh (II. 2.) *ring*; F. bague: from beógan, búgan *to bow, bend.* Rings whether for the arm (earm-beáh), or neck (heals-beáh), were usual gifts from an A. S. or Scandinavian chief or prince to his followers.

(³) Láf (II. 3.) *leaving, relic, heir-loom,* as swords often were.

(⁴) Wræt *embossed or carved ornament.*

(⁵) Wǽg (II. 3.) *wave;* G. woge, F. vague: *adorned with wavy lines* as blades still are.   (⁶) Ecg (II. 3.) *edge;* G. ecke.

(⁷) Hrunting was the name of Beówulf's famous sword.

Weder-Geáta leód   *the* Weder-Geáts' prince
éfste mid elne (¹),   hastened with boldness,
ná-læs and-sware   nor answer
bidan wolde: would bide:
brim-wylm on-feng   *the* ocean-tide received
hilde-rince (²).   *the* man of war.

Part of Canto XXVII. (³)

Cwom (⁴) þá tó flóde   Came then to *the* floor
fela módigra   many proud
hæg-stealdra (⁵),   bachelors,
hring net (⁶) bǽron,   *who* ring-nets bore,
locene leoðo-syrcan (⁸).   locked limb-shirts.
Land-weard on-fand   *The* land-guard found out
eft-síð eorla,   *the* return of the warriors,
swá he ǽr dyde;   as he ere had done;
nó he mid hearme   not with insult did he
of hliðes (⁸) nosan (⁹)   from *the* cape's point
gæstas ne grétte,   *the* guests greet,
ac him tó-geanes rád;   but to meet them rode,

(¹) Ellen (II. 1.) *courage, valour.*

(²) Rinc (II. 2.) *man, warrior.*   (³) Line 3772—38·5.

(⁴) Fela usually governs a genitive plural, while the verb often stands in the singular.

(⁵) Hæg-steald (II. 2.) G. hage-stolz; the genitive plural in ·ra seems to show that this word was originally a participle past; and "hæg-steald mon" occurs.

(⁶) Another allusion to the *ring* 'heir mail.

(⁷) Lið, leoð (III. 1.) G. glied, D. lid.

(⁸) Hlið (II. 1.) *lid, covering, cliff.*   (⁹) Nose I. 3.

cwæð þæt wil-cuman   quoth that welcome
Wedera leódum,   to *the* people of *the* Wed-
                               ers,
scalcas(¹) on scír-hame(²)   men in bright mail
tó scipe fóron.   to *their* ship went.
þá wæs on sande   There was on *the* sand
sǽ-geáp naca(³)   *the* sea-curved bark
hladen here-wǽdum,   laden with war-weeds,
hringed stefna(⁴),   *the* ringed vessel,
mærum and máðmum;   with horses and gifts;
mæst hlifade   *the* mast lifted itself
ofer Hróð-gáres   over Hróthgár's
hord-ge-streónum(⁵):   hoarded treasures:
he þǽm bát-wearde(⁶)   he to the boat-ward
bunden golde   bound with gold
swurd ge-sealde,   *a* sword gave,
þæt he síð-þán wæs   *so* that he afterwards was
on meodu-bence(⁷)   on *the* mead-bench
máðma þý weorðre,   for *the* gifts the worthier,
yrfe-láfe.   *the* heir-loom.
Ge-wát him on nacan   *He* departed in *the* ship

(¹) Scealc, scalc *man, servant* &c.; G. schalk *rogue*. Mearh-scealc *officer* &c. *having the care of the horses* (mearh *horse*); hence *mar-shal.*

(²) Ham (hama) *covering,* here *armour.*

(³) Comp. G. nachen, F. nacelle.

(⁴) Stefn (stemn) (II. 2.) *stem, prow;* stefna *ship having a stem: ship with the stem adorned with rings.*

(⁵) Hord (II. 2.) *hoard, treasure;* ge-streón (II. 3.) *acquisition, wealth* &c.; streónan, strýnan *to acquire, get, beget;* hence *strain, breed.*

(⁶) Bát (II. 1.) G. boot.

(⁷) Meodo, medo (-u) (III. 2.) G. meth, D meede.

dréfan deóp wæter; to urge *the* deep water;
Dena land of-geaf: the Danes' land *he* left:
þá wæs be mæste there was by *the* mast
mere-hrægla sum, a certain sea-vest,
segl(¹) sále-fæst(²); a sail fast by *a* rope;
sund-wudu(³) þunede(⁴); the sea-wood thundered;
nó þær wǽg-flotan(⁵) not there *the* wave-floater
        did

wind ofer ýðum *the* wind over *the* billows
síðes ge-twǽfde(⁶); from *its* course hinder;
sǽ-genga fór, *the* sea-goer went,
fleát fámig-heals(⁷) floated *the* foamy-necked
forð ofer ýðe, forth over *the* wave,
bunden(⁸) stefna *the* bounden ship
ofer brim-streámas, over *the* ocean-streams,
þæt híe Geáta clifu(⁹) *so* that they *the* Geats'
        cliffs

on-gitan meahton, could make out,
cúðe næssas(¹⁰). *the* known headlands.

(¹) Segel (II. 2.) G. segel.

(²) Sál (II. 2.) *string*, &c. G. seil; hence sǽlan below *to bind, make fast.*

(³) From sund, comes *sound (strait)* G. sund.

(⁴) Þunian; comp. L. tonare; þunor (II. 2.) *thunder;* L. tonitru, G. donner, D. donder. Hence Þór *Thor*, the *thunderer*, (Jupiter) Tonans.

(⁵) Flota *floater, ship, sailor;* from fleótan (III. 3.) *to float, fleet;* F. flotter.   (⁶) Ge-twǽfan *to divide*, &c.; from twá.

(⁷) Heals (II. 2.) *neck;* G hals.

(⁸) With ornaments *bound* or *wound* round the prow.

(⁹) Clif (III. 1.) *rock, cliff;* L. clivus, G. klippe, D. klip.

(¹⁰) Næs *nose, promontory;* L. nasus, G. nasc: hence *-ness* in Dungeness and the like.

Ceól(¹) úp-ge-sprang	*The* ship up-sprang
lyft-ge-swenced(²),	air-compelled,
on lande stód.	on *the* land stood.
Hraðe wæs æt holme	Quickly was at *the* sea
hýð-weard(³) geara,	*the* shore-guard ready,
se-þe ǽr lange tíd	who long time ere
leófra manna,	*the* dear men's,
fús æt faroðe,	ready at *the* strand,
fær wlátode:	journey had watched:
sǽlde tó sande	*he* tied to *the* sand
síd-fæðme(⁴) scip	*the* wide-bosomed ship
oncer-bendum(⁵) fæst,	with anchor-bands fast,
þý-læs hine ýð-þrym,	lest it *the* force of *the* waves,
wudu wynsuman,	*the* winsome wood,
for-wrecan(⁶) meahte.	might damage.

(¹) Ceól (II. 2.) *keel*, *vessel* (= L. carina) G. kiel: vessels called *keels* are still in use on the Humber.

(²) Lyft (II. 3.) G. luft, O. lift; swencan *to drive, urge.*

(³) Hýð (II. 3.) *haven*, &c.; hence -*hythe* in Queen-*hythe*, &c.

(⁴) Fæðm II. 2.   (⁵) Oncer, ancer (II. 2.) G. anker.

(⁶) For-wrecan (II. 1.) *to banish, injure*, &c. hence to *wreck.*

APPENDIX.

1.—*Words spelt alike, but differing in accent, pronunciation, and meaning.*

₊ This list, in addition to what is stated at p. 2, will prove the great importance of attention to the quantity of A. S. vowels, if only as a mean of distinguishing words otherwise of the same aspect, but in truth differing in every respect but spelling. Other spellings, by which some of the words may be further known from each other, are given between brackets.

Ac (ah) *but.*
ác (II. 3.) *oak;* G. eiche, D. eik.
a-gán *a-gone, a-go.*
ágan (anom.) *to own, possess, have.*
a-gen ([1]) (a-(on-)gean) *a-gain, a-gainst;* G. gegen, D. te-gen.
ágen *own;* G. and D. eigen.
an (on) *on, in;* ἐν, L. in, G. an, D. aan ([2]).
an (ann) (*I*) *grant,* from unnan.

([1]) P. *agen* or *agin.*
([2]) The Dutch sometimes, as here, has lengthened a short vowel; on the whole however it will perhaps be found as safe a guide to the A. S. quantity as any modern language can be. In D. a double vowel or diphthong, in G. a diphthong, a vowel with h before or after it, or a double vowel, in general answers to an A. S. long vowel.

án *one, a;* G. ein, D. een: L. ūn-us, εἰς(¹).
ar (II. 2.) *messenger.*
ár (II. 3.) *honour;* G. ehre, D. eer.
aras; plur. of ar.
a-rás *a-rose,* from a-rísan.
ædre *instantly, forthwith.*
ædre (I. 3.) *vein;* G. and D. ader.
æl (II. 2.) *awl;* G. ahl, D. els.
ǽl (II. 2.) *eel;* G. and D. aal.
ban (ge-bann) (II. 2.) *ban, edict;* G. bann, D. ban.
bán (II. 1.) *bone;* G. bein, D. been.
bær (II.) *bare;* G. bar.
bær (*I*) *bare;* G. (ge-)bar.
bǽr (II. 3.) *bier;* G. bahre, D. baar.
ben (benn) (II. 3.) *wound.*
bén (II. 3.) *prayer.*
blæd (II. 2.) *fruit;* G. blatt, D. blad (*leaf, blade.*)
blǽd (II. 3.) *blast;* G. blasen.
brid (bridd) (II. 2.) (*young*) *bird.*
bríd (brýd) (II. 3.) *bride;* G. braut, D. brijd.
bude; 2nd pers. imperf. of beódan *to bid.*
búde; imperf. of búan *to cultivate,* &c. G. baute.
cneow (III. 1.) *knee;* G. and D. knie.
cneów (*I*) *knew.*
coc (cocc) (II. 2.) *cock.*
cóc (II. 2.) *cook.*
feol(²) (feoll) (*I*) *fell;* G. fiel.

(¹) Here and often else, the *ν* has evidently been dropped before *σ*; it appears in the neut. *ἲν*, and in the oblique cases *ἲνος*, &c. See Additions, &c.

(²) Quantity doubtful; if long, both words should be shifted to II. below.

feól (fýl) (II. 3.) *file*; G. feile, D. vijl.([1])
floc (flocc) (II. 2.) *flock (of sheep &c.)*
floc (flocc) (II. 3.) *flock (of wool &c.)*; G. flocke, D. vlok.
flóc (II. 3.) *flook, (flat-fish, of an anchor.)*
for- (prefix) *for-*; G. ver-.
for *for*; G. für, D. voor.
fór (II. 3.) *going, journey.*
fór; imperf. of faran; G. fuhr, D. voer.
fore *be-fore*; G. vor, D. voor, L. pro, προ.
fóre; 2nd pers. imperf. of faran.
ful (full) (II. 1.) *cup.*
ful (full) *full*; G. voll, D. vol.
fúl *foul*; G. faul, D. vuil.
fyl (fyll) (II. 2.) *felling, slaughter.*
fyl (fyll) (II. 3.) *fill, glut*; G. fülle.
fýl (feól) (II. 3.) *file*; G. feile, D. vijl.
fyr *further.*
fýr (II. 1.) *fire*; G. feuer, D. vuur: πῦρ.
geat (III. 1.) *gate*; D. gat *hole, opening.*
geát; imperf. of geótan *to pour*; G. goss, D. goot.
geoc (II. 1.) *yoke*; G. joch, D. juk, L. jŭgum, ζυγον.
geóc (II. 3.) *consolation.*
geong *young*; G. jung, D. jong.
geóng; imperf. of gán; G. gieng.
God (II. 2.) *God*; G. Gott, D. God.
gód *good*; G. gut, D. goed.
heaf (III. 1.) *ocean, deep*; G. haf-en, D. hav-en *hav-en*, F. hav-re.
heáf (heóf) (II. 2.) *grief.*

([1]) D. v is = f.

ham *ham;* D. ham.
ham (hama) (II. 2.) *covering, skin.*
hám(¹) (II. 2.) *home, dwelling;* G. heim, D. heem.
hama (homa, ham); see above.
háma *grasshopper.*
hig (II. 1.) *hay;* G. heu.
hig *hey! oh!*
híg (hí) *they:* oí, L. ei, ii.
hof (II. 2.) *court, dwelling;* G. and D. hof.
hóf (*I*) *hove;* G. hub, D. hief.
hwæte *eager, brave.*
hwǽte (II. 2.) *wheat;* G. weizen, D. weit.
hyrde (II. 2.) *herd;* G. hirt.
hýrde (*I*) *heard;* G. hörte.
hyre (hire) *her;* G. ihr.
hýre (heóre) *gentle, mild;* G. (un-ge-)heuer.
is *is;* G. ist, D. is: ἐστι, L. est.
ís (II. 1.) *ice;* G. eis, D. ijs.
lam *lame;* G. lahm, D. lam.
lám (II. 2.) *loam;* G. lehm, D. leem.
leoð (lið) (III. 1.) *limb;* G. glied, D. lid.
leóð (II. 1.) *lay, song;* G. and D. lied.
lim (III. 1.) *limb.*
lím (II. 2.) *lime, s-lime*(²); G. (sch-)leim, D. (s-)lijm.
man (mann) (III. 2.) *man;* G. mann, D. man.
mán (II. 1.) *sin, crime;* comp. G. mein-eid, D. mijn-eed *perjury,* and our *man*-sworn.

(¹) Hence *ham*-let, and *ham* (*hamp*-) in local names; comp. G. Blind-heim, D. Gorinc-hem &c. (²) See p. 105, n. 9.

mæst (II. 2.) *mast* ; G. mast.
mǽst *most* ; G. meist, D. meest.
men (menn) *men* ; G. männer.
mén *necklace*, &c. L. mon-ile.
metan (II. 1.) *to mete, measure* ; G. messen, D. meeten
metan (I. 2.) *to paint*.
métan (I. 2.) *to meet* ; D. moeten.
ne *not*, O. *ne* ; L. and F. ne.
né (for ne-ge) *nor* ; L. nec, G. noch, F. ni.
nið (II. 2.) *man, warrior*.
níð (II. 2.) *envy, malice* ; G. neid.
sæd *sated*, hence *sad* ; G. satt: comp. L. săt-is *enough*.
sæd (ge-sæd, -sægd) *said* ; G. ge-sagt.
sǽd (II. 1.) *seed* ; G. saat, D. zaad([1]).
sæl (sel, sal, sele) *hall* ; G. saal, F. salle: αὐλη.
sǽl (II. 2.) *time*.
sǽl (sél) *good, excellent*.
spræc (I) *spake* ; G. sprach, D. sprak.
sprǽc (II. 3.) *speech* ; G. sprache, D. spraak.
syn (synn) (II. 3.) *sin* ; G. sünde, D. zonde.
sýn (seón) (II. 3.) *sight*.
sýn (sín) *his*, &c.; G. sein, D. zijn.
to- (prefix) G. zer-([2]).
tó *to* ; G. zu, D. te, toe, tot.
tó *two* ; G. zu, D. te.
tol (toll) (II. 1.) *toll* ; G. zoll, D. tol.
tól (II. 1.) *tool*.
uton *let us*— ; L. utin-am ?

([1]) D. z often answers to A. S., E. and G. s.
([2]) G. z (= ts) answers to A. S., E., and D. t.

úton *without;* G. aussen, D. b-uiten.
wæg (II. 3.) *dish, wey, weight, balance;* G. wage, D. waag.
wǽg (II. 2.) *wave;* G. woge, F. vague.
wende (*I*) *turned, went;* G. wandte, D. wende.
wénde (*I*) *weened;* G. wähnte, D. waande.
werig *spiteful.*
wérig *weary.*
westan *from the west.*
wéstan (I. 2.) *to waste, ravage;* G. ver-wüsten.
win (ge-winn) (II. 2.) *war, labour, gain;* G. ge-winn.
win (wyn) (II. 3.) *pleasure;* G. wonne.
win (II. 1.) *wine;* G. wein, D. wijn: οἶν-ος, L. vīn-um.
þa *the &c.;* G. die, D. de : τἄ.
þá *then, when ;* G. da.
þara (þar, þær) *there;* G. dar.
þára (þǽra) *of the &c.;* G. der.

II.—*Words spelt and accented alike, but differing in meaning.*

Aldor (ealdor) ([1]) (II. 2.) *chief, prince;* hence aldor-man.
aldor (ealdor) (II. 2.) *life.*
a′r (II. 1.) *brass;* G. eher, erz, L. æs, ær-is.
ǽr *ere;* G. eher, D. eer.
æt (II. 2.) *food, eating.*
æt (*I*) *ate;* G. ass, D. at
æt *at;* L. ad.

([1]) The A. S. has a tendency to insert e (y) before a : hence the frequent modern pronunciation of *kyart* for *cart* and the like.

bát (II. 1.) *boat;* G. boot.
bát (*I*) *bit;* G. biss, D. beet.
beáh (II. 2.) *ring;* F. bague.
beáh; imperf. of búgan *to bow, bend;* G. bieg, D. boog.
beó (I. 3.) *bee;* G. biene, D. bij.
beó (*I*) *be;* G. bin, D. ben.
beón *bees.*
beón *to be.*
bere (II. 2.) *bere, bar-ley.*
bere (*I*) *bear.*
bil (II. 1.) *bill, faulchion;* G. beil, D. bijl.
bil *bill, beak.*
blác *pale, bleak,* hence *black;* G. bleich, D. bleek.
blác; imperf. of blícan *to shine, blink;* G. blinken.
bóc (III. 3.) *book;* G. buch, D. boek.
bóc; imperf. of bacan *to bake;* D. biek.
byre (II. 2.) *son, child.*
byre (II. 2.) *event, time.*
byrne (I. 3.) *corslet,* O. birnie.
byrne (birne) (*I*) *burn* (neut.) G. brenne.
cin (cinn) (II. 1.) *chin,* G. kinn.
cin (cynn) (II. 1.) *kin, race.*
cyst (cist) (II. 3.) *chest;* P. kist, G. kiste, D. kist.
cyst (II. 3.) *choice;* D. keus.
cyst; 3rd pers. pres. of cyssan *to kiss;* G. küsst.
deór (II. 1.) *animal, deer;* G. thier, D. dier.
deór (dýr) *dear;* G. theuer, D. duur.
ealdor; see aldor above.
earm (II. 2.) *arm;* G. arm, L. arm-us.
earm *poor;* G. arm.

éce (II. 2.) *ache.*
éce *eternal.*
fáh *hostile;* hence *foe.*
fáh *variegated, stained, discoloured.*
fær (II. 2.) *stratagem.*
fær (II. 3.) *carriage, going;* hence *fare.*
fæsten (III. 1.) *fastness;* G. feste.
fæsten (II. 1.) *fast;* G. fasten.
fæt (III. 1.) *vat, fat;* L. vas, G. fass, D. vat.
fæt *fat;* G. fett, D. vet.
from (fromm) *bold, pious;* G. fromm.
from (fram) *from.*
fyllan (II. 2.) *to fill;* G. füllen, D. vullen.
fyllan (II. 2.) *to fell;* G. fällen, D. vellen.
fyrst (first) (II. 3.) *period, space of time;* G. frist.
fyrst (fyrmest) *first, chief;* G. fürst.
ge *ye;* D. gij.
ge *both &c.*
gif *if,* O. *gif;* G. ob.
gif *give;* G. gieb.
git (gyt, get, iet) *yet.*
git (gyt) *ye two.*
healt *halt, lame.*
healt (hylt, healded) *holdeth.*
hrán (hrón) (II. 2.) *whale.*
hrán; imperf. of hrínan *to touch.*
hund (II. 2.) *hound, dog;* G. hund, D. hond.
hund (II. 1.) *hundred &c.;* D. hond.
hylt (hilt) (II. 1.) *hilt.*
hylt = healt, healded; (see above) G. hält.

hyrst(¹) (II. 2.) *forest.*
hyrst (II. 3.) *ornament.*
in (inn) (II. 1.) *dwelling, inn*
in (on) *in;* ἐν, G. and L. in.
leáf (II. 1.) *leaf;* G. laub, D. loof.
leáf (II. 2.) *leave;* G. ur-laub, D. ver-lof(²).
leán (II. 1.) *reward;* G. lohn, D. loon.
leán (II. 3.) *to reproach, blame.*
leás *false, loose;* G. loos, L. lax-us.
leás; imperf. of leósan *to lose.*
list (lyst, lust) (II. 2.) *lust, desire, pleasure;* G. lust.
list (II. 3.) *craft;* G. list.
lið (leoð) (III. 1.) *limb;* G. glied, D. lid.
lið *fleet, navy.*
lið (licgeð) (*he*) *lieth;* G liegt.
mæg (II. 2.) *son, kin's-man;* D. maag.
mæg (*I*) *may;* G. and D. mag.
mægð (II. 3.) *maid;* G. magd, maid, D. mcid.
mægð (II. 3.) *tribe, kindred, generation.*
mǽl (II. 3.) *time &c.* G. mahl, D. maal.
mǽl (III. 1.) *spot;* G. mahl, D. maal.
mǽl *picture, image.*
mǽnan (I. 2.) *to mean;* G. meinen, D. meenen.
mǽnan (I. 2.) *to moan.*
mearh (mear)(³) (II. 2.) *horse.*
mearh (mearg) (II. 3.) *marrow;* G mark, D. merg.

(¹) Hence *Hurst,* Lynd-*hurst* &c.; comp G. Delmen-*horst* &c.
(²) Hence *fur-lough;* or there may have been an A. S. for-leáf.
(³) There are traces of the E. masc. *mare* in local names and old sayings; night-*mare* and G. nacht-*mahr* are properly masc answering to L. incubus, *i*ncubo; G. mühre *mare,* answers to A. S. mvre, D. merrie.

mót (ge-mót) (II. 1.) *mote, meeting.*
mót (*I*) *must, may;* G. muss, D. moet.
næs (nose) (II. 2.) *nose, ness, headland;* G. nase, D. neus, L. nas-us.
næs (ne wæs) *was not.*
næs (nas) *not.*
neát (II. 1.) *neat, nout, ox.*
neát; imperf. of neótan *to use.*
nest (II. 1.) *nest;* G. nest.
nest (nist, nyst) (II. 3.) *food, provision.*
ofer (ufor) (II. 2.) *shore, bank;* G. ufer, D. oever.
ofer *over;* ὑπερ, L. super, G. über, D. over.
odde *or,* O. *other;* G. oder, L. aut.
odde (for od-þæt) *until.*
rǽdan (I. 2.) *to read, guess;* G. er-rathen, D. raaden.
rǽdan (I. 2.) *to rede, advise;* G. rathen, D. raaden.
ríce (III. 1.) *realm, empire;* G. reich, D. rijk.
ríce *powerful, rich;* G. reich, D. rijk.
sæc (II. 2.) *sack;* σακκος, L. saccus, G. sack, D. zak.
sæc (II. 3.) *war, battle.*
sǽl (II. 2.) *time, occasion.*
sǽl (sél) *good.*
sceaft (II. 2.) *shaft, spear;* G. schaft.
sceaft (ge-sceaft) (II. 3.) *creature, creation.*
scír (II. 3.) *shire, division.*
scír *bright, clear, sheer;* G. schier.
scyld (scild) (II. 2.) *shield;* G. schild.
scyld (II. 3.) *debt &c.;* G. schuld.
segen (II. 2.) *sign, ensign;* L. signum.
segen (II. 3.) *saw, saying;* G. sage.

seld (II. 1.) *seat, throne.*
seld (seldan) *seldom;* G. selten, D. zelden.
seó si͜ht, *pupil of the eye.*
seó *the, who;* G. sie, D. zij: ἡ, L. ea.
síde (I. 3) *side;* G. seite, D. zijde.
síde (I. 3.) *silk;* G. seide, D. zijde.
síde *widely.*
sið (II. 2.) *time, journey &c.*
sið *late.*
s'ð *since,* O. *sith;* G. seit.
s'ege (slecge) (II. 2.) *sledge (hammer).*
slege (III. 1.) *slaying.*
span (II. 3.) *span;* G. spanne, D. span.
span (*I*) *span;* G. spann.
stefn (II. 2.) *stem, prow;* G. steven, D. steeven.
stefn (stemn) (II. 3.) *voice;* G. stimme, D. stem.
stician *to stich, stab;* G. stechen ⎫
stician *to stich, cleave;* G. stecken ⎬ D. steeken.
treówe (¹) (trýwe) *true, faithful;* G. treu, D. trouw.
treówe (trýwe, treówð) (I. 3.) *truth, troth, faith;* G. treue, D. trouw.
tyn (tin) (II. 1.) *tin;* G. zinn, D. tin, L. s-tannum.
tyn (tyne) (²) *ten;* G. zehn, D. tien.
wan (won) *dark, dusky;* hence *wan.*

(¹) Treówe (adj.) and treówe or treówð (noun) with the G. and D. synonyms, never have the modern sense of our *true, truth,* L. verus, veritas, G. wahr, wahrheit, D. waar, waarheid; these are in A. S. sóð and sóð-fæstnis: sóð-fæst (used chiefly of persons) conveys both notions, as also that of *justice, veracity*—" honest and *true.*" It need hardly be added that anyhow *Truth* is neither in word nor in deed " that which one *troweth.*"

(²) Tyne seems rarely used except absolutely; see p. 34.

wan (wann) (*I*) *won*; G. ge-wann.

weal(¹) (wealh, wala) (II. 2.) *Gael, Celt, stranger, one not of Gothic race.*

weal (weall) (II. 2.) *wall*; G. wall.

weard (II. 2.) *ward-en, guard-ian, keeper.*

weard (II. 3.) *ward, guard, keeping.*

wel (well, wyll) (II. 3.) *well, spring*; G. quelle, D. wel

wel *well*; G. wohl, D. wel.

weorđe (wyrđe) *worth, worthy*; G. werth, würdig.

weorđe (wurđe) from weorđan; G werde, D. worde.

wit (ge-witt) III. 1. *wit, sense*; G. witz.

wit (wyt) *we two.*

wítan (anom.) *to know*; O. wit, wis, wot; G. wissen, D. weeten.

wítan (²) *to punish, blame*; O. wite, D. wijten.

wód *wood, mad.*

wód imperf. of wadan *to go, wade*; L. vadere.

wráđ (II. 3.) *wreath.*

wráđ *wroth.*

wyllan (welan, weallan) (II 2.) *to boil*; G. wallen.

wyllan (willan) *to will*; G. wollen, L. velle.

þanc (II. 2.) *thank*; G. dank.

þanc (ge-þanc) (II. 2.) *thought*; G. ge-danke, D. gedagte.

þe *that, which.*

þe *or.*

þe *than.*

(¹) Hence *Wal*-es, Corn-*wall*, *Wall*-oon, *wal*-nut (P. *welsh*-nut) G. *wall*-nuss (*wülsche*-nuss) *wall*-fahrt *foreign journey, pilgrimage* &c. See p. 118. n. 3. (²) From æt-wítan, ed-wítan comes t-*wit*.

þe *thee;* Dor. τε, L. te, G. dich.
þeáh *though;* G. doch.
þeáh (þáh) imperf. of þeón *to thrive;* G. ge-dieg.

III.—*Other words likely to be confounded by learners.*

Æl- for eal; as æl-mihtig *almighty.*
æl- (el-) ; as, æl-þeódig *foreign.*
beran (II. 1.) *to bear.*
berian ([1]) *to bare.*
birnan ([2]) (byrnan) (III. 1.) *to burn,* (neut.) G. brennen.
bærnan (bernan) (I. 2.) *to burn,* (act) G. brennen.
búgan (beógan) (III. 3.) *to bow, bend,* (neut.) G. biegen, D. buigen.
bígan (I. 2.) *to bow, bend,* (act.)
búgian (= búan) *to inhabit &c.*
cleófan (clúfan) (III. 3.) *to cleave, split;* G. klieben, D. klieven, klooven.
clifian *to cleave, stick;* G. kleben, D. kleeven.
cunnan (anom.) *to know, be able.*
cunnian *to try, tempt, attempt.*

([1]) The conjugation of verbs in -ian is not marked here or in the later notes above, as they can only be I. 1.

([2]) Here and in the other instances below the neuter verb is complex, conj. II. or III., while the active is simple, conj. I., usually I. 2. ; the latter is commonly formed from the imperf. of the former; as, hirne, barn; bærnan, and the like: the E., G., and D. synonyms on the whole answer closely to the A. S. *Fall* for *fell, lay* for *lie, set* for *sit* are as wrong as *drink* for *drench,* or *drench* for *drink* would be. Comp. L. pendēre *to hang,* (neut.) pendĕre *to hang* (act.) &c.

cwelan (II. 1.) *to die, perish*; hence *quail.*
cwellan (I. 3.) *to quell, kill*; G. quälen *to vec* &c.
denn (II. 1.) *den.*
denu (III. 3.) *vale, dean.*
drincan (III. 1.) *to drink*; G. trinken, D. drinken.
drencan (I. 2.) *to drench, drown* (act.); G. tränken, D. drenken.
a-drincan (III. 1.) *to drown* (neut.); G. er-trinken, D. ver-drinken.
faran (II. 2.) ⎱
feran (I. 2.) ⎰ *to go, fare*; G. fahren, D. vaaren.
ferian *to convey, carry*, also *go*; G. führen, D. voeren
feallan (II. 2.) *to fall*; G. fallen, D. vallen.
fyllan (I. 2.) *to fell*; G. fällen, D. vellen.
fleógan (fleón) (III. 3.) *to flee, fly.*
fl'gan (a-fligan) (I. 2.) *to put to flight.*
fúlian *to rot, grow foul*; G. ver-faulen.
fullian *to baptise.*
grétan (greótan) (I. 2.) *to greet, weep*; D. krijten.
grétan (I. 2.) *to greet, salute*; G. grüssen, D. groeten.
hangian *to hang* (neut.); G. hangen.
hangan (hón) (II. 2.) *to hang* (act.); G. hängen.
hátan (II. 2.) *to command, call*; G. heissen, D. heeten.
hatian *to hate*; G. hassen, D. haaten.
hæbban (habban) *to have*; G. haben, D. hebben.
hebban (II. 3.) *to heave*; G. heben, D. heffen.
heort (heorot) (II. 2.) *hart*; G. hirsch, D. hert.
heorte (I. 3.) *heart*; G. herz, D. hart.
hlast (last) (II. 3.) *foot-step.*
hlæst (II. 1.) *lust, load*; G. last.

hnígan (III. 2.) *to stoop;* D. nijgen, G. neigen (act.)
hnǽgan (I. 2.) *to make stoop.*
hrím *rime, frost.*
rím (II. 2.) *rime, number;* G. reim, D. rijm.
hýran (I. 2.) *to hear;* G. hörèn, D. hooren.
hýrian *to hire;* G. heuern, D. huuren.
herian *to praise.*
hergian *to harry, ravage;* G. ver-heeren.
inc *you two.*
inca ([1]) *ill-will.*
irnan (yrnan) (III. 1.) *to run;* G. rinnen, D. rennen.
ærnan (ernan) (I. 2.) *to let run.*
lág (II. 3.) *law;* L. lex, lēg-is.
lagu (III. 3.) *water;* comp. L. lăc-us, G. lache *lake* &c.
leán (II. 2.) *reward;* G. lohn, D. loon.
lǽn (II. 1.) *loan;* G. lehen.
leom (lim) (III. 1.) *limb.*
leóma *light;* L. lūm-en.
leósan (III. 3.) *to lose;* G. ver-lieren, D. ver-liezen.
losian *to be lost, escape from, perish.*
lýsan (a-lýsan) (I. 2.) *to loose, re-lease, re-deem;* G. er-lösen.
letan (lettan) (I. 2.) *to let, hinder.*
lætan (II. 2.) *to let, leave;* G. lassen, D. laaten.
liccian *to lick;* λειχειν, L. lingere, G. lecken, D. lekken.
lician *to please, like.*
licgan (II. 1.) *to lie;* G. liegen, D. liggen.
lecgan (I. 3.) *to lay;* G. legen, D. leggen.

([1]) The declension of nouns in -a here, and in the later notes to the Extracts, is not marked, as they can be only I. 1.

be-lífan (III. 2.) *to remain;* G. b-leiben, D. b-lijven.
lǽfan (I. 2.) *to leave, make remain.*
a lýfan (lýfan) (I. 2.) *to al-low;* G. er-lauben, F. al-louer.
ge-lýfan (I. 2.) *to be-lieve;* G. g-lauben, D. ge-looven.
liðan (III. 2.) *to go, voyage.*
lǽdan (I. 2.) *to lead, make go;* G. leiten, D. leiden.
locc (II. 2.) *lock (of hair &c.);* D. lok.
loca *locker, fold, place locked or shut up.*
locu (III. 2.) *lock, fastening;* also *locker* &c.
lutian *to lurk;* L. lăt-ere.
lútan (leótan) (III. 3.) *to lout, bow.*
mǽd (II. 1.) *math, mead;* G. mahd, matte.
méd (II. 3.) *meed, reward.*
medo (-u, meodo) (III. 2.) *mead;* G. meth, D. meede.
mæg (mæcg, mecg) (II. 2. plur. magas) *son, kin's-man.*
mǽg (II. 2. plur. mágas) } *kin's-man;* D. maag.
maga (plur. magan)
mæge (I. 3.) *kin's-woman.*
metan } See I. above.
métan }
mætan (I. 2.) *to paint.*
múð (II. 2.) *mouth (of an animal);* G. mund, D. mond.
múða *mouth (of a river);* G. münd-ung.
a-rísan (III. 2.) *to a-rise;* D. rijzen.
a-rǽran (I. 2.) *to rear.*
sáwan (II. 2.) *to sow;* G. sähen, D. zaaijen.
seówian (sýwian) *to sew.*

sincan (III. 1.) *to sink* (neut.); G. sinken, D. zinken.
sencan (I. 2.) *to sink* (act.); G. senken, D. zenken.
sittan (II. 1.) *to sit*; G. sitzen, D. zitten.
settan (I. 2.) *to set*; G. setzen, D. zetten.
sígan (III. 2.) *to sink, fall down.*
sǽgan (I. 2.) *to throw down, subdue.*
springan (III. 1.) *to spring, burst* (neut.); G. springen.
sprengan (I. 2.) *to spring, burst* (act.); G. sprengen. (¹)
swefan (II. 1.) *to sleep.*
swebban *to put to sleep.*
swefnian *to dream.*
swincan (III. 1.) *to labour*; O. swink.
swencan (I. 2.) *to make labour, oppress.*
swindan (III. 1.) *to vanish*; G. schwinden.
swendan (I. 2.) *to make vanish, dissipate*; G. verschwenden.
treów (III. 1.) *tree.*
treówe (trýwe) *true, truth*; see II. above.
wacan (II. 3.) (wacian) *to wake, watch* (neut.); G. wachen, D. waaken.
weccan (I. 2.) *to wake* (act.); G. wecken, D. wekken.
weder (II. 1.) *weather*; G. wetter, D. weder.
weder (II. 2.) *wether*; G. widder.
wíc (II. 1.) *dwelling*; οἶκ-ος: see p. 103, n. 12.
wicg (II. 1.) *horse.*
wíg (II. 2.) *war.*
windan (III. 1.) *to wind, turn* (neut.); G. and D. winden.
wendan (I. 3.) *to turn* (act.), *wend, go*; G. and D. wenden.

(¹) *To spring (a mine), blow up or open.*

wíse (I. 3.) *wise, manner;* G. weise, D. wijze.
wísa *wise man, guide;* G. weiser, D. wijzer.
wítan (anom.) *to know* &c.: see I. above.
ge-wítan *to depart.*
witian *to decide.*
wíte (III. 1.) *punishment;* O. wite.
wita *counsellor;* hence witena ge-mót *parliament.*
wræð *wrath, anger.*
wráð *wroth, angry.*
þincan (I. 3.) *to seem;* G. dünken, D. dunken.
þencan (I. 3.) *to think, make seem to one-self;* G. and D. denken. (¹)

(¹) Comp. δοκεω *I think, seem,* δοκει μοι *me-thinks.*

IV.—*Additional Notes.*

Page 1.—Æ is not a diphthong, but a modification of a in the other dialects, for which it is substituted in certain cases, as before a mute, or a consonant followed by e; thus dæg, dæge, but plur. dagas, dagum; so also fæt, sæd, &c. : é answering to Goth. é, is not changed.

The A. S. wrote ı without a dot, ẏ with one.

Ꝥ probably gave rise to the O. abbreviations ye for *the* (þe), yt for *that* (þt), &c.

Page 2.— ⁊ was also written for oð ð|e *or*, sóð⁊ for sóð-lice *truly, verily*. Examples of the use of n̄ are þā for þám *to the* &c., þoñ for þonne *then, when*.

In later times ȝ occurs for g, originally most likely a guttural, afterwards = y: hence the O. z still retained in some S. names, as Dalzell, Menzies, pronounced *Dalyell, Menyies*.

A long vowel is sometimes written double without the accent; as, wiid, good, gees, for wíd, gód, gés, like D. wijd &c.; in G. also the vowel is sometimes doubled in like manner. Where A. S. vowels are made long by contraction the dropt consonant sometimes appears, sometimes not in the modern Teutonic dialects; as, (sleahan) sleán, G. schlagen, D. slaan; gangan, gán, G. gehen, D. gaan; hangan, hón, G. and D. hangen. N has been often dropt and the vowel lengthened before other consonants, above all before s, (Note 1.) while it remains in kindred tongues; as, ést (*love, favour*), Goth. ansts; gós, G. gans, L. ans-er; ós (*god, hero*)Goth.ans; sóft, G. sanft; fús (*prompt*), Goth. funs; ús, Goth. and G. uns, L. nos, &c. This seems the case in Greek too, where ns is in like manner avoided; as, δοὺς, δοῦσα (L. dans), στας, στᾶσα (L. stans), Σιμοεις, and many other words, in some of which the circumflex, as elsewhere, marks the contraction; the ν appears as soon as the σ is removed: neut. δον, σταν; gen. δοντος, σταντος, Σιμοεντος &c. In A. S. í, ẏ, ó, and ú before ð, often answer to a cognate short vowel followed by nd, nt, or nth, in the other languages; as, líðe, (*lithe, soft*) G. linde; síð (*time*) Goth. sinths, Dan. sinde; swíð, Goth. swinths; hrýðer, G. rind, D. rund; ýð, L. unda; óðer, Goth. anthars, G. ander; teóðe (*tenth*), G. zehnte; cúð, G. kund; gúð (*war*), Goth. gunths, O. G. kund.

In the imperfects stód, bróhte, þúhte, þóhte, n is likewise dropt, and the vowel made long, g or c in the three last becoming h, as often else; cunnan and unnan also make cúðe, úðe instead of cunde (G. konnte), unde: bohte *bought* should most likely be short, not being so contracted. Something like these changes now and then appears in L.; as, fundo, fūdi, fūsus; tundo, tūsus, where the vowel in the present is long for prosodical purposes only. On the whole, though the Gr. and L. quantity sometimes agrees with the A. S., and the D. and G. very often, the Gothic is the only sure guide, or failing that, the Icelandic, or other old kindred dialects.

Page 4.—Sometimes too g is added before e, as geów for eów, with little or no change of sound (see p. 41); with a soft vowel before or after it, g seems to have been but lightly sounded, as y, or as a fine guttural.

Page 5.—Other changes are io for eo, and ió for eó; seofon, siofon, heó, hió: u for o, and ú for ó, especially after ge, which sometimes becomes i; geong, (giung) iung; geó, (giú) iú, ió; Iótas, Iútas *Jutes*: ie for y, gyld, gield *payment, tax* &c. U occurs medievally for v in foreign names, as Dauid *David*; hence also for f, as luuian for lufian *to love*. Some of these spellings and those p. 5. are the variations of different times, some of different dialects, of which as yet but little is known with certainty.

Page 8.—A. S. d has sometimes become E. th (soft), often G. t; fæder *father*, G. vater. Þ and ð usually answer to G. and D. d; þreo, G. drei, D. drie; bróðer, G. bruder, D. broeder; ð sometimes to G. and D. t; forð, G. fort, D. voort. See also p. 2 and addition thereto. The loss of these letters in E. and the substitution of the one unmeaning combination th for both the hard and soft sound is much to be regretted. The A. S. had seemingly no rule but custom for the use of these two letters and sounds, as we for the latter, respectively, but as þ is found oftenest at the beginning, and ð at the end of a syllable, they are here so printed throughout.

Page 8—9.—The following are likewise exceptions to the general rule that the A. S. gender agrees with the German:

Neut. clif	G. klippe (f.)	*cliff*, *rock*.
— líc	G. leiche (f.)	*corpse*.
— sǽd	G. saat (f.)	*seed*.
— sceorp	G. schärpe (f.)	*scarf*.
— big-spel	G. bei-spiel (m.)	*example*.
— toll	G. zoll (m.)	*toll*.
Masc. næs	G. nase (f.)	*nose, ness*.
— sál	G. seil (n.)	*cord*.
— tear	G. zähre (f.)	*tear*.
— an-(ge-)weald	G. ge-walt (f.)	*power*.
Fem. blǽd	G. blatt (n.)	*fruit, leaf*.
— nyt	G. nutz (m.)	*use*.

L. has clivus masc. and clivum neut.; nasus is masc.

Page 9.—Swefen *dream* is fem. II. 3., and neut. III. 1.

Sc|eó *shoe* (G. schuh masc.) is masc. II. 2. (plur. sceós), or fem. I. 3. (plur. sceón O. *shoon*), or III. 3. (plur. (ge-)scý.)

Page 10.—But few certain rules can be given for the genders, especially from the terminations, of which several, as -e, -u, -el, -en, -er, contain nouns of all three. To some of the rules given above the following are exceptions and there may be more: setl *seat*, and wered *host* are masc.; -oð and -uð are interchangeable, and when from an adjective, fem.; as, geógoð(·uð) *youth*, from geong: -ð after a consonant is fem. chiefly when from an adjective, as, strengð from strang; otherwise sometimes neut. as, morð *murder*, or masc. as monð (monað) *month*.

Compounds in -lác are neut., in -rǽden feminine.

Nouns of the 1st declension are called Simple from the simplicity of their inflection, having but four endings for the eight cases of the two numbers, and also from the close likeness of the three genders; the 2nd and 3rd declensions are termed Complex, as having in general more case-endings, and wider distinctions of gender. The former kind answer to the Gr. nouns making their dative plural in -σι, and the L. in -bus, the latter to the Gr. which form it in -οις or -αις, and the L. in -is. The terms Weak and Strong for Simple and Complex have greater *seeming* propriety when applied to other Gothic tongues, Gr. and L. for instance, than to A. S., since in the former case they in general need the help of another syllable to form their inflection, while A. S. needs only -n, and in the latter they have oftener the power of forming their cases without an additional syllable, than the A. S. has. Gr. and L. synonyms sometimes correspond with the A. S. in declension as well as in meaning and etymon; thus, simple: οὑς, aur-is, eár-e; ὁ-νομ-α, nom-en, n a m-a; hom-o, g u m-a; complex: ἐργ-ον, w e o r c; πυργ-ος, b u r h; via, w e g; vir, w e r. Some nouns have both forms without a change of meaning; as, heofon, heofone *heaven*, mann, manna *man*, þeów, þeówa *slave;* some with; as, múð *month (animate)*, múða *mouth (inanimate)*, see List III. above; lufu and lufe are sometimes used indifferently, but usually the former stands for *love, affection* (amor), the latter for *love, sake* (gratia): Godes lufu *love of God;* for sames gódes lufan *for the sake of some good.*

Page 11.—The neuter is placed first in the declension of nouns, adjectives, and pronouns, as the simplest and purest form of the word, the masculine next as agreeing with it usually in three or four cases out of the five, and the feminine last as generally unlike both. The accusative stands next after the nominative as agreeing with it always in the neut., and sometimes in the masc., while in the fem. it is derived from it; the ablative next as in some words derived from the accus.; and the genitive after the dative as sometimes derived from it, and last of all, as being in neuters and masculines in general most changed from the nominative. This applies more or less to Gr., L., G. &c.: in A. S. it is more apparent in complex than in simple nouns, more still in the indefinite inflection of adjectives, and most of all in demonstrative pronouns. As regards the genders, twá, bá, and þreo are noticeable exceptions.

Page 13.—The plural ending -an (G. -en) became in time -en which in *ox-en* (ox-an) is yet rightly used; *hos-en* (hós-a), and P. *hous-en* (hús), and *furz-en* (fyrs-as) are wrong. To *brethr-en* (bróðr-u), and *childr-en* (cildr-u) too it has been wrongly added; O. was *child-er* still in P. use: see p. 18, n. 3. *Chick-en* (G. küch-en) whence *chick* is shortened, is no more a plural than *maid-en* or *vix-en*; see p. 66.

Proper names in -a whether A. S. or foreign are thus declined; as Gota *Goth*, Beda, Anna: Europa follows the L. making accus. Europam; dat. and gen. Europe (the medieval form of Europæ): Donua *Danube* (G. Donau; well called by Milton *Donaw*), and sometimes Sicilia and the like are not declined. There are no A. S. fem. names in -a; all nouns in -a being masc., those now so written end either in a consonant or in -u, (II. 3. or III. 3.); as, Mæð-hild, Eád-gifu, since latinised to *Mathilda*, *Edgiva*. Other foreign names sometimes take the L. cases except the vocative; as, He ge-seáh Simonem *he saw Simon*. Fram Decapoli *from Decapolis*. Iacobus Zebedei *James (son) of Zebedee*. Lazarus gá út! *Lazarus come forth!* Masculines ending in a consonant often follow II. 2., as, Salomon, Salomones, Salomone; Petrus, Petre, and the like.

The now anomalous genitives in -ens of some G. simple nouns, as herz-ens, nam-ens, will-ens, lieb-ens(-würdig), are derived from the Goth. gen., hairt-ins, nam-ins (L. nom-inis) wilj-ins &c. A. S. heort-an, nam-an, will-an, luf-an. Glaub-ens is the only gen. of this kind which had a nom. in -en, glauben, (complex) Goth. ga-láubeins, A. S. (simple) ge-leáfa. Herz-e (Goth. hairto, A. S. heorte) is still in P. and poetical use: other G. simple nouns, as hert (A S. hearra) have lost the final vowel. Feminines have in general lost the oblique -n in the singular, except in some phrases, as auf erden (*on earth*), vor freuden (*for joy*) &c. Many feminines and a few masculines properly complex now form the plural in -n, and in general the two orders have come to be much mixed.

Page 15.—Nouns in -e (II. 2.) sometimes keep the e in the plural; as, end-eas, end-eum &c.

Freónd and feónd being originally participials, derived, the former from freógan (G. freien) *to court, honour*, the latter from a lost verb akin to fáh *hostile* (whence *foe*), properly made the nom. and accus. sing. and plur. alike, but in time came to be inflected as II. 2.

ADDITIONAL NOTES.

It is only in monosyllables before one consonant that æ is changed to a; otherwise not; as, wæstm, pl. wæstmas (*fruit*) æcer, pl. æceras, æcras: thus too in adjectives; smæl, þæt smale, smalor, but fæst, þæt fæste, fæstor and the like.

Feld and ford originally belonged to III. 2; feld-u, ford-u like sun-u.

Page 17.—Hand belongs to a lost class of complex feminines in -u: hand-u.

Page 20.—Wædla *poor* hitherto called an adjective having the definite inflection only, seems rather a noun (I. 2.) *a beggar*; wædlian *to beg*: þearfa *poor* is commonly if not always used as a noun—*a poor man*: wana *wanting* seems indeclinable.

Page 24.—The comparative and superlative endings -or, -ost (-oste), and -er, -est (-este) are sometimes used indifferently, but it would seem that the former oftener follow a, o, and u, the latter e, i, or y. see addit. note on p. 42

Page 25.—Several of these adjectives form adverbs regularly in -e and -lice (p. 70.) as lang-e, lang-lice, strang-e, strang-lice, hræd-lice, heág-e, heá-lice, eáð-e, eáðe-lice, sceort-lice, sóft-e, yfel-e, lytl-e.

Page 26.—*Lesser* for *less* is as wrong as *least-est* for *least* would be, or as *wors-er* for *worse* is. *Lest* is (þý-)læs(-þe), t being added as in *against* &c. The ending -mest has no connexion with mæst *most*, though it also has become -*most*: our *upper-most*, *after-most* &c. have arisen from the wrong notion that *most* was added to the comparative.

Page 27.—*Ye* is therefore the true nom., *you* the accus. &c. "If any man say ought to *you, ye* shall say."

Page 29.—*Mine* and *thine* are therefore the older forms, from which *my* and *thy* are shortened; the former were long retained before vowels.

Page 30.—Þissere and þissera are older forms than þisse and þissa.

Page 32.—The á- in á-wiht &c. must not be confounded with the common prefix a- for on-, an- (p. 73); á is *ever, aye, æi*, Goth. áiw-, G. je, whence *aiwv*, Goth. áiws, L. ævum, *age, eternity*. A'- or æg- (p. 65) gives a *general* sense like G. je, in je-mand *some one*; á-hwær *some-, any-, every-where*, á-hwænne *some time, any time*, P. *some-when, any-when*: with the negative it becomes ná *never, no*; nú-hwider *no-whither*: ná-wiht is more regular than nán-wiht. A'wðer and áðer (if true readings) are contractions of á-hwæðer, and = ægðer, æg-hwæðer: náwðer is nú-hwæðer = L. ne-uter; hence rightly comes O. and P. *nother neither* has arisen from *either*.

Page 33.—Our *one* and *a* are both descended from án; in *an* before a vowel the n has been restored; most languages use the same word in both senses: in A. S. sum is commoner for the article than án.

Page 37.—Verbs of the first conjugation are called Simple from the simplicity of their inflection, and its likeness in the three classes, or Weak as needing the help of another syllable to form their imperfect; those of the second and third are termed Complex from the various changes of vowel &c. they undergo, and the greater diversity of their classes, or Strong, as having in themselves the power of forming their imperfect. The analogy of the A. S. simple with the Gr. contracted verbs, and the L. 1st, 2nd, and 4th conjugations, and of the A. S. complex with the Gr. regulars, and L. 3rd conj. is worthy of attention. Some of the Gr. and L. synonyms agree in conjugation, as well as in meaning and etymology with the A. S.; as, simple: ceall-ian, καλ-εειν, cal-are *to call*; tem-ian, δαμ-αειν, dom-are *to tame*; lix-an, L. luc-ere *to shine*: complex; graf-an, γραφ-ειν; *to (en-)grave, write*; brec-an, ῥηγ-ειν, frang-ere, *to break*; ter-an, τειρ-ειν, ter-ere *to tear* &c.; flów-an, flu-ere *to flow*; drag-an, trah-ere *to draw, drag*. Simple verbs are now in E. and G. usually called regular, complex irregular; in both many complex verbs have in course of time become simple, and this change is still going on. Thus *bake, sleep, leap, sweep, weep, fare, wield, fold, step, starve, creep, reek, lye*

wreak, dive, shove, row, flow, swallow, brook &c. from A. S. complex forms have become simple: others are in a fair way to do so, retaining only a complex imperf. or part. past, some of which are either gone or going out of use; as, *hung, hove, stood, shove, clomb, glode, bet, shod; waxen, hewn, laden, graven, shapen, washen, strewn, holpen, bursten, foughten, swollen* &c.

G. walten (*to rule*), wallen (*to boil*), sähen (*to sow*), krähen (*to crow*), kauen (*to chew*), wachen (*to watch*), wathen (*to wade*), reuen (*to rue*), lachen (*to laugh*), as also most of the E. synonyms, have become simple; others, as backen (*to bake*), hauen (*to hew*), sieden (*to seethe*) &c. are in the transition state. A few E. verbs from A. S. I. 2., and I. 3. have assumed imperfects (but not participles past) of a *seeming* complex form; as, *meet, met; lead, led; send, sent; build, built;* from métan, lǽdan, sendan, byldan. A very few A. S. verbs have both forms without change of meaning; as, bringan; bringe, bróhte, bróht, or bringe, brang, brungen; the latter however is rare.

Page 38.—Attention should be paid to the quantity of the complex or strong imperfects, both as compared with that of the present, and as to whether it is long throughout, or short throughout, or short in the first and third persons singular, and long in the 2nd, and the whole plural, or long in the first and third pers., and short in the rest. Thus II. 2. from presents some short, some long, and II. 3. from presents all short, make it long throughout, except some doubtful in the former; as, healde; heóld, heólde &c. drage; dróh &c. III. 1. has the present short, and the imperf. short throughout with a change of vowel; binde; band, bunde, band, bundon. II. 1. short in the pres. has the imperf. short and long; brece; bræc, bræce, bræc, bræcon; except the f w in ea; as, geaf, geafe &c., together with com, come &c., and nam, name &c. which are short throughout. III. 2. and III. 3. with long pres. have the imperf. long and short with a change of vowel; drífe; dráf, drife, dráf, drifon; clúfe; cleáf, clufe, cleáf, clufon. Complex participles past are all short but some of II. 2.

Page 41.—Verbs in -igan (for -iau) are often conjugated regularly like I. 2.; as, fylígan *to follow*, imperf. fylígde, imper. fylig, but part. past fyligd: see p. 42.

Page 42.—There seem to have been originally two distinct classes of verbs in -ian, both now included in I. 1., the one forming its imperf. and part. past in -óde, -ód, the other in -ede, -ed; the former answering closely to the Gr. contracted verbs, and the L. in -āvi, -ātus, ēvi, ēt-us, and -īvi, īt-us, the latter to the L. in -ui, ĭt-us &c. In time -óde, ód were shortened, and then came to be confounded with -ede, -ed, many verbs being found with both forms; -ode, -od however seems to occur oftenest when the root-vowel is a, o, or u, -ede, ed when it is e, i, or y; see addit. note on p. 25: -ade, -ad is a modification of -ode, -od. The -de, -ed (-d) of I. 2. 3. is contracted from -ede, -ed, I. 1.; when the d is thus brought next a hard consonant it becomes t.

The characteristic c is not changed if l, n, or s stand before it; as, elce (*delay*) imperf. elcte; drence (*drench*) drencte; wisce (*wish*) wiscte; unless the n be dropt, as in þince, þúhte, and the like: it else commonly (in simple verbs) becomes h, as in tǽce, p. 42, &c.

Page 43 —The original form of the 2nd and 3rd persons sing. of I. 2, 3, II. and III. was hýrest, hýreð, tellest, telleð, brecest, breceð, healdest, healdeð, dragest, drageð, bindest, bindeð, drífest, drífeð, clúfest, clúfeð and the like, which often occur, especially in poetry: the shortened and modified forms hýrst, hýrð, telst, bricst &c. given in the grammar are more modern, and commonest in prose.

Page 44.—All verbs seem at first to have formed their 1st pers. pres. in -o or -u; comp. -ω and L. -o : haf-o = L. hab-eo.

Page 50.—Most of the verbs in II. 2., and some in II. 3. are derived from the Goth. reduplicative verbs, which repeat the long syllable; the A. S. has kept only what may be called the literal augment, and that in but a few verbs; as, héht, leólc, reórd, from hátan, lúcan (*to play, deceive*), rǽdan (G. reden *to discourse*), where the Goth.

has háí-háit, láí-láik, rái-ród from háitan &c. Some only alter the vowel, as sceape, sceóp, where the Goth. has sái-skáp.

Page 54.—Verbs in -án form their part. pres. in -ánde; sleán, sleánde.

Page 58.—Wríðan is an exception to the general rule that complex verbs change ð into d in the 2nd pers. sing., and in the plural of the imperf., and in the past part.: see cweðan p. 50, weorðan p. 57, and seóðan p. 60, which are all regular.

Page 62.—Complex participles past sometimes agree like adjectives with a noun, sometimes do not; as, þa þing þe him ge-sende wǽron *the things that were sent him*. Seó óðre naman wæs Tate háten *who by another name was hight Tate*.

The part. past in the pluperfect is sometimes governed in the accus. by the auxiliary bæbban, as, þá híg hæfdon hyra lof-sang ge-sungenne *when they had sung their song of praise*.

Page 63.—Un- sometimes, as in G., is not merely negative, but implies badness; un-þeáw *bad habit*, un-weder (G. un-ge-witter) *storm, bad weather*.

The prefix to- must be carefully distinguished from the preposition tó in composition; as, to-gán *to go asunder, separate*, tó-gán *to go to*; G. zer-gehen, zu-gehen: to- implies *division, dispersion of parts*, and hence often *destruction*.

Page 64.—For- gives in general a negative or bad sense, or is intensive, much like κατα-; déman *to judge*, for-déman '*to condemn*, κρινειν, κατα-κρινειν, G. ur-theilen, ver-urtheilen; bernan *to burn*, for-bernan *to burn up, consume*, καιειν, κατα-καιειν, G. brennen, ver-brennen; dón *to do, make*, for-dón *to un-do, ruin, destroy*; scyppan *to form*, for-scyppan *to trans-form, de-form*; for-fela *very many*. This prefix must not be confounded with the prepositions for and fore; (probably of the same origin, = L. pro); thus for-seón is *to over-look, de-spise*, G. ver-sehen; for-seón, fore-seón *to fore-see*, G. vor-sehen; for-gún *to for-go, do without, perish*, G. ver-gehen, L. per-ire; fore-gán *to fore-go, go before*, G. vor-gehen, L. præ-ire. It is as wrong to write *fore*-go for *for*-go, as *fore*-give for *for*-give.

And- answers closely to ἀντι-, denoting opposition, reciprocity &c.; and-saca *denier;* and-wyrdan, and-swarian, ἀντ-ερειν *to answer;* and-wlítan, ἀντι βλεπειν, *to gaze at, look in the face.*

The prefix ge- is in A. S. used oftener and more indiscriminately than in any kindred language old or new. Though originally conveying no notion of past time, it seems gradually to have acquired it, and to have become a kind of syllabic augment to imperfects, but especially to participles past, as in Dutch and German. In the formation of English it was by degrees dropt before all but participles past, where it first became i- or y-, and has since been lost altogether, surviving only as a- in some P. words. In G. and D. it is still in use before nouns, adjectives &c., but in general with a distinct effect on their meaning, referible to its original collective force. A. S. ge- sometimes denotes *the result of doing a thing;* as, Ge-slóh þín fæder fæhðe mæste *thy father by striking avenged the greatest of feuds.* His feorh ge-faran oððe ge-irnan *to save his life by going or running* (*to a sanctuary*).

Page 65.—The prefix or- (left out in the right place) denotes want of a thing; as, or-mæte *im-mense, measure-less,* or-trúwian *to de-spair,* or-sorh *care-less, se-cure:* it must not be confounded with or- in or-eald *very old,* (G. ur-alt), from or, ord *beginning, point,* connected with L. or-ior, or-igo &c.

The ending -el, -ol, answers sometimes to L. -ul-um; gyrd-el, L. cing-ulum, *girdle.*

The primary meaning of -ing is *young,* and hence it forms patronymics, and terms of contempt &c.: -ling has been supposed to be derived from -ing.

Page 66.—Other feminines in -en are menn-en from man, G. mann, männin; gyd-en from god, G. gott, gött-in, D. god, god-in: in -e; fyl-e, *filly,* from fol-a *foal;* wal-e from wealh or wal-a, *Celt, stranger;* webb-e (or webb-estre *web-ster*), from webb-a *weaver.*

The ending -estre (like D. -ster) is feminine only, and the notion of thus forming nouns of contempt &c., as pun-*ster*, trick-*ster*, road-*ster* is modern.

The ending dóm is properly a noun (II. 2.) *doom, judgment, authority, dignity;* hád is also a noun (II. 2.) *state, condition, rank, Holy Orders.*

Page 67.—scipe (not occurring alone) is related to scapan, (sceapan), *to shape, form, create,* and denotes *form, mode, condition;* land-*scape,* or land-*skip,* (land-scipe) G. land-schaft, D. land-schap, should in rule be land-*ship,* unless borrowed, like a few other words, directly from the Dutch.

The adjective ending -ig answers to ικ-ος, L. -ic-us.

Page 68.—A. S. -isc had often a bad sense, which E., G., and D. -ish, -isch, -sch almost always have, except when added to local names; the three former often contrast with -líc, -*like* or -*ly,* G. -lich, which convey a good or indifferent notion; as, folc-isc *vulgar* (Chaucer has *pepl-ish*), folc-líc *popular;* cild-isc *child-ish,* G. kind-isch, cild-líc *child-like,* G. kind-lich; compare also *mann-ish, man-like, man-ly,* G. männ-isch, männ-lich; *woman-ish, woman-ly,* G. weib-isch, weib-lich; *girl-ish, maiden-ly* &c.

While -ol (-ul) answers in form to L. -ul-us, in sense it is more like -ax, commonly denoting a wrong propensity; as, sprec-ol, cwid-ol, L. loqu-ax, dic-ax *talkative, evil-tongued;* et-ol, L. ed-ax *greedy.* Sometimes as in sóð-sag-ol *truth-telling,* deóp-þanc-ol *deep-thinking,* it expresses a good quality.

-en (G. -ern, -en) usually denotes the material of which a thing is made; as, stæn-en *of stone,* G. stein-ern; treów-en *treen, wood-en;* gyld-en *gold-en,* G. gold-en; lin-en *lin-en, of lin or flax,* G. lein-en; from stán, treów, gold, lin. Several words thus formed are now obsolete; *ston-en, brick-en* &c. are still in P. use.

-cond answers to L. -cund-us.

Some adjectives are formed in -ed or -d like simple participles past, as, ge-hyrned *horn-ed,* (G. ge-hörn-t); ge-sceód *shod* (G. ge-schuh-t); the rest of the verb, if any, is here wanting.

Page 69.—-c-, -n-, -s-, in these and the like verbs represent lost syllables; therefore swin-s-ian (*to make melody*) is no exception to the rule against ns in the same syllable; see p. 2. n. 1.

The verbal endings -ian and -an (-ειν, G. and D. -an) became in time -en and -e, the latter of which has in many cases been dropt, in all has lost its sound. Such verbs as *whit-en*, *black-en* are of modern use, *to white* and the like being the older form.

Page 71.—Other adverbs in common use are: á *aye, always*, æfre (G. and D. immer) *ever*, næfre (G. and D. nimmer) *never*, ædre *straightway*, recene *instantly*, eft-sona *eft-soon, forth-with*, en demes *at length*, þær-rihte (forð-rihte) *forthwith*, elles *else, otherwise*, elles-hwider *else-whither*, ellor *elsewhere*, þus (D. dus) *thus*, georne (G. gerne) *earnestly, willingly*, þearle *very, exceedingly*, geara *well, accurately*, (lyt-)hwon *a little* (S. *a wheen*), hugu (hwegu), hwæt-(hwylc)-hugu &c. *somewhat, a little*, þances *gratis*, ágnes þances *of one's own accord*, his &c. willan, unwillan *with, against his &c. will*, semninga *suddenly*, hrædinga *quickly*, áninga (æninga) *alone, only*, on bæc-ling *backward*. Sona is construed with a genitive; as, Sona þæs *soon after that*. Sona þæs wintres *early in the winter*.

Page 72.—It seems likely that the first part of the word *Oxena*-ford is not from oxa *ox*, but from the Celtic root meaning *water, river*, (A. S. wos is *ooze, liquid*) which appears in Ouse (many) Isis, Ex, Ax, Usk, Esk, Oise, Aisne, Yssel, Oxus, and so many other names of rivers; and this is confirmed by *Ousn-ey* in the neighbourhood. *Ford of oxen* is however the strict meaning of the A. S. name, and doubtless the one then attached to it; Βος-πορος, Schwein-furt, Swin-ford and the like supply fair analogies.

Ofer- sometimes conveys the same idea as for-; ofer-gitan (= for-gitan) *to forget*, ofer-hycgan = for-hycgan *to despise*.

Of- beside its intensive force (p. 105. n. 2.) sometimes has a bad one; as, me þincð *me thinks*, me of-þincð *it repenteth me, I take it ill*.

Page 73.—Our prefix a- has in general sprung from the A. S. on- (an-, a-), and on is still sometimes used for it; as, *a-float*, A. S. on-flote; *a-live*, A. S. on-life (G. am leben); *a-two (in-two)*, A. S. on-twá; *a-feared*, A. S. a-fered; O. on flote, on life, on two, also on sleep, on row &c. now *a-sleep* &c.; we yet say *on board*, or *a-board, on fire*, or *a-fire* and the like: see also p. 69—71, 73.

In some words a- is from A. S. of-; as, of-dúne (a-dúne, a-dún) *a-down, down* (= G. berg-ab); of-þyrst *a-thirst*; we say too *of kin* or *a-kin*; it is therefore not unlikely that in other cases A. S. a- may, as the sense would imply, have sprung from of-; thus a-faran *to depart*, a-wendan *to turn away*, a-weorpan *to cast off*, answer to G. ab-fahren, and G. and D. ab-wenden, af-wenden, ab-werfen, af-werpen: so ἀπο, ἀπ' became L. ab, and that in time a. Once or twice E. a- is from A. S. ge-; as ge-líc (O. y-like), *a-like*; ge-mang (O. e-mong), *a-mong*.

Page 77.—Adjectives also take an abl. or dat. of the cause &c., which commonly stands first; as, I ú-dædum fáh *stained with (my) former deeds*. Wundum wérig *weary with wounds*.

Likewise of the person &c. by whom the action implied is done; as, His freóndum or-wéne *despaired of by his friends*. Wurð-full þám cyningum *to be honoured by kings*. Un-a-secgend-líc ænigum *unspeakable by any*.

Adjectives in general govern the object to which they have relation in the dative; as, Ic eom ge-trýwe mínon hláf-orde *I am true to my lord*. He wæs me yrre *he was angry with me*. Dryhten wæs þám folce gram (*the*) *Lord was wroth with the people*.

Adjectives denoting nearness also govern the dative; as, A'n biscop þe him þá hendest wæs *a bishop that was then nearest (handiest) to him*.

Some adverbs take the same case as the adjectives whence they are formed: Nænig him ge-líce þæt dón meahte *none could do that like him*.

Page 79.—The following verbs also govern the dative of the far object: **secgan** *to say, tell,* **bodian** *to preach, announce,* **beódan** *to offer,* **and-wyrdan, and-swarian** *to answer,* **gifan** *to give,* **for-gifan** *to give away, forgive,* **syllan** *to give, sell* (of which examples need not be given), **wið-metan** *to compare, measure with,* **ge-an-lícian** *to liken, make like;* **yrsian** *to be angry with,* **œt-filhan** *to approach, apply to,* **wísian (wissian)** *to guide, direct,* **fore-wesan** (L. præ-esse) *to govern, be over,* **be-sárgian** *to pity, be sorry for,* have a dative of the near object; **losian** *to be lost, escape from,* one of the person affected; as, **Hire fær is wið-meten fyrd-lícum truman** *her going is compared to an army on the march.* **Ic eom yslum and axum ge-an-lícod** *I am made like cinders and ashes.* **Se-þe yrsað his bréðer** *he that is angry with his brother.* **Nó ic him þæs georne œt-fealh** *I did not therefore willingly approach him.* **Þœt híg mihton þám folce wel wissian** *that they might guide the people well.* **Mid-þý heó þá feala geara þissum mynstre fore-wæs** *when she then many years had ruled this convent.* **Þá be-sárgode he þære sorh-fullan méder** *then pitied he the sorrowful mother.* **Him losade án sceáp** *he had lost one sheep.*

Some of the verbs having a dative &c. of the object to which the action is directed, govern the thing done in the accusative; as, **Démað rihtne dóm** *judge right judgment.*

Page 81.—The following verbs are sometimes used in the usual reflective way with the pronoun in the accusative: **ge-biddan** *to pray,* **warnian** *to be ware,* **belgan** *to be angry,* **ge-wraðian** *to be wroth;* as, **Þonne þú þe ge-bidde** *when thou prayest.* **Warniað eów fram mannum** *be ware of men.* **Warniað wið þa bóceras** *be ware of the scribes.* **Þá bealh he hine** *then was he angry.* **Ge belgað wið me** *ye are angry with me.* **Þá ge-wraðede hine se arce-biscop Landfranc** *then was the archbishop Lanfranc wroth.*

Likewise some compounds of **seón**; as, **Hine** &c. **for-seón** (G. sich ver-sehen) *to err, commit an oversight, sin.* **Gif he hine under-bœc be-sáwe** *if he should look back.*

Page 81—3.—Wealdan, on-fón, éhtan, bídan, and earnian sometimes govern the accusative.

Page 83.—On-þracian *to dread, feel horror at* governs the genitive like on-drædan; as, An-þraciende þæs un-ge-limpes *feeling horror at the misfortune.*

Page 87.—Be and tó sometimes govern the ablative; as, Be þý mæg œlc mon wítan *by that may each man know.* Tó-þý-þæt (= tó-þón-þœt) *in order that.* Tó-hwý *why?*

As æt is sometimes *to,* so is tó sometimes *at;* the two are now and then confounded in E., and G. zu stands for both. Tó and æt (the latter in composition often) sometimes mean *from,* the former especially with wilnian and sécan; as, Ealle tó þe œtes wilniaþ *all from thee desire food.* Manna ge-hwylc se-þe séceþ tó him *every man that seeketh from him.* He þæt ful ge-þeah æt Wealh-þeón *he took the cup from (at the hand of) Wealhtheó.*

Tó meaning *motion to,* has sometimes, though seldom, an accusative: He fór tó Samariam þæt land *he went to the land of Samaria.*

Page 88.—Tó-emnes (a rare word) rather *by, along-side, over-against* than *along,* is from efen (efn, emn) *even, equal;* on-efn (-emn) is the same; Him on-efn ligeþ ealdor-ge-winna *by him lieth (his) deadly foe.* Emn-, em- are common in composition; emn-lang (G. eben (so) lang) *of the same length;* em-leóf (G. eben (so) lieb) *equally dear;* em-þeów *fellow-slave.*

Page 90.—Innon, úton, and úppon should not be divided,-on (-an) being here only an ending and not the preposition on, serving in the two last to change the adverb into a preposition.

Page 93.—Þenden *while* sometimes has a subjunctive; as, þenden hit hát sý *while it be hot.*

Page 95.—For-standan (or fore-standan) *to defend, stand before*, likewise for-standan (G. ver-stehen) *to understand* govern the accusative; as, Hine God for-stód *him God defended*.

Page 96.—Other conjunctions are swá-same-swá *the same as—, in like manner as—*, ná-læs þæt án ac— *not (that) only but—*, nates-hwón *by no means*, nóht-þón-læs *never-(nought)-theless*, gea *yea*, ná *nay*, gese *yes*, nese *no*, næs (nas) *not*, huru *moreover, chiefly*, huru-þinga *at least*, þæs-þe *since, after that, because*, for-hwón, tó-hwón (= for-hwý) *hwy*, þæs(-for) *for that, therefore*, gen, gena *yet*.

Comp. οὐκ ἐχομεν εἰ μη—*we have (not) but—*, one only of the many instances of likeness between the Gr. and A. S. syntax.

Weorðe too may be either expressed or understood; as, Wá (weorðe) þám men! *wo worth the man!*

Page 97.—*Lo!* has no more to do with *look* than O. *gif* has with gifan: our vulgar *law!* and *lawk!* may also be derived from lá!

Page 98.—Which Latin translation the A. S. versions of the Holy Scripture are taken from is hard to say; this only is certain that the A. S. Gospels follow the Vulgate more closely than the Heptateuch does. The Latin MSS. doubtless varied much, and the A. S. is now and then seemingly not an accurate rendering of any one. Ælfríc was a common name; among those who bore it, were an Archbishop of Canterbury, and one of York, of whom the latter is believed to have translated the parts of the O. Testament known as the Heptateuch.

Page 133.—Teóhhian (from teóh, p. 152. n. 3.) means also *to furnish, provide, fit out*, and perhaps should be so rendered in the extract from Boëthius, where its meaning is not very clear.

Page 140.—Tó- in tó-geanes sometimes does not rime (see p. 158, last line) though seemingly always in other combinations: to- on the other hand never rimes.

THE END.

VALUABLE AND INTERESTING BOOKS,

PUBLISHED OR SOLD BY

JOHN RUSSELL SMITH,

36, SOHO SQUARE, LONDON.

A Compendious Anglo-Saxon and English Dictionary, by the Rev. JOSEPH BOSWORTH, D.D., Anglo-Saxon Professor in the University of Oxford, &c. 8vo. *closely printed in treble columns, cloth*, 12s

This may be considered quite a new work from the author's former Dictionary; it has been entirely remodelled and enlarged, bringing it down to the present state of Anglo-Saxon literature both at home and abroad.

Anglo-Saxon Delectus; serving as a first Class-Book to the Language. By the Rev. W. BARNES, B.D., of St. John's Coll. Camb. 12mo. *cloth*, 2s 6d

"To those who wish to possess a critical knowledge of their own Native English, some acquaintance with Anglo-Saxon is indispensable; and we have never seen an introduction better calculated than the present to supply the wants of a beginner in a short space of time. The declensions and conjugations are well stated, and illustrated by references to the Greek, Latin, French and other languages. A philosophical spirit pervades every part. The Delectus consists of short pieces on various subjects, with extracts from Anglo-Saxon History and the Saxon Chronicle. There is a good Glossary at the end."—*Athenæum*, Oct 20, 1849.

The Anglo-Saxon Version of the Life of St. Guthlac, Hermit of Croyland. Printed for the first time, from a MS. in the Cottonian Library, with a Translation and Notes, by CHARLES WYCLIFFE GOODWIN, M.A., Fellow of Catherine Hall, Cambridge, 12mo. *cloth*, 5s

An Introduction to Anglo-Saxon Reading; comprising Ælfric's Homily on the Birthday of St. Gregory, with a copious Glossary, &c. by L. LANGLEY, F.L.S. 12mo. *cloth*, 2s 6d

Ælfric's Homily is remarkable for beauty of composition, and interesting as setting forth Augustine's mission to the "Land of the Angles."

Analecta Anglo-Saxonica. — Selections, in Prose and Verse, from Anglo-Saxon Literature, with an Introductory Ethnological Essay, and Notes, Critical and Explanatory, by LOUIS F. KLIPSTEIN, of the University of Giessen, 2 thick vols. post 8vo. *cloth*, 12s (*original price*, 18s)

Containing an immense body of information on a language which is now becoming more fully appreciated, and which contains fifteen-twentieths of what we daily think, and speak, and write. No Englishman, therefore, altogether ignorant of Anglo-Saxon, can have a thorough knowledge of his own mother-tongue; while the language itself, to say nothing of the many valuable and interesting works preserved in it, may, in copiousness of words, strength of expression, and grammatical precision, vie with the modern German.

Anglo-Saxon Version of the Hexameron of St Basil, and the Anglo-Saxon Remains of St. Basil's Admonitio ad Filium Spiritualem; now first printed from MSS. in the Bodleian Library, with a Translation and Notes, by the Rev. H. W. NORMAN, 8vo. SECOND EDITION, *enlarged, sewed*, 4s

Anglo-Saxon Version of the Holy Gospels. Edited from the original MSS. by BENJAMIN THORPE, F.S.A., post 8vo. *cloth*, 8s (*original price*, 12s)

Anglo-Saxon Version of the Story of Apollonius of Tyre;—upon which is founded the Play of Pericles, attributed to Shakespeare;—from a MS., with a Translation and Glossary, by BENJAMIN THORPE, 12mo. *cloth*, 4s 6d (*original price*, 6s)

Analecta Anglo-Saxonica.—A Selection in Prose and Verse, from Anglo-Saxon Authors of various ages, with a Glossary, by BENJAMIN THORPE, F.S.A. *a new edition, with corrections and improvements*, post 8vo. *cloth*, 8s (*original price*, 12s)

Popular Treatises on Science, written during the Middle Ages, in Anglo-Saxon, Anglo-Norman, and English. Edited by THOS. WRIGHT, M.A., 8vo. *cloth*, 3s

Contents:—An Anglo-Saxon Treatise on Astronomy, of the TENTH CENTURY, *now first published from a MS. in the British Museum, with a Translation;* Livre des Creatures, by Phillippe de Thaun, *now first printed with a translation,* (*extremely valuable to Philologists, as being the earliest specimens of Anglo-Norman remaining, and explanatory of all the symbolical signs in early sculpture and painting*); the Bestiary of Phillippe de Thaun, *with a translation;* Fragments on Popular Science from the Early English Metrical Lives of the Saints, (*the earliest piece of the kind in the English language.*)

Fragment of Ælfric's Anglo-Saxon Grammar, Ælfric's Glossary, and a Poem on the Soul and Body of the XIIth Century, discovered among the Archives of Worcester Cathedral, by Sir THOMAS PHILLIPS, Bart., folio, PRIVATELY PRINTED, *sewed*, 1s 6d

A Philological Grammar, grounded upon English, and formed from a comparison of more than Sixty Languages. Being an Introduction to the Science of Grammars of all Languages, especially English, Latin, and Greek, by the Rev. W. BARNES, B.D., of St John's College, Cambridge, author of "Poems in the Dorset Dialect," "Anglo-Saxon Delectus," &c. &c. pp. 322, *cloth*, 9s

Biographia Britannica Literaria, or Biography of Literary Characters of Great Britain and Ireland, ANGLO SAXON PERIOD, by THOMAS WRIGHT, M.A., F.S.A., &c., Membre de l'Institute de France, thick 8vo. *cloth*, 6s (*original price*, 12s)

——— THE ANGLO-NORMAN PERIOD, thick 8vo. *cloth*, 6s (*original price*, 12s)

Published under the superintendence of the Council of the Royal Society of Literature. There is no work in the English Language which gives the reader such a comprehensive and connected History of the Literature of these periods.

Philological Proofs of the Original Unity and Recent Origin of the Human Race, derived from a Comparison of the Languages of Europe, Asia, Africa, and America, by A. J. JOHNES, 8vo. *cloth*, 6s (*original price*, 12s 6d)

Printed at the suggestion of Dr. Pritchard, to whose works it will be found a useful supplement.

Essays on the Literature, Popular Superstitions,
and History of England in the MIDDLE AGES, by THOMAS WRIGHT, M.A., F.S.A,, 2 vols. post 8vo. *elegantly printed, cloth*, 16s

Contents:—Essay I. Anglo-Saxon Poetry. II. Anglo-Norman Poetry. III. Chansons de Geste, or Historical Romances of the Middle Ages. IV. On Proverbs and Popular Sayings. V. On the Anglo-Latin Poets of the Twelfth Century. VI. Abelard and the Scholastic Philosophy. VII. On Dr. Grimm's German Mythology. VIII. On the National Fairy Mythology of England. IX. On the Popular Superstitions of Modern Greece, and their connection with the English. X. On Friar Rush, and the Frolicsome Elves. X¹. On Dunlop's History of Fiction. XII. On the History and Transmission of Popular Stories. XIII. On the Poetry of History. XIV. Adventures of Hereward the Saxon. XV. The Story of Eustace the Monk. XVI. The History of Fulke Fitzwarine XVII. On the Popular Cycle of Robin-Hood Ballads. XVIII. On the Conquest of Ireland by the Anglo-Normans. XIX. On Old English Political Songs. XX. On the Scottish Poet Dunbar.

Literature of the Troubadours. Histoire de la
Poésie Provençale, par M. FAURIEL, publié par J. MOHL, Membre de l'Institut de France, 3 vols. 8vo. *new, sewed*, 14s (*original price*, £1. 4s)

A valuable work, and forms a fit companion to the Literary Histories of Hallam, Ticknor, and Ginguene. J. R. S. is the only agent in London for the sale of it, at the above moderate price.

Skelton's (John, *Poet Laureat to Henry VIII.*)
Poetical Works: the Bowge of Court, Colin Clout, Why come ye not to Court? (his celebrated Satire on Wolsey), Philip Sparrow, Elinour Rumming, &c.; with Notes and Life, by the Rev. A. DYCE, 2 vols. 8vo. *cloth*, 16s (*original price*, £1. 12s)

"The power, the strangeness, the volubility of his language, the audacity of his satire, and the perfect originality of his manner, made Skelton one of the most extraordinary writers of any age or country."—*Southey.*

"Skelton is a curious, able, and remarkable writer, with strong sense, a vein of humour, and some imagination; he had a wonderful command of the English language, and one who was styled, in his turn, by as great a scholar as ever lived (Erasmus), 'the light and ornament of Britain.' He indulged very freely in his writings ,in censures on monks and Dominicans: and, moreover, had the hardihood to reflect, in no very mild terms, on the manners and life of Cardinal Wolsey. We cannot help considering Skelton as an ornament of his own time, and a benefactor to those who come after him."

A New Life of Shakespeare, including many particulars
respecting the Poet and his Family, never before published, by J. O. HALLIWELL, F.R.S., in one handsome vol., 8vo. *illustrated with 76 engravings on wood, of objects, most of which are new, from drawings by* FAIRHOLT, *cloth*, 15s

This work contains upwards of forty documents respecting Shakespeare and his Family, never before published, besides numerous others indirectly illustrating the Poet's Biography. All the anecdotes and traditions concerning Shakespeare are here, for the first time collected, and much new light is thrown on his personal history, by papers exhibiting him as selling Malt and Stone, &c. Of the seventy-six engravings which illustrate the volume, more than fifty have never before been engraved.

It is the only Life of Shakespeare to be bought separately from his Works.

Archæological Index to Remains of Antiquity of
the Celtic, Romano-British, and Anglo-Saxon Periods, by JOHN YONGE AKERMAN, *Fellow and Secretary to the Society of Antiquaries*, 8vo. *illustrated with numerous engravings, comprising upwards of five hundred objects, cloth*, 15s

"One of the first wants of an incipient Antiquary, is the facility of comparison, and here it is furnished him at one glance. The plates, indeed, form the most valuable part of the book, both by their number and the judicious selection of types and examples which they contain. It is a book which we can, on this account, safely and warmly recommend to all who are interested in the antiquities of their native land."—*Literary Gazette.*

Ancient Coins of Cities and Princes, geographically
arranged and described, HISPANIA, GALLIA, BRITANNIA, by J. Y. AKER-
MAN, F.S.A., 8vo. *with engravings of many hundred coins from actual
examples, cloth*, 10s

Introduction to the Study of Ancient and Modern
Coins, by J. Y. AKERMAN, *Secretary of the Society of Antiquaries*, fcap.
8vo. *with numerous wood engravings from the original coins, (an excellent
introductory book), cloth*, 6s 6d

CONTENTS: SECT. 1. Origin of Coinage.—Greek Regal Coins. 2. Greek Civic Coins. 3. Greek Imperial Coins. 4. Origin of Roman Coinage—Consular Coins. 5. Roman Imperial Coins. 6. Roman British Coins. 7. Ancient British Coinage. 8. Anglo-Saxon Coinage. 9. English Coinage from the Conquest. 10. Scotch Coinage. 11. Coinage of Ireland. 12. Anglo-Gallic Coins 13. Continental Money in the Middle Ages. 14. Various representations of Coinage. 15. Forgeries in Ancient and Modern Times. 16. Table of Prices of English Coins realized at Public Sales.

Tradesmen's Tokens struck in London and its Vici-
nity, from 1648 to 1671, described from the originals in the British
Museum, &c. by J. Y. AKERMAN, F.S.A., 8vo. *with 8 plates of numerous
examples, cloth*, 15s—LARGE PAPER, in 4to. *cloth*, £1. 1s

This work comprises a list of nearly three thousand Tokens, and contains occasional illustrative topographical and antiquarian notes on persons, places, streets, old tavern and coffee-house signs, &c. &c. with an introductory account of the causes which led to the adoption of such a currency.

Coins of the Romans relating to Britain, described
and illustrated, by J. Y. AKERMAN, F.S.A. SECOND EDITION, greatly
enlarged, 8vo. *with plates and woodcuts*, 10s 6d

The "Prix de Numismatique" was awarded by the French Institute to the author for this work.

"Mr. Akerman's volume contains a notice of every known variety, with copious illustrations, and is published at a very moderate price; it should be consulted, not merely for these particular coins, but also for facts most valuable to all who are interested in the Romano-British History."—*Archæological Journal.*

Numismatic Illustrations of the Narrative Portions
of the New Testament, by J. Y. AKERMAN, 8vo. *numerous woodcuts from
the original coins in various public and private collections, cloth*, 5s

"The New Testament has, it appears, in the compass of the Gospel and Acts, no less than 32 allusions to the coinage of Greece, Rome, and Judæa; and these beautifully engraved, and learnedly described, give Mr. Akerman an opportunity of serving the good cause of truth in the way of his peculiar avocation."—*Church of England Journal.*

English Surnames. An Essay on Family Nomen-
clature, Historical, Etymological, and Humourous; with several illustrative
Appendices, by MARK ANTONY LOWER, M.A., 2 vols. post 8vo. THIRD
EDITION, ENLARGED, *woodcuts, cloth*, 12s

This new and much improved Edition, besides a great enlargement of the Chapters contained in the previous editions, comprises several that are entirely new, together with Notes on Scottish, Irish, and Norman Surnames. The "Additional Prolusions," besides the articles on Rebuses, Allusive Arms, and the Roll of Battel Abbey, contain dissertations on Inn signs, and Remarks on Christian Names: with a copious INDEX of many thousand Names. These features render "English Surnames" rather a new work than a new edition.

Remains of Pagan Saxondom, principally from
Tumuli in England. Drawn from the Originals. Described and illustrated by J. Y. AKERMAN, Fellow and Secretary of the Society of Antiquaries, 4to. 40 FINE COLOURED PLATES, *half morocco*, £2. 12s 6d

The plates are admirably executed by Mr. Basire, and coloured under the direction of the Author. It is a work well worthy the notice of the Archæologist.

Curiosities of Heraldry, with Illustrations from Old
English Writers, by MARK ANTONY LOWER, M.A., author of "Essays on English Surnames," *with illuminated Title-page, and numerous engravings from designs by the author*, 8vo. *cloth*, 14s

"Mr. Lower's work is both curious and instructive, while the manner of its treatment is so inviting and popular, that the subject to which it refers, which many have hitherto had too good reason to consider meagre and unprofitable, assumes, under the hands of the writer, the novelty of fiction with the importance of historical truth."—*Athenæum.*

A Grammar of British Heraldry, consisting of
"Blazon" and "Marshalling," with an Introduction on the Rise and Progress of Symbols and Ensigns, by the Rev. W. SLOANE EVANS, B.A., 8vo. *with 26 plates, comprising upwards of 400 figures, cloth*, 5s

One of the best introductions ever published.

Genealogical and Heraldic History of the Extinct
and Dormant Baronetcies of England, Ireland, and Scotland, by J. BURKE, Esq., medium 8vo. SECOND EDITION, 638 *closely printed pages, in double columns, with about* 1000 *arms engraved on wood, fine portrait of* JAMES I. *cloth*, 10s (*original price*, £1. 8s)

This work engaged the attention of the author for several years, comprises nearly a thousand families, many of them amongst the most ancient and eminent in the kingdom, each carried down to its representative or representatives still existing, with elaborate and minute details of the alliances, achievements, and fortunes; generation after generation, from the earliest to the latest period.

Handbook to the Library of the British Museum,
containing a brief History of its Formation, and of the various Collections of which it is composed; Descriptions of the Catalogues in present use; Classed Lists of the Manuscripts, &c.; and a variety of Information indispensable for Literary persons; with some Account of the principal Public Libraries in London, by RICHARD SIMS, of the Department of Manuscripts, Compiler of the "Index to the Heralds' Visitations," small 8vo. pp. 438, *with map and plan, cloth,* 5s

It will be found a very useful work to every literary person or public institution in all parts of the world.

What Mr. Antonio Panizzi, the keeper of the department of printed books, says *might be done*, Mr. Richard Sims, of the department of manuscripts, says *shall be done*. His Hand-book to the Library of the British Museum is a very comprehensive and instructive volume. I have the sixtieth edition of "Synopsis of the Contents of the British Museum" before me—I cannot expect to see a sixtieth edition of the *Hand-book,* but it deserves to be placed by the side of the Synopsis, and I venture to predict for it a wide circulation.
Mr. Bolton Corney, in Notes and Queries, No. 213.

Wiltshire Tales, illustrative of the Manners, Customs, and Dialect of that and adjoining Counties, by JOHN YONGE AKERMAN. 12mo. *cloth*, 2s 6d

Contributions to Literature, Historical, Antiquarian,
and Metrical, by MARK ANTONY LOWER, M.A., F.S.A., author of "Essays on English Surnames," "Curiosities of Heraldry," &c., post 8vo. *woodcuts,* cloth, 7s 6d

CONTENTS:—1. On Local Nomenclature. 2. On the Battle of Hastings, an Historical Essay. 3. The Lord Dacre, his mournful end; a Ballad. 4. Historical and Archæological Memoir on the Iron Works of the South of England, *with numerous illustrations.* 5. Winchelsea's Deliverance, or the Stout Abbot of Battayle; in Three Fyttes. 6. The South Downs, a Sketch; Historical, Anecdotical, and Descriptive. 7. On Yew Trees in Churchyards. 8. A Lyttel Geste of a Greate Eele; a pleasaunt Ballade. 9. A Discourse of Genealogy. 10. An Antiquarian Pilgrimage in Normandy, *with woodcuts.* 11. Miscellanea, &c. &c. &c.

Retrospective Review (New Series); consisting of
Criticisms upon, Analysis of, and Extracts from curious, useful, valuable, and scarce Old Books, 2 vols. 8vo. *cloth,* 10s 6d

These two volumes form a good companion to the old series of the *Retrospective,* in 16 vols.; the articles are of the same length and character.

The Nursery Rhymes of England, collected chiefly
from Oral Tradition. Edited by J. O. HALLIWELL. The FIFTH EDITION, enlarged, with many Designs, by W. B. SCOTT, *Director of the School of Design, Newcastle-on-Tyne,* 12mo. *cloth, gilt leaves,* 4s 6d

Popular Rhymes and Nursery Tales, with Historical Elucidations, by J. O. HALLIWELL, 12mo. *cloth,* 4s 6d

This very interesting volume on the traditional Literature of England, is divided into Nursery Antiquities, Fireside Nursery Stories, Game Rhymes, Alphabet Rhymes, Riddle Rhymes, Nature Songs, Proverb Rhymes, Places, and Families, Superstition Rhymes, Custom Rhymes and Nursery Songs; *a large number are here printed for the first time.* It may be considered a sequel to the preceding article.

Old Songs and Ballads.—A Little Book of Songs
and Ballads, gathered from Ancient Music Books, MS. and Printed, by E. F. RIMBAULT, LL.D., F.S.A., &c., *elegantly printed in* post 8vo. pp. 240, *half morocco,* 6s

"Dr. Rimbault has been at some pains to collect the words of the Songs which used to delight the Rustics of former times."—*Atlas.*

Anecdotes and Characters of Books and Men.
Collected from the Conversation of Mr. Pope and other eminent Persons of his Time, by the Rev. JOSEPH SPENCE, with Notes, Life, &c. by S. W. SINGER. The second edition, fcap. 8vo. *portrait, elegantly printed by Whittingham, cloth,* 6s

"The 'Anecdotes' of kind-hearted Mr. Spence, the friend of Pope, is one of the best books of ana in the English language."—*Critic.*

The Table Talk of John Selden. With a Biogra-
phical Preface and Notes by S. W. SINGER, fcap. 8vo. *third edition, portrait, cloth,* 5s

There are few volumes of its size so pregnant with sense, combined with the most profound learning; it is impossible to open it without finding some important fact or discussion, something practically useful and applicable to the business of life. Coleridge says, "There is more weighty bullion sense in this book than I ever found in the same number of pages in any uninspired writer."

Life, Progresses, and Rebellion of James, Duke of
Monmouth, &c. to his Capture and Execution, with a full account of the "Bloody Assize," under Judge Jefferies, and copious Biographical Notices, by GEORGE ROBERTS, 2 vols. post 8vo. *plates and cuts, cloth,* 7s 6d (*original price,* £1. 4s)

Two very interesting volumes, particularly so to those connected with the West of England.

A Dictionary of Old English Plays, existing either
in print or in manuscript, from the earliest times to the close of the 17th century, including also Notices of Latin Plays written by English Authors during the same period, with particulars of their Authors, Plots, Characters, &c. by JAMES ORCHARD HALLIWELL, Esq., F.R.S., 8vo. *cloth,* 12s

*** Twenty-five copies have been printed on thick paper, price £1. 1s.

Anecdota Literaria; a Collection of Short Poems
in English, Latin, and French, illustrative of the Literature and History of England in the XIIIth Century; and more especially of the Condition and Manners of the different Classes of Society, by T. WRIGHT, M.A., F.S.A., &c. 8vo. *cloth, only* 250 *copies printed,* 5s

Dictionary of Archaic and Provincial Words, Obsolete
Phrases, Proverbs, and Ancient Customs, from the Reign of Edward I., by JAMES ORCHARD HALLIWELL, F.R S., F.S.A., &c. 2 vols. 8vo. containing upwards of 1000 pages, *closely printed in double columns, cloth, a new and cheaper edition,* 15s

It contains above 50,000 words (embodying all the known scattered glossaries of the English language), forming a complete key for the reader of our old Poets, Dramatists, Theologians, and other authors, whose works abound with allusions, of which explanations are not to be found in ordinary Dictionaries and books of reference. Most of the principal Archaisms are illustrated by examples selected from early inedited MSS. and rare books, and by far the greater portion will be found to be original authorities.

A Glossary; or, Collection of Words, Phrases,
Customs, Proverbs, &c., illustrating the Works of English Authors, particularly Shakespeare and his Contemporaries, by ROBERT NARES, Archdeacon of Stafford, &c., a new Edition, with considerable Additions, both of Words and Examples, by JAMES O. HALLIWELL, F.R.S., and THOMAS WRIGHT, M.A., F.S.A., 2 thick vols. 8vo. *cloth,* £1. 8s

The Glossary of Archdeacon Nares is by far the best and most useful work we possess for explaining and illustrating the obsolete language and the customs and manners of the sixteenth and seventeenth centuries, and it is quite indispensable for the readers of the literature of the Elizabethan period. The additional words and examples are distinguished from those in the original text by a † prefixed to each. The work contains between *five and six thousand* additional examples, the result of original research, not merely supplementary to Nares, but to all other compilations of the kind.

A Glossary of Northamptonshire Words and Phrases;
with examples of their colloquial use, with illustrations, from various Authors; to which are added, the Customs of the County, by Miss A. E. BAKER, 2 vols. post 8vo. *cloth,* 16s (*original price,* £1. 4s)

"We are under great obligations to the lady, sister to the local historian of Northamptonshire, who has occupied her time in producing this very capital Glossary of Northamptonshire provincialisms."—*Examiner.*

Poems of Rural Life, in the Dorset Dialect, with a
Dissertation and Glossary, by the Rev. WM. BARNES, B.D., *second edition, enlarged and corrected*, royal 12mo. *cloth*, 10s

Hwomely Rhymes; a Second Collection of Poems
in the Dorset Dialect, by the Rev. W. BARNES, royal 12mo. *cloth*, 5s 1859

"The author is a genuine poet, and it is delightful to catch the pure breath of song in verses which assert themselves only as the modest vehicle of rare words and Saxon inflections. We have no intention of setting up the Dorset patois against the more extended provincialism of Scotland, still less of comparing the Dorsetshire poet with the Scotch; yet we feel sure that these poems would have delighted the heart of Burns, that many of them are not unworthy of him, and that (at any rate) his best productions cannot express a more cordial sympathy with external nature, or a more loving interest in human joys and sorrows."—*Literary Gazette.*

Dialect of South Lancashire; or, Tim Bobbin's
Tummus and Meary; revised and corrected, with his Rhymes, and an enlarged Glossary of Words and Phrases, chiefly used by the Rural Population of the Manufacturing Districts of South Lancashire, by SAMUEL BAMFORD, 12mo. *second edition, cloth,* 3s 6d

Barnes (Rev. W.) Notes on Ancient Britain and
the Britons, fcap. 8vo. *cloth*, 3s

"A little book in exactly inverse proportion to its great merit; its contents might have been amplified into a huge octavo. As it is, it is an invaluable manual; and to any thoughtful individual, disposed to the preparation of a series of lectures on our early history, it would be a difficult task to point out a more suggestive book in the English tongue."—*Manchester Advertiser.*

Views of Labour and Gold, by the Rev. W. BARNES,
B.D., Author of "Poems in the Dorset Dialect," "Notes on Ancient Britain," &c. 12mo. *cloth*, 3s

"Mr. Barnes is a reader and a thinker. He has a third and a conspicuous merit—his style is perfectly lucid and simple. If the humblest reader of ordinary intelligence desired to follow out the process by which societies are built up and held together, he has but to betake himself to the study of Mr. Barnes's epitome. The title, 'Views of Labour and Gold,' cannot be said to indicate the scope of the Essays, which open with pictures of primitive life, and run on, through an agreeable and diversified range of topics, to considerations of the rights, duties, and interests of Labour and Capital, and to the inquiry—what constitutes the utility, wealth, and positive well-being of a Nation? Subjects of this class are rarely handled with so firm a grasp and such light and artistic manipulations."
Athenæum.

Biblia Pauperum, reproduced in facsimile from one
of the Copies in the British Museum, with an Historical and Bibliographical Introduction by J. PH. BERJEAU, royal 4to. *with* 40 *plates, half morocco,* £2. 2s

As a specimen of the earliest Woodcuts, and of printed Block-books, destined to supersede the Manuscripts anterior to the valuable Invention of Guttenburg, the "Biblia Pauperum" (executed between 1420 and 1430) is well worthy the attention of the Amateur of the Fine Arts, as well as of the Bibliographer. It is printed uniformly with Mr. S. Leigh Sotheby's "Principia Typographica."

www.ingramcontent.com/pod-product-compliance
Lightning Source LLC
Chambersburg PA
CBHW031813220426
43662CB00007B/625